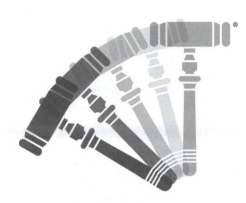

Casenote® Legal Briefs

CONTRACTS

Keyed to Courses Using

Burton's
Principles of Contract Law

Fourth Edition

Published by Wolters Kluwer Law & Business in New York.

Wolters Kluwer Law & Business serves customers worldwide with CCH, Aspen Publishers, and Kluwer Law International products. (www.wolterskluwerlb.com)

No part of this publication may be reproduced or transmitted in any form or by any means, electronic or mechanical, including photocopy, recording, or utilized by any information storage and retrieval system, without written permission from the publisher. For information about permissions or to request permission online, visit us at wolterskluwerlb.com or a written request may be faxed to our permissions department at 212-771-0803.

To contact Customer Service, e-mail customer.service@wolterskluwer.com, call 1-800-234-1660, fax 1-800-901-9075, or mail correspondence to:

Wolters Kluwer Law & Business
Attn: Order Department
P.O. Box 990
Frederick, MD 21705

Printed in the United States of America.

1 2 3 4 5 6 7 8 9 0

ISBN 978-1-4548-2460-2

Certified Chain of Custody
Product Line Contains At Least
20% Certified Forest Content
www.sfiprogram.org
SFI-00756

THIRD-PARTY RIGHTS

THIRD-PARTY BENEFICIARIES

The third party must have been present at the formation of the contract. If third party was added later, look into assignment or delegation.

THIRD-PARTY BENEFICIARIES

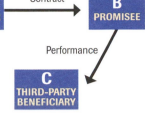

ENFORCEMENT

- A creditor beneficiary may sue the promisor OR the promisee (not both). *Lawrence v. Fox*, 20 N.Y. 268 (1859).
- A donee beneficiary may sue the promisor but may NOT sue the promisee unless there was detrimental reliance.

INTENDED BENEFICIARIES

Only intended beneficiaries have contractual rights. Incidental beneficiaries do not. Intended beneficiaries are usually:
1. Identified in the contract; OR
2. There is some indication by the original parties to intend a benefit.

VESTING

A third-party beneficiary may only enforce a contract if her rights have vested.
1. Three ways a third party vests her rights:
   a. Detrimental reliance.
   b. Filing of a lawsuit (can only assert rights at time of suit).
   c. Third party accepts in a manner expressly invited by the original contracting parties
2. If not vested, original parties may freely modify.
3. Third-party beneficiary has no greater rights than original contracting parties.

ASSIGNMENT OF RIGHTS

IN GENERAL

1. Assignor must adequately describe rights to be assigned and manifest an intention to presently vest those rights in the assignee.
2. Certain tasks may NOT be assigned:
   a. Rights in a future contract are generally not assignable.
   b. Assignment of rights is banned if it will substantially change the obligor's duty.
   Common Law: Requirements contracts are not assignable, substantially changes the obligor's duty.
   UCC: Assignment is permissible if reasonable.

---

3. Consideration is not needed; a gratuitous assignment is effective. *Speelman v. Pascal*, 10 N.Y.2d 313, 178 N.E.2d 723 (1961).
4. Subsequent assignments revoke the former assignment. However, an assignment becomes irrevocable if there is one of the following:
   a. Consideration.
   b. Writing.
5. A valid assignment creates privity of contract between the obligor and the assignee while extinguishing privity between the obligor and the assignor.

ENFORCEMENT

Assignee may sue the obligor. Obligor cannot raise any defenses that the assignor may have against the assignee.

ASSIGNMENT

DELEGATION OF DUTIES

IN GENERAL

1. Most duties may be delegated with the following exceptions:
   a. Duties involving personal judgment and skill.
   b. Changes the obligee's expectancy (such as requirements and output contracts).
   c. There is a contractual prohibition on delegation.
2. Generally, a delegator remains liable on the contract, even if delegate has expressly assumed the duty.
3. When obligee consents (expressly) to a transfer of duties, then this is an offer of novation, and the original delegator is relieved of any liability.

Note: This is different from a novation.

DELEGATION

DAMAGES

MEASURE OF DAMAGES

1. Contracts for the Sale of Land

   Contract price
   – Fair market value
   _____
   Damages

   Specific performance may be requested, since land is unique. *Parker v. Twentieth Century-Fox Film Corp.*, 89 Cal. Rptr. 737, 474 P.2d 689 (1970).
2. Employment Contracts
   a. Employer breach:

      Full contract price
      – Wages earned elsewhere after breach
      _____
      Damages
   b. Employee breach:

      Cost of replacement
      (to find another employee)
      – Wages due to the employee
      _____
      Damages
3. Construction Contracts: *Jacob & Youngs v. Kent*, 230 N.Y. 239, 129 N.E. 889 (1921).
   a. Builder breach:
      i. Non-performance: owner recovers cost of completion.
      ii. Deficient performance: diminution in market value is the measure of damages. (Cost of completion would unjustly enrich the owner.)
   b. Owner breach:

      Cost
      + Expected profit
      _____
      Damages

OTHER DAMAGES

1. Consequential Damages: Damages must have been foreseeable at the time of entering the contract. *Hadley v. Baxendale*, 9 Exch. 341, 156 Eng. Rep 145 (1854).
2. Punitive Damages: Usually reserved for tort and are unusual in a commercial contract case, but have been applied in cases by insureds against their insurance companies for failure to settle or defend in good faith (*Comunale v. Traders & General Ins. Co.*, 50 Cal.2d 654, 328 P.2d 198 (1958)), and in other limited contexts. *Nicholson v. United Pacific Ins. Co.*, 219 Mont. 32, 710 P.2d 1342 (1985).
3. Specific Performance: Available for land and unique goods, but not for services.

QUICK COURSE OUTLINE
CONTRACTS

FORMATION

IN GENERAL

The parties must form an agreement by consenting to the same terms at the same time. They accomplish this by the process of offer and acceptance. *Lonergan v. Scolnick*, 129 Cal. App. 2d 179, 276 P.2d 8 (1954).

Once there is an offer and an acceptance, the parties have arrived at mutual assent.

OFFER

An offer is the manifestation of willingness to enter into a bargain, so made as to justify a reasonable person in the position of the offeree in understanding that her assent to that bargain is invited and will conclude it.

INTENT

Intent must be manifested through such words or acts that a reasonable person would believe an offer is being made. *Lucy v. Zehmer*, 196 Va. 493, 84 S.E.2d 516 (1954).

ESSENTIAL TERMS OF AN OFFER (COMMON LAW)

1. Identification of the parties.
2. Description of the subject matter.
3. Time for performance.
4. Price.

    Note: Silence on some of the terms above may be interpreted to mean that reasonable terms may be determined at a later date.

    (Article 2 of the UCC, which governs the sale of goods, only requires that quantity be an essential term of the contract—all other terms will be filled in appropriately.)

DURATION OF THE OFFER

1. Merchant's Firm Offer (UCC § 2-205): Usually irrevocable.
2. Option Contract:
    a. Money is paid to keep the offer open for a certain period of time.
    b. Counteroffer does not terminate the power to accept, unless the buyer detrimentally relies on it.

"INVITATION TO DEAL"

Do not confuse an offer with an "invitation to deal." The latter is more of the type that would be found in catalogs.

Note: Crossing offers in the mail that are identical are void and do NOT form a contract.

OFFER TERMINATION

1. An offeree's power of acceptance may be terminated by:
    a. Rejection or counter-offer by the offeree.
    b. Lapse of time.
    c. Revocation by the offeror.
    d. Death or incapacity of the offeror or offeree.
    e. Non-occurrence of any condition of acceptance under the terms of the offer.
2. Detrimental reliance makes an offer irrevocable for a reasonable time (modern view).
    a. Common Law: No such thing (must go to the UCC—merchant firm offer).
3. Termination by operation of law:
    a. Incapacitation of the offeror.
    b. Destruction of the subject matter prior to an effective acceptance.

CONSIDERATION

A contract is enforceable only if it is supported by consideration. *Kirksey v. Kirksey*, 8 Ala. 131 (1845). Consideration must be a bargained-for exchange and of legal value.

1. Bargained-for exchange:
    a. Parties must exchange something, even if it is a peppercorn.
    b. Gifts are not "bargained for" and thus do not qualify as consideration (see promissory estoppel).
    c. Forbearance will be sufficient if it benefits the promisor.
    d. Past or moral consideration is not valid.
2. Legal value.
    a. A party must bear a detriment.
    b. A pre-existing legal duty is not consideration.
3. Substitutes for consideration.
    a. Promissory estoppel.
    b. Detrimental reliance.
    c. Modification under the UCC.

ACCEPTANCE

1. Unilateral:
    a. Acceptance can be done only through performance. *Ragosta v. Wilder*, 156 Vt. 390, 592 A.2d 367 (1991).
    b. Once performance has started, offeror may not revoke the offer.
    c. Offeree must be aware that the offer exists.

2. Bilateral (see Mailbox Rule Chart below):
    a. Requires an exchange of promises.
    b. A valid acceptance (for a bilateral contract) requires that there be an offeree with the power to accept, unequivocal terms of acceptance, and communication of acceptance.

POWER TO ACCEPT

Generally, the entity to whom the offer has been addressed has the power of acceptance.

UNEQUIVOCAL TERMS OF ACCEPTANCE

Acceptance must mirror the offeror's terms exactly. Otherwise, the "new" offer with additional or modified terms becomes a new offer.

(Under the UCC, the rule is different. An acceptance need not be an exact mirror of the original offer.)

COMMUNICATION OF ACCEPTANCE

1. Mailbox Rule: A contract is formed upon the moment of dispatch of the acceptance. This assumes that it is properly sent (i.e., properly addressed, stamped, and deposited in a mailbox). If the acceptance has not been properly sent, then acceptance is effective upon receipt.

    Note: The Mailbox Rule only applies to acceptances. Other acts (e.g., rejection) are only effective upon receipt.
2. Exceptions to the Mailbox Rule:
    a. If the offer stipulates that the acceptance is not effective until received. (The parties may contract out of the Mailbox Rule.)
    b. Option contracts are immune to the Rule.
    c. If the offeree sends a rejection and then sends an acceptance, whichever arrives first is effective.
    d. If the offeree sends an acceptance and then a rejection, the Mailbox Rule would normally apply. If the rejection arrived first and the offeror detrimentally relies on it, the Rule would be inapplicable.

THE MAILBOX RULE

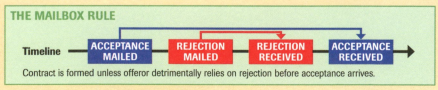

Contract is formed unless offeror detrimentally relies on rejection before acceptance arrives.

VARIATIONS OF THE MAILBOX RULE

Scenario 1. Rejection arrives first = rejection controls and no contract is formed.

Scenario 2. Acceptance arrives first = acceptance controls and contract is formed.

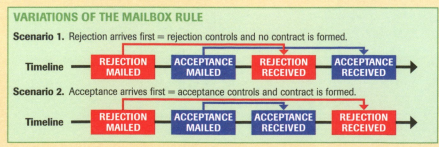

ELEMENTS OF CONTRACTS

ELEMENTS OF A CONTRACT

A contract, to be properly formed, needs an offer and an acceptance with consideration.

TYPES OF CONTRACTS

1. Express contracts are formed when the offer and acceptance are manifested by oral or written words.
2. Implied contracts are formed if the mutual assent of the parties is manifested by conduct. *Wood v. Lucy, Lady Duff-Gordon*, 222 N.Y. 88, 118 N.E. 214 (1917).
3. Quasi-contracts ("implied-at-law") are not technically contracts, but devices created to avoid unjust enrichment.

DEFENSES TO FORMATION

STATUTE OF FRAUDS

The following types of contracts require the contract to be in writing in order to be valid:
1. Marriage.
2. Contract cannot be performed within a year.
3. Executor/administrator.
4. Surety.
5. Interest in land.
6. Contract for the sale of goods at a price of $500 or more.

5. PART PERFORMANCE FOR A LAND SALE CONTRACT

- Part performance on a land sale contract will waive the Statue of Frauds and allow a land sale to be performed without fulfilling the written requirements of the Statute of Frauds.
- Part performance will be satisfied for a land sale contract if buyer does TWO of the following three:
  1. Part payment.
  2. Possession.
  3. Improvements on the land.
  Winternitz v. Summit Hills Joint Venture, 312 Md. 127, 538 A.2d 778 (1988).

6. SALE OF GOODS FOR $500 OR MORE

In order to be valid, a contract for a sale of goods requires the following elements:
1. Some writing (at least the quantity); and
2. Be signed by the party to be charged.

To qualify under the Statute of Frauds, the writing presented can be informal in nature (e.g., a scribbled note that contains the quantity amount or a check), and may be spread out over many documents. *Crabtree v. Elizabeth Arden*, 305 N.Y. 48, 110 N.E.2d 551 (1953).

EXCEPTIONS TO THE STATUTE OF FRAUDS

1. Confirmatory Memo Rule (Between Merchants).
   a. This rule applies only between merchants.
   b. There is a written confirmation sent (within a reasonable time) after the two merchants have come to an oral agreement. If the recipient of the memo does not object to the contents of the memo, then the contract is valid (despite the requirements of the Statute of Frauds). UCC § 2-201(2)
2. Goods are specifically made for the buyer (the goods must only be usable by the buyer).
3. An ADMISSION by one of the parties that a contract was made.
4. The contract has already been performed (the goods have been received and accepted or paid for). *Buffaloe v. Hart*, 114 N.C. App. 52, 441 S.E.2d 172 (1994).

INCAPACITY, MINORITY

1. Incapacity: Insane persons lack the capacity to enter into a valid contract. Intoxicated people as well.
2. Minority (under the age of 18):
   a. A contract made during one's legal minority may be disaffirmed at any time before or after the attainment of a legal majority. Unless and until the contract is disaffirmed, it remains binding.
   b. Other considerations for minority:
      i. If the contract involves necessities (food, clothes, or medical attention), the minor is still liable for the reasonable market value of the items.
      ii. Once the minor reaches the age of legal majority, the contract may be ratified, and thus be made binding.

DUTY TO MITIGATE

In most cases, the suing party has a duty to mitigate damages. If the duty has been breached, it merely serves to reduce (does not bar) recovery.

DURESS

1. Physical Duress: Coercive acts (can be to others beside the victim, i.e., family members) may be a valid personal defense to avoid the obligations of a contract or the forced rescission of a contract.
2. Economic Duress: No defense when one of the parties is in dire need of the subject matter and the other takes advantage of the circumstances to drive an overly harsh bargain.

MISTAKE

1. Unilateral Mistake: A unilateral mistake of a material fact will not be a defense to contract formation. The contract will be enforceable despite the mistake of one of the parties. *Exception:* The non-mistaken party had reason to know of the mistake by the other party. Only then, does a unilateral mistake become a defense to contract formation. *Market St. Associates v. Frey*, 941 F.2d 588 (7th Cir.1991).
2. Mutual Mistake: If there is a mutual mistake of a material fact concerning the bargain, the parties may engage in a rescission of the contract. *Sherwood v. Walker*, 66 Mich. 568, 33 N.W. 919 (1887).
3. Mistake in Transmission: "Scrivener's error." If there is an error in transmission differing from the parties' original intent, then they may reform the contract to reflect the original terms of the intended bargain. If one party is aware of the mistake (to an essential term) or should have known of the mistake in transmission, then the other party may use the mistake as a defense to formation.

UNCONSCIONABILITY

If a contract is deemed "unconscionable," a court will attempt to strike the offending clause(s) from the contract and enforce the rest of the contract.

ILLEGALITY

If the subject matter of the bargain is illegal, the contract is void. *R.R. v. M.H. & Another*, 426 Mass. 501, 689 N.E.2d 790 (1998). However, a few things should be considered:
1. If the subject matter or participation of parties is declared illegal when the offer is made, the offer is revoked as a matter of law.
2. If the subject matter or participation of the parties is declared illegal AFTER formation, BUT BEFORE performance, then the duties of both parties are discharged under the doctrine of impossibility.

FRAUD

Misrepresentation of a fact or promise of future performance at the time the contract was made which induces party to enter into the contract.

PERFORMANCE

CONDITIONS

1. Promise v. Condition: A promise is a commitment to do or not to do an act that is at the heart of the contract. A condition is an event which will modify the underlying promise (such as when and if the promise must be performed).
2. Effects of Condition v. Promise:
   Failure of a promise = Breach.
   Failure of a condition = Relief from the obligation to perform.

TYPES OF CONDITIONS

1. Categorized by timing: condition precedent, conditions concurrent, condition subsequent.
2. Categorized by source: express conditions, implied-in-fact, implied-at-law conditions.

CONDITION PRECEDENT

Condition must occur before performance is due. Once condition occurs, then performance must happen. *Oppenheimer & Co. v. Oppenheim, Appel, Dixon & Co.*, 86 N.Y.2d 685, 660 N.E.2d 415 (1995).

CONDITIONS CONCURRENT

Conditions to occur at the same time. If one condition has occurred, then the other must occur as well.

CONDITION SUBSEQUENT

Condition cuts off already existing duty. Once this occurs, duty to perform is excused.

Example: In a contract, a clause containing a condition subsequent will state: "I am liable to perform this promise until (the occurrence)."

Performance continues on page 3 ▶

IMPLIED-IN-FACT CONDITION

Implied-in-fact conditions arise by physical or moral inference from what the parties have expressed (i.e., reasonable expectations of parties). *Jacob & Youngs, Inc. v. Kent*, 230 N.Y. 239, 129 N.E. 689 (1921).

IMPLIED-AT-LAW (CONSTRUCTIVE) CONDITION

"Constructive" conditions function to fix the order of performance when the express terms of the bargain are silent in this region.

DUTY OF PERFORMANCE

Once a condition has been met, a duty of performance arises.

SATISFACTION OF DUTY

Performance is the most desirable way to "discharge" a duty that arises from a contract. Once a party performs a duty required by a contract, that duty is "discharged."

DISCHARGE OF DUTY

Duty to perform may be discharged by one of the following methods:

1. Impossibility: As measured by the objective standard, the impossibility must arise after the contract was entered into. The destruction of the subject matter of the contract gives rise to an impossibility, as does the subsequent passing of a law that renders the contract matter illegal. And if the services required in the contract were unique to one person (such as an artist or performer), then the death of the person will give rise to impossibility and discharge the duty inherent in the contract.
2. Impracticability: Occurs when subsequent factors have rendered the cost of performing a contract grossly in excess of what was foreseen. The key is whether the unreasonable increase in price was foreseeable. If it was foreseeable, the impracticability may NOT be used to discharge the duty.
3. Frustration of purpose: Occurs when a subsequent development not foreseeable at the time of entering the contract completely destroys the purpose of the contract (as understood by both parties).
4. Rescission: Duties to a contract may be re-scinded by mutual agreement of both parties.
5. Novation:
   a. Novation substitutes a new party for an original party to the contract.
   b. All parties must assent to the substitution.
   c. Once the substitution occurs, then the original party is released from the contract.
6. Accord and Satisfaction: An accord and satisfaction releases debtor from a disputed debt through a new agreement. A valid accord and satisfaction must have consideration and the amount paid to satisfy the debt must be less than the debtor was originally entitled to.
   a. If the debt is undisputed, there is no accord and satisfaction.
   b. There is no consideration involved in releasing someone from a debt that is agreed upon—the debtor may seek additional payment.
   c. If the debt is disputed, then there is a valid accord and satisfaction.

EXCUSE OF CONDITIONS

However, there are intervening factors that may prematurely "discharge" a duty, thus relieving a party of fulfilling the earlier promise.

1. Anticipatory Repudiation (applies only to bilateral contracts). *Hochster v. De La Tour*, 2 Ellis. & Bl. 678 (1853).
   a. The anticipatory repudiation must be unequivocal, definite, and communicated before the time of performance (must be more than a mere expression of doubt).
   b. Upon the anticipatory repudiation, the non-repudiating party may:
      i. Suspend own performance and sue other party immediately, OR
      ii. Affirm the contract and await the due date for performance.
2. Waiver: A party may voluntarily relinquish a known contract right, such as a condition or a contract, thus excusing the underlying condition or promise. *Clark v. West*, 193 N.Y. 349, 86 N.E. 1 (1908).
3. Estoppel: If a party who has the protection of a condition precedent or concurrent creates an impression that she will NOT insist upon its satisfaction, and the other party reasonably relies on such, the advantaged party will be estopped from insisting upon satisfaction.
4. Prevention or Failure to Cooperate: If a party wrongfully prevents a condition from occurring, whether by prevention or failure to cooperate, she will no longer be given the benefit of it.
5. Substantial Performance:
   a. Only applies to where implied-at-law (constructive) conditions are involved.
   b. Where a party has almost completely performed her duties, but has breached in a minor way, forfeiture of a return performance may be avoided by this rule.

   [Remember, substantial performance does not apply in the sale of goods (Article 2) context; the "perfect tender" rule applies.]
6. Conditions may also be excused by impossibility, impracticability, or frustration.

CROSSING OFFERS

If there are two crossing offers that are identical and are mailed at the same time to the other party in such a way that they cross in the mail, a contract is not formed.

PAROL EVIDENCE RULE

INTERPRETATION OF TERMS

1. Ignorant party wins against knowing party. Restatement § 201.
2. When both parties knew of the differing intent, there is no contract
3. In order of preference:
   a. Express terms.
   b. Course of performance (negotiations).
   c. Course of dealing (previous contracts).
   d. Usage of trade.

PAROL EVIDENCE RULE

1. Prior or contemporaneous negotiations and agreements that contradict or modify contractual terms are legally irrelevant if the written contract is intended as a complete and final expression of the parties.
   a. "Merger clause": A clause included in the contract intended to buttress the presumption that the written contract is a complete and final expression of the parties. *ARB Inc. v. E-Systems, Inc.*, 663 F.2d 189 (D.C. Cir. 1980).
   b. Such a contract outlined above is said to be "integrated."
2. Exceptions to the Parol Evidence Rule (evidence of the following may be admitted despite the Parol Evidence Rule):
   a. Subsequent modifications to the contract.
   b. Collateral agreement.
   c. Formation defects.
   d. Ambiguous terms.
   e. Existence of a condition precedent.
   f. Partial integration.

SUBSEQUENT ASSIGNMENTS

Subsequent assignments automatically revoke the former assignment; an assignment in writing is, however, irrevocable. If the assignments are "equal," then usually one applies the "American Rule": first in line is first in right.

BREACH OF CONTRACT

MATERIAL v. MINOR BREACH

1. Material breach: One may suspend performance AND sue for damages. *K & G Contr. Co. v. Harris*, 223 Md. 305, 164 A.2d 451 (1960).
2. Minor breach: One may only sue for damages (which may be nominal). It is important to remember that this does NOT suspend the duty to perform. *Walker & Co. v. Harrison*, 347 Mich. 630, 81 N.W.2d 352 (1957).
3. The test for materiality for a breach weighs several factors:
   a. The benefit received by the injured (non-breaching) party.
   b. Adequacy of compensation for the injured party.
   c. The extent to which the non-injured (breaching) party has partly performed.
   d. Hardship to the non-injured party.
   e. Negligence or willful behavior of the breaching party.
   f. The likelihood that the breaching party will perform the remainder of contract.

LATE PERFORMANCE

1. Usually a minor breach.
2. May become a material breach only where:
   a. Contract requires timely performance (usually UCC).
   b. Contract contains language such as "time is of the essence."

About Wolters Kluwer Law & Business

Wolters Kluwer Law & Business is a leading global provider of intelligent information and digital solutions for legal and business professionals in key specialty areas, and respected educational resources for professors and law students. Wolters Kluwer Law & Business connects legal and business professionals as well as those in the education market with timely, specialized authoritative content and information-enabled solutions to support success through productivity, accuracy and mobility.

Serving customers worldwide, Wolters Kluwer Law & Business products include those under the Aspen Publishers, CCH, Kluwer Law International, Loislaw, Best Case, ftwilliam.com and MediRegs family of products.

CCH products have been a trusted resource since 1913, and are highly regarded resources for legal, securities, antitrust and trade regulation, government contracting, banking, pension, payroll, employment and labor, and healthcare reimbursement and compliance professionals.

Aspen Publishers products provide essential information to attorneys, business professionals and law students. Written by preeminent authorities, the product line offers analytical and practical information in a range of specialty practice areas from securities law and intellectual property to mergers and acquisitions and pension/benefits. Aspen's trusted legal education resources provide professors and students with high-quality, up-to-date and effective resources for successful instruction and study in all areas of the law.

Kluwer Law International products provide the global business community with reliable international legal information in English. Legal practitioners, corporate counsel and business executives around the world rely on Kluwer Law journals, looseleafs, books, and electronic products for comprehensive information in many areas of international legal practice.

Loislaw is a comprehensive online legal research product providing legal content to law firm practitioners of various specializations. Loislaw provides attorneys with the ability to quickly and efficiently find the necessary legal information they need, when and where they need it, by facilitating access to primary law as well as state-specific law, records, forms and treatises.

Best Case Solutions is the leading bankruptcy software product to the bankruptcy industry. It provides software and workflow tools to flawlessly streamline petition preparation and the electronic filing process, while timely incorporating ever-changing court requirements.

ftwilliam.com offers employee benefits professionals the highest quality plan documents (retirement, welfare and non-qualified) and government forms (5500/PBGC, 1099 and IRS) software at highly competitive prices.

MediRegs products provide integrated health care compliance content and software solutions for professionals in healthcare, higher education and life sciences, including professionals in accounting, law and consulting.

Wolters Kluwer Law & Business, a division of Wolters Kluwer, is headquartered in New York. Wolters Kluwer is a market-leading global information services company focused on professionals.

Format for the Casenote® Legal Brief

Nature of Case: This section identifies the form of action (e.g., breach of contract, negligence, battery), the type of proceeding (e.g., demurrer, appeal from trial court's jury instructions),or the relief sought (e.g., damages, injunction, criminal sanctions).

Fact Summary: This is included to refresh your memory and can be used as a quick reminder of the facts.

Rule of Law: Summarizes the general principle of law that the case illustrates. It may be used for instant recall of the court's holding and for classroom discussion or home review.

Facts: This section contains all relevant facts of the case, including the contentions of the parties and the lower court holdings. It is written in a logical order to give the student a clear understanding of the case. The plaintiff and defendant are identified by their proper names throughout and are always labeled with a (P) or (D).

Palsgraf v. Long Island R.R. Co.

Injured bystander (P) v. Railroad company (D)

N.Y. Ct. App., 248 N.Y. 339, 162 N.E. 99 (1928).

NATURE OF CASE: Appeal from judgment affirming verdict for plaintiff seeking damages for personal injury.

FACT SUMMARY: Helen Palsgraf (P) was injured on R.R.'s (D) train platform when R.R.'s (D) guard helped a passenger aboard a moving train, causing his package to fall on the tracks. The package contained fireworks which exploded, creating a shock that tipped a scale onto Palsgraf (P).

🏛 RULE OF LAW
The risk reasonably to be perceived defines the duty to be obeyed.

FACTS: Helen Palsgraf (P) purchased a ticket to Rockaway Beach from R.R. (D) and was waiting on the train platform. As she waited, two men ran to catch a train that was pulling out from the platform. The first man jumped aboard, but the second man, who appeared as if he might fall, was helped aboard by the guard on the train who had kept the door open so they could jump aboard. A guard on the platform also helped by pushing him onto the train. The man was carrying a package wrapped in newspaper. In the process, the man dropped his package, which fell on the tracks. The package contained fireworks and exploded. The shock of the explosion was apparently of great enough strength to tip over some scales at the other end of the platform, which fell on Palsgraf (P) and injured her. A jury awarded her damages, and R.R. (D) appealed.

ISSUE: Does the risk reasonably to be perceived define the duty to be obeyed?

HOLDING AND DECISION: (Cardozo, C.J.) Yes. The risk reasonably to be perceived defines the duty to be obeyed. If there is no foreseeable hazard to the injured party as the result of a seemingly innocent act, the act does not become a tort because it happened to be a wrong as to another. If the wrong was not willful, the plaintiff must show that the act as to her had such great and apparent possibilities of danger as to entitle her to protection. Negligence in the abstract is not enough upon which to base liability. Negligence is a relative concept, evolving out of the common law doctrine of trespass on the case. To establish liability, the defendant must owe a legal duty of reasonable care to the injured party. A cause of action in tort will lie where harm,

though unintended, could have been averted or avoided by observance of such a duty. The scope of the duty is limited by the range of danger that a reasonable person could foresee. In this case, there was nothing to suggest from the appearance of the parcel or otherwise that the parcel contained fireworks. The guard could not reasonably have had any warning of a threat to Palsgraf (P), and R.R. (D) therefore cannot be held liable. Judgment is reversed in favor of R.R. (D).

DISSENT: (Andrews, J.) The concept that there is no negligence unless R.R. (D) owes a legal duty to take care as to Palsgraf (P) herself is too narrow. Everyone owes to the world at large the duty of refraining from those acts that may unreasonably threaten the safety of others. If the guard's action was negligent as to those nearby, it was also negligent as to those outside what might be termed the "danger zone." For Palsgraf (P) to recover, R.R.'s (D) negligence must have been the proximate cause of her injury, a question of fact for the jury.

▶ ANALYSIS
The majority defined the limit of the defendant's liability in terms of the danger that a reasonable person in defendant's situation would have perceived. The dissent argued that the limitation should not be placed on liability, but rather on damages. Judge Andrews suggested that only injuries that would not have happened but for R.R.'s (D) negligence should be compensable. Both the majority and dissent recognized the policy-driven need to limit liability for negligent acts, seeking, in the words of Judge Andrews, to define a framework "that will be practical and in keeping with the general understanding of mankind." The Restatement (Second) of Torts has accepted Judge Cardozo's view.

▬

Quicknotes
FORESEEABILITY A reasonable expectation that change is the probable result of certain acts or omissions.

NEGLIGENCE Conduct falling below the standard of care that a reasonable person would demonstrate under similar conditions.

PROXIMATE CAUSE The natural sequence of events without which an injury would not have been sustained.

▬

Party ID: Quick identification of the relationship between the parties.

Concurrence/Dissent: All concurrences and dissents are briefed whenever they are included by the casebook editor.

Analysis: This last paragraph gives you a broad understanding of where the case "fits in" with other cases in the section of the book and with the entire course. It is a hornbook-style discussion indicating whether the case is a majority or minority opinion and comparing the principal case with other cases in the casebook. It may also provide analysis from restatements, uniform codes, and law review articles. The analysis will prove to be invaluable to classroom discussion.

Issue: The issue is a concise question that brings out the essence of the opinion as it relates to the section of the casebook in which the case appears. Both substantive and procedural issues are included if relevant to the decision.

Holding and Decision: This section offers a clear and in-depth discussion of the rule of the case and the court's rationale. It is written in easy-to-understand language and answers the issue presented by applying the law to the facts of the case. When relevant, it includes a thorough discussion of the exceptions to the case as listed by the court, any major cites to the other cases on point, and the names of the judges who wrote the decisions.

Quicknotes: Conveniently defines legal terms found in the case and summarizes the nature of any statutes, codes, or rules referred to in the text.

Wolters Kluwer Law & Business is proud to offer *Casenote® Legal Briefs*—continuing thirty years of publishing America's best-selling legal briefs.

Casenote® Legal Briefs are designed to help you save time when briefing assigned cases. Organized under convenient headings, they show you how to abstract the basic facts and holdings from the text of the actual opinions handed down by the courts. Used as part of a rigorous study regimen, they can help you spend more time analyzing and critiquing points of law than on copying bits and pieces of judicial opinions into your notebook or outline.

Casenote® Legal Briefs should never be used as a substitute for assigned casebook readings. They work best when read as a follow-up to reviewing the underlying opinions themselves. Students who try to avoid reading and digesting the judicial opinions in their casebooks or online sources will end up shortchanging themselves in the long run. The ability to absorb, critique, and restate the dynamic and complex elements of case law decisions is crucial to your success in law school and beyond. It cannot be developed vicariously.

Casenote® Legal Briefs represents but one of the many offerings in Legal Education's Study Aid Timeline, which includes:

- *Casenote® Legal Briefs*
- *Emanuel® Law Outlines*
- Emanuel® *Law in a Flash* Flash Cards
- Emanuel® *CrunchTime®* Series
- *Siegel's Essay and Multiple-Choice Questions and Answers Series*

Each of these series is designed to provide you with easy-to-understand explanations of complex points of law. Each volume offers guidance on the principles of legal analysis and, consulted regularly, will hone your ability to spot relevant issues. We have titles that will help you prepare for class, prepare for your exams, and enhance your general comprehension of the law along the way.

To find out more about Wolters Kluwer Law & Business' study aid publications, visit us online at *www.wolterskluwerlb.com* or email us at *legaledu@wolterskluwer.com*. We'll be happy to assist you.

A. Decide on a Format and Stick to It

Structure is essential to a good brief. It enables you to arrange systematically the related parts that are scattered throughout most cases, thus making manageable and understandable what might otherwise seem to be an endless and unfathomable sea of information. There are, of course, an unlimited number of formats that can be utilized. However, it is best to find one that suits your needs and stick to it. Consistency breeds both efficiency and the security that when called upon you will know where to look in your brief for the information you are asked to give.

Any format, as long as it presents the essential elements of a case in an organized fashion, can be used. Experience, however, has led *Casenote® Legal Briefs* to develop and utilize the following format because of its logical flow and universal applicability.

NATURE OF CASE: This is a brief statement of the legal character and procedural status of the case (e.g., "Appeal of a burglary conviction").

There are many different alternatives open to a litigant dissatisfied with a court ruling. The key to determining which one has been used is to discover *who is asking this court for what.*

This first entry in the brief should be kept as *short as possible.* Use the court's terminology if you understand it. But since jurisdictions vary as to the titles of pleadings, the best entry is the one that addresses who wants what in this proceeding, not the one that sounds most like the court's language.

RULE OF LAW: A statement of the general principle of law that the case illustrates (e.g., "An acceptance that varies any term of the offer is considered a rejection and counteroffer").

Determining the rule of law of a case is a procedure similar to determining the issue of the case. Avoid being fooled by red herrings; there may be a few rules of law mentioned in the case excerpt, but usually only one is *the* rule with which the casebook editor is concerned. The techniques used to locate the issue, described below, may also be utilized to find the rule of law. Generally, your best guide is simply the chapter heading. It is a clue to the point the casebook editor seeks to make and should be kept in mind when reading every case in the respective section.

FACTS: A synopsis of only the essential facts of the case, i.e., those bearing upon or leading up to the issue.

The facts entry should be a short statement of the events and transactions that led one party to initiate legal proceedings against another in the first place. While some cases conveniently state the salient facts at the beginning of the decision, in other instances they will have to be culled from hiding places throughout the text, even from concurring and dissenting opinions. Some of the "facts" will often be in dispute and should be so noted. Conflicting evidence may be briefly pointed up. "Hard" facts must be included. Both must be *relevant* in order to be listed in the facts entry. It is impossible to tell what is relevant until the entire case is read, as the ultimate determination of the rights and liabilities of the parties may turn on something buried deep in the opinion.

Generally, the facts entry should not be longer than three to five *short* sentences.

It is often helpful to identify the role played by a party in a given context. For example, in a construction contract case the identification of a party as the "contractor" or "builder" alleviates the need to tell that that party was the one who was supposed to have built the house.

It is always helpful, and a good general practice, to identify the "plaintiff" and the "defendant." This may seem elementary and uncomplicated, but, especially in view of the creative editing practiced by some casebook editors, it is sometimes a difficult or even impossible task. Bear in mind that the *party presently* seeking something from this court may not be the plaintiff, and that sometimes only the cross-claim of a defendant is treated in the excerpt. Confusing or misaligning the parties can ruin your analysis and understanding of the case.

ISSUE: A statement of the general legal question answered by or illustrated in the case. For clarity, the issue is best put in the form of a question capable of a "yes" or "no" answer. In reality, the issue is simply the Rule of Law put in the form of a question (e.g., "May an offer be accepted by performance?").

The major problem presented in discerning what is *the* issue in the case is that an opinion usually purports to raise and answer several questions. However, except for rare cases, only one such question is really the issue in the case. Collateral issues not necessary to the resolution of the matter in controversy are handled by the court by language known as *"obiter dictum"* or merely *"dictum."* While dicta may be included later in the brief, they have no place under the issue heading.

To find the issue, ask *who wants what* and then go on to ask *why did that party succeed or fail in getting it.* Once this is determined, the "why" should be turned into a question.

The complexity of the issues in the cases will vary, but in all cases a single-sentence question should sum up the issue. *In a few cases,* there will be two, or even more rarely, three issues of equal importance to the resolution of the case. Each should be expressed in a single-sentence question.

Since many issues are resolved by a court in coming to a final disposition of a case, the casebook editor will reproduce the portion of the opinion containing the issue or issues most relevant to the area of law under scrutiny. A noted law professor gave this advice: "Close the book; look at the title on the cover." Chances are, if it is Property, you need not concern yourself with whether, for example, the federal government's treatment of the plaintiff's land really raises a federal question sufficient to support jurisdiction on this ground in federal court.

The same rule applies to chapter headings designating sub-areas within the subjects. They tip you off as to what the text is designed to teach. The cases are arranged in a casebook to show a progression or development of the law, so that the preceding cases may also help.

It is also most important to remember to *read the notes and questions* at the end of a case to determine what the editors wanted you to have gleaned from it.

HOLDING AND DECISION: This section should succinctly explain the rationale of the court in arriving at its decision. In capsulizing the "reasoning" of the court, it should always include an application of the general rule or rules of law to the specific facts of the case. Hidden justifications come to light in this entry: the reasons for the state of the law, the public policies, the biases and prejudices, those considerations that influence the justices' thinking and, ultimately, the outcome of the case. At the end, there should be a short indication of the disposition or procedural resolution of the case (e.g., "Decision of the trial court for Mr. Smith (P) reversed").

The foregoing format is designed to help you "digest" the reams of case material with which you will be faced in your law school career. Once mastered by practice, it will place at your fingertips the information the authors of your casebooks have sought to impart to you in case-by-case illustration and analysis.

B. Be as Economical as Possible in Briefing Cases

Once armed with a format that encourages succinctness, it is as important to be economical with regard to the time spent on the actual reading of the case as it is to be economical in the writing of the brief itself. This does not mean "skimming" a case. Rather, it means reading the case with an "eye" trained to recognize into which "section" of your brief a particular passage or line fits and having a system for quickly and precisely marking the case so that the passages fitting any one particular part of

the brief can be easily identified and brought together in a concise and accurate manner when the brief is actually written.

It is of no use to simply repeat everything in the opinion of the court; record only enough information to trigger your recollection of what the court said. Nevertheless, an accurate statement of the "law of the case," i.e., the legal principle applied to the facts, is absolutely essential to class preparation and to learning the law under the case method.

To that end, it is important to develop a "shorthand" that you can use to make marginal notations. These notations will tell you at a glance in which section of the brief you will be placing that particular passage or portion of the opinion.

Some students prefer to underline all the salient portions of the opinion (with a pencil or colored underliner marker), making marginal notations as they go along. Others prefer the color-coded method of underlining, utilizing different colors of markers to underline the salient portions of the case, each separate color being used to represent a different section of the brief. For example, blue underlining could be used for passages relating to the rule of law, yellow for those relating to the issue, and green for those relating to the holding and decision, etc. While it has its advocates, the color-coded method can be confusing and time-consuming (all that time spent on changing colored markers). Furthermore, it can interfere with the continuity and concentration many students deem essential to the reading of a case for maximum comprehension. In the end, however, it is a matter of personal preference and style. Just remember, whatever method you use, underlining must be used sparingly or its value is lost.

If you take the marginal notation route, an efficient and easy method is to go along underlining the key portions of the case and placing in the margin alongside them the following "markers" to indicate where a particular passage or line "belongs" in the brief you will write:

N   (NATURE OF CASE)
RL (RULE OF LAW)
I   (ISSUE)
HL (HOLDING AND DECISION, relates to the RULE OF LAW behind the decision)
HR (HOLDING AND DECISION, gives the RATIONALE or reasoning behind the decision)
HA (HOLDING AND DECISION, APPLIES the general principle(s) of law to the facts of the case to arrive at the decision)

Remember that a particular passage may well contain information necessary to more than one part of your brief, in which case you simply note that in the margin. If you are using the color-coded underlining method instead of marginal notation, simply make asterisks or checks in the margin next to the passage in question in the colors that indicate the additional sections of the brief where it might be utilized.

The economy of utilizing "shorthand" in marking cases for briefing can be maintained in the actual brief writing process itself by utilizing "law student shorthand" within the brief. There are many commonly used words and phrases for which abbreviations can be substituted in your briefs (and in your class notes also). You can develop abbreviations that are personal to you and which will save you a lot of time. A reference list of briefing abbreviations can be found on page xii of this book.

C. Use Both the Briefing Process and the Brief as a Learning Tool

Now that you have a format and the tools for briefing cases efficiently, the most important thing is to make the time spent in briefing profitable to you and to make the most advantageous use of the briefs you create. Of course, the briefs are invaluable for classroom reference when you are called upon to explain or analyze a particular case. However, they are also useful in reviewing for exams. A quick glance at the fact summary should bring the case to mind, and a rereading of the rule of law should enable you to go over the underlying legal concept in your mind, how it was applied in that particular case, and how it might apply in other factual settings.

As to the value to be derived from engaging in the briefing process itself, there is an immediate benefit that arises from being forced to sift through the essential facts and reasoning from the court's opinion and to succinctly express them in your own words in your brief. The process ensures that you understand the case and the point that it illustrates, and that means you will be ready to absorb further analysis and information brought forth in class. It also ensures you will have something to say when called upon in class. The briefing process helps develop a mental agility for getting to the *gist* of a case and for identifying, expounding on, and applying the legal concepts and issues found there. The briefing process is the mental process on which you must rely in taking law school examinations; it is also the mental process upon which a lawyer relies in serving his clients and in making his living.

Abbreviations for Briefs

acceptance	acp	offer	O
affirmed	aff	offeree	OE
answer	ans	offeror	OR
assumption of risk	a/r	ordinance	ord
attorney	atty	pain and suffering	p/s
beyond a reasonable doubt	b/r/d	parol evidence	p/e
bona fide purchaser	BFP	plaintiff	P
breach of contract	br/k	prima facie	p/f
cause of action	c/a	probable cause	p/c
common law	c/l	proximate cause	px/c
Constitution	Con	real property	r/p
constitutional	con	reasonable doubt	r/d
contract	K	reasonable man	r/m
contributory negligence	c/n	rebuttable presumption	rb/p
cross	x	remanded	rem
cross-complaint	x/c	res ipsa loquitur	RIL
cross-examination	x/ex	respondeat superior	r/s
cruel and unusual punishment	c/u/p	Restatement	RS
defendant	D	reversed	rev
dismissed	dis	Rule Against Perpetuities	RAP
double jeopardy	d/j	search and seizure	s/s
due process	d/p	search warrant	s/w
equal protection	e/p	self-defense	s/d
equity	eq	specific performance	s/p
evidence	ev	statute	S
exclude	exc	statute of frauds	S/F
exclusionary rule	exc/r	statute of limitations	S/L
felony	f/n	summary judgment	s/j
freedom of speech	f/s	tenancy at will	t/w
good faith	g/f	tenancy in common	t/c
habeas corpus	h/c	tenant	t
hearsay	hr	third party	TP
husband	H	third party beneficiary	TPB
injunction	inj	transferred intent	TI
in loco parentis	ILP	unconscionable	uncon
inter vivos	I/v	unconstitutional	unconst
joint tenancy	j/t	undue influence	u/e
judgment	judgt	Uniform Commercial Code	UCC
jurisdiction	jur	unilateral	uni
last clear chance	LCC	vendee	VE
long-arm statute	LAS	vendor	VR
majority view	maj	versus	v
meeting of minds	MOM	void for vagueness	VFV
minority view	min	weight of authority	w/a
Miranda rule	Mir/r	weight of the evidence	w/e
Miranda warnings	Mir/w	wife	W
negligence	neg	with	w/
notice	ntc	within	w/i
nuisance	nus	without	w/o
obligation	ob	without prejudice	w/o/p
obscene	obs	wrongful death	wr/d

Table of Cases

The Autonomy and Security Principles

Quick Reference Rules of Law

Hawkins v. McGee

Injured patient (P) v. Surgeon (D)

N.H. Sup. Ct., 84 N.H. 114, 146 A. 641 (1929).

NATURE OF CASE: Action in assumpsit for the breach of an alleged warranty.

FACT SUMMARY: McGee (D), a surgeon, performed an unsuccessful operation on Hawkins's (P) hand after having guaranteed to make the hand 100 percent perfect. Hawkins (P) was awarded damages for pain and suffering and for "what injury he has sustained over and above the injury he had before."

RULE OF LAW

The purpose of awarding damages for breach of contract is to put the plaintiff in as good a position as he would have been in had the defendant kept his contract.

FACTS: McGee (D), a surgeon, performed an operation on Hawkins's (P) hand. Before the operation, McGee (D) had repeatedly solicited an opportunity to perform the operation and had guaranteed to make the hand 100 percent perfect. The operation was not successful, and Hawkins (P) sought to recover on the basis of McGee's (D) warranty. The trial court instructed the jury that Hawkins (P) would be entitled to recover for his pain and suffering and for "what injury he has sustained over and above the injury he had before."

ISSUE: Is the measure of damages for breach of a contract what the defendant contracted to give the plaintiff?

HOLDING AND DECISION: (Branch, J.) Yes. McGee's (D) words, if taken at face value, indicate the giving of a warranty. Coupled with the evidence that McGee (D) repeatedly solicited the opportunity to perform the operation, there is a reasonable basis for a jury to conclude that McGee (D) spoke the words with the intention that they be taken at face value as an inducement for Hawkins's (P) submission to the operation. The jury instruction on damages was erroneous. The purpose of awarding damages is to put a plaintiff in as good a position as he would have been in had the defendant kept his contract. The measure of recovery is what the defendant should have given the plaintiff, not what the plaintiff has given the defendant or otherwise expended. Hence, the measure of Hawkins's (P) damages is the difference between the value of a perfect hand, as promised by McGee (D), and the value of his hand in its present condition. Hawkins's (P) pain is not relevant to this determination. Also, damages might be assessed for McGee's (D) failure to improve the hand, even if there was no evidence that the operation had made it worse. New trial ordered.

ANALYSIS

The measure of damages is the actual loss sustained by reason of the breach, which is the loss of what the promisee would have made if the contract had been performed, less the proper deductions. The plaintiff may recover damages not only for the net gains which were prevented by the breach, but also for expenses incurred in reliance on the defendant's performance of his contract promise. In a proper case, prospective profits which were lost because of the breach are also recoverable.

Quicknotes

ASSUMPSIT An oral or written promise by one party to perform or pay another.

MONEY DAMAGES Monetary compensation sought by, or awarded to, a party who incurred loss as a result of a breach of contract or tortious conduct on behalf of another party.

SOLICITATION Contact initiated by an attorney for the purpose of obtaining employment.

WARRANTY An assurance by one party that another may rely on a certain representation of fact.

Lucy v. Zehmer

Purchaser of farm (P) v. Owners of farm (D)

Va. Sup. Ct. App., 196 Va. 493, 84 S.E.2d 516 (1954).

NATURE OF CASE: Action for specific performance of a land sale contract.

FACT SUMMARY: Zehmer (D) claimed his offer to sell his farm to Lucy (P) was made in jest.

🏛 RULE OF LAW
If a person's words and acts, judged by a reasonable standard, manifest a certain intent, it is immaterial what may be the real but unexpressed state of that person's mind.

FACTS: Zehmer (D) and his wife (D) contracted to sell their 471-acre farm to Lucy (P) for $50,000. Zehmer (D) contended that his offer was made in jest while the three of them were drinking and that Zehmer (D) only desired to bluff Lucy (P) into admitting he did not have $50,000. Lucy (P) appeared to have taken the offer seriously by discussing its terms with Zehmer (D), by rewriting it to enable Mrs. Zehmer (D) to sign also, by providing for title examination, and by taking possession of the agreement. Lucy (P) offered $5 to bind the deal and the next day sold a one-half interest to his brother (P) in order to raise money.

ISSUE: Does the law impute to a person an intention corresponding to the reasonable meaning of his words and acts?

HOLDING AND DECISION: (Buchanan, J.) Yes. The existence of an offer depends upon the reasonable meaning to be given the offeror's acts and words. For the formation of a contract, the mental assent of the parties is not required. If the words and acts of one of the parties have but one reasonable meaning, his undisclosed intention is immaterial except when an unreasonable meaning which he attaches to his manifestations is known to the other party. Accordingly, one cannot say he was merely jesting when his conduct and words would warrant reasonable belief that a real agreement was intended. Reversed and remanded.

▌ ANALYSIS

Note that it is not what is said but how it is heard and reasonably understood. Mutual assent of the parties is required for the formation of a contract, but mental assent is not. Where one party can reasonably believe from the other party's acts and words that a real agreement is intended, the other party's real but unexpressed intention is immaterial. Mutual assent is an objective determination based upon what a reasonable man would believe. An offer is an expression of will or intention creating a power of acceptance upon the offeree. If the offer to sell the farm had been for a price of $50, the court could judge the ridiculousness of the offer in determining whether a reasonable man would believe it to be serious.

Quicknotes

MUTUAL ASSENT A requirement of a valid contract that the parties possess a mutuality of assent as manifested by the terms of the agreement and not by a hidden intent.

OFFER A proposed promise to undertake performance of an action, or to refrain from acting, that is to become binding upon acceptance by the offeree.

Embry v. Hargadine, McKittrick Dry Goods Co.

Employee (P) v. Employer (D)

St. Louis Ct. App., 127 Mo. App. 383, 105 S.W. 777 (1907).

NATURE OF CASE: Action to enforce renewal of employment contract.

FACT SUMMARY: Embry (P) was allegedly rehired by Hargadine, McKittrick (D) after his employment contract had expired. Hargadine, McKittrick (D) denied the rehiring.

🏛 RULE OF LAW

The secret feelings, intentions, or beliefs of a party will not affect the formation of a contract if their words and acts indicate that they intend to enter into a binding agreement.

FACTS: Embry (P) was working for Hargadine, McKittrick (D) under a written employment contract. After its expiration, Embry (P) approached McKittrick (D) and demanded a new contract or he would immediately quit. According to Embry (P), McKittrick (D) agreed to rehire him. Embry (P) was terminated in February of the next year. He brought suit to recover the amount due him under the contract. McKittrick (D) swore that the conversation never took place and that Embry (P) had not been rehired. The judge instructed the jury that even if the conversation occurred as related by Embry (P), to form a contract both parties must have intended to enter into a binding agreement. The jury found against Embry (P). He appealed on the basis that the judge's instruction was incorrect, that if McKittrick (D) conveyed by word and deed his intent to rehire Embry (P), a binding contract was formed regardless of McKittrick (D)'s secret intention.

ISSUE: Will a hidden, undisclosed intention affect the formation of a contract?

HOLDING AND DECISION: (Goode, J.) No. If the other party reasonably relies on the promise, an undisclosed intention will not affect the formation of a binding contract. Therefore, the trial judge's instructions were erroneous. If the jury reasonably believed that McKittrick (D) had promised to rehire Embry (P), it is immaterial whether McKittrick (D) meant his promise or not. It is obvious that Embry (P) believed a valid contract had been formed because he remained on the job. His reliance was reasonable since McKittrick (D) was the president of the company and had the authority to rehire him. Therefore, the case must be remanded for a new trial since it cannot be determined on what basis the jury found for McKittrick (D). The same holding applies where a reasonable person would interpret the meaning of a conversation as the formation of a binding contract. The fact that McKittrick (D) did not intend to rehire Embry (P) is immaterial if the natural interpretation of the conversation is that he was being rehired. Again, McKittrick's (D) undisclosed intent is immaterial. Reversed and remanded.

▶ ANALYSIS

In order to analyze the manifest intentions of the parties, there are several standards of interpretation which may be applied to their words. First, there is the generally accepted meaning of the terms used. Then, there is the meaning of the term according to trade or custom. Finally, there is the meaning the parties may have assigned to the term in the course of past dealings. By utilizing these methods, a court attempts to determine what the parties thought they were doing and to give effect to their legitimate expectations.

━━■

Quicknotes

DETRIMENTAL RELIANCE Action by one party, resulting in loss, that is based on the conduct or promises of another.

REASONABLE PERSON STANDARD The standard of care exercised by a hypothetical person who possesses the intelligence, education, knowledge, attention, and judgment required by society of its members when governing behavior; the standard applies to a person's judgment when determining breach of a duty under the theory of negligence.

━━■

Oswald v. Allen

Buyer (P) v. Seller (D)

417 F.2d 43 (2d Cir. 1969).

NATURE OF CASE: Appeal from judgment in favor of defendant in breach of contract case.

FACT SUMMARY: Oswald (P) brought an action against Allen (D) to enforce a contract for the sale of Allen's (D) Swiss coin collection.

RULE OF LAW

A contract does not exist when the terms used to express an agreement are ambivalent, the parties understand the terms in different ways, and neither party should have reasonably been aware of the other party's understanding.

FACTS: Allen (D) owned two coin collections—the "Swiss Coin Collection" and the "Rarity Coin Collection"—and Oswald (P) was interested in purchasing some of the coins. After meeting with Allen (D) and reviewing the coins, Oswald (P) offered to purchase certain coins from each collection, referring to all of them as the "Swiss Coins." After some negotiation, Allen (D) agreed to the sale, thinking "Swiss Coins" referred only to the coins in her "Swiss Coin Collection." Oswald (P) believed he was purchasing all the Swiss coins, including those in the "Rarity Coin Collection." Allen (D) later realized that she had miscounted the number of coins in her "Swiss Coin Collection" and offered Oswald (P) a re-evaluation time. Oswald (P) could not re-evaluate, as he was out of the country, and wrote to Allen (D) to proceed with the sale. Oswald (P) and Allen (D) exchanged correspondence until Allen (D) finally withdrew from the sale at her children's request. Oswald (P) sued Allen (D) to enforce the contract and the trial court found no contract existed, as the parties' minds had not met as to the terms of the contract; specifically, the term "Swiss Coins" was ambiguous. Oswald (P) appealed.

ISSUE: Does a contract exist when the terms used to express an agreement are ambivalent, the parties understand the terms in different ways, and neither party should have reasonably been aware of the other party's understanding?

HOLDING AND DECISION: (Moore, J.) No. A contract does not exist when the terms used to express an agreement are ambivalent, the parties understand the terms in different ways, and neither party should have reasonably been aware of the other party's understanding. Here, Oswald (P) and Allen (D) agreed to the sale of the "Swiss Coins." Oswald (P) understood the term to mean the sale of all Swiss coins, including the Swiss Coin Collection and the Swiss coins in the Rarity Coin Collection. Allen (D)

understood the term to mean only those in the Swiss Coin Collection. None of the parties' correspondences clarified the term "Swiss Coins" and the trial court found the term to be ambiguous. The trial court further found that the different understandings were reasonable and neither party should have reasonably been aware of the other party's understanding. As a result, there is no reasonable basis for choosing between the conflicting understandings. Affirmed.

ANALYSIS

One unique note to this case is that it was decided by a federal court. Usually contract cases such as this are decided by state courts, but federal law allows contract cases in excess of a statutory minimum sum of money to be heard in federal court when the parties are from different states or one party is from a foreign state. Since Oswald (P) was from Switzerland and Allen (D) was an American citizen, Oswald (P) was permitted to invoke federal court jurisdiction by virtue of 28 U.S.C. 1332(a)(2), providing for so-called alienage jurisdiction over actions between aliens and citizens of a state.

■━■

Quicknotes

AMBIGUOUS TERMS Contract terms that are capable of more than one interpretation.

MEETING OF THE MINDS A requirement of a valid contract that the parties possess a mutuality of assent as manifested by the terms of the agreement and not by a hidden intent; enforceability of the contract is limited to those terms to which the parties assented.

■━■

Mesaros v. United States

Consumers (P) v. Federal government (D)

845 F.2d 1576 (Fed. Cir. 1988).

NATURE OF CASE: Breach of contract class action suit.

FACT SUMMARY: Mesaros (P) and other similarly situated plaintiffs brought suit seeking damages for an alleged breach of contract by the Government (D) in failing to deliver Statue of Liberty commemorative coins the plaintiffs had ordered pursuant to an advertisement.

🏛 RULE OF LAW
Where one party solicits and receives an order or other expression of agreement from another, clearly specifying that there is to be no contract until ratification or assent by some officer or representative of the solicitor, the solicitation itself is not an offer, it is a request for an offer.

FACTS: Mesaros (P) and other similarly situated plaintiffs brought suit seeking damages for an alleged breach of contract by the Government (D) in failing to deliver Statue of Liberty commemorative coins the plaintiffs had ordered pursuant to an advertisement. The Government (D) passed an act to raise funds for the restoration of the Statue of Liberty and facilities used for immigration at Ellis Island. Demand for the coins greatly exceeded the Government's (D) expectations. Mesaros's (P) credit card order was rejected on the basis that the Mint (D) was unable to process the order. Investigation revealed that Mesaros's (P) financial institution was not responsible for rejection of the order. Plaintiffs filed suit seeking damages. Summary judgment was granted to the Government (D) and plaintiffs appealed.

ISSUE: Where one party solicits and receives an order or other expression of agreement from another, clearly specifying that there is to be no contract until ratification or assent by some officer or representative of the solicitor, is the solicitation itself an offer?

HOLDING AND DECISION: (Skelton, J.) No. Where one party solicits and receives an order or other expression of agreement from another, clearly specifying that there is to be no contract until ratification or assent by some officer or representative of the solicitor, the solicitation itself is not an offer, it is a request for an offer. The Mint (D) advertisement materials were not an offer of sale of the coins that could be accepted by the plaintiffs to create a contract, and no contract was made between the plaintiffs and the Government (D) with reference to the coins. Affirmed.

▶ ANALYSIS

The rationale behind the rule announced here is explained in Williston's treatise that such advertisements are regarded as "a mere invitation to enter into a bargain rather than an offer." In determining whether an offer has been made, it must be objectively reasonable that the alleged offeree believe that the advertisement or solicitation was intended as an offer. It is unreasonable for persons to believe that advertisements constitute offers that are binding upon the advertiser, since it is conceivable the offeror could be bound by contracts requiring the delivery of goods far in excess of the advertiser's supply.

Quicknotes

CLASS ACTION A suit commenced by a representative on behalf of an ascertainable group that is too large to appear in court, who shares a commonality of interests and who will benefit from a successful result.

OFFER A proposed promise to undertake performance of an action, or to refrain from acting, that is to become binding upon acceptance by the offeree.

SOLICITATION Contact initiated by an attorney for the purpose of obtaining employment.

Academy Chicago Publishers v. Cheever

Publisher (P) v. Widow of author (D)

Ill. Sup. Ct., 578 N.E.2d 981 (1991).

NATURE OF CASE: Appeal from affirmance of judgment for plaintiff in an action to determine the validity of a publishing contract.

FACT SUMMARY: Academy Chicago Publishers (P) filed suit against Mary Cheever (D), the widow of author John Cheever, when she changed her mind after agreeing to the publishing of an anthology of her husband's short stories.

RULE OF LAW
In order for a valid contract to be formed, an offer must be so definite as to its material terms, or require such definite terms in the acceptance, that the promises and performances to be rendered by each party are reasonably certain.

FACTS: The widow of author John Cheever, Mary Cheever (Mrs. Cheever) (D), entered into an agreement with Academy Chicago Publishers (Academy) (P) for the publication of a collection of John Cheever's short stories that had never before been published in a single anthology. However, many terms in the agreement were left unresolved, including the date the final anthology would be delivered to Academy (P), the date the collection would be published, the price it would sell for, the length of the book, and the stories it would contain. After Academy (P) had procured and delivered some sixty stories to Mrs. Cheever (D) to review, and sent her an advance payment, she informed Academy (P) in writing that she objected to the publication of the book, and she attempted to return her advance. Academy (P) filed suit seeking a declaratory judgment compelling Mrs. Cheever's (D) compliance with the agreement. The trial court entered judgment for Academy (P), entering an order that declared that: the contract was enforceable; Mrs. Cheever (D) was entitled to select the stories to be included in the manuscript; she would comply with her obligations if she delivered at least 10 to 15 stories totaling at least 140 pages; and Academy (P) controlled the work's design and format, subject to cooperation with Mrs. Cheever (D). The state's intermediate appellate court affirmed. Academy (P) appealed the rulings favorable to Mrs. Cheever (D), and the state's highest court granted review.

ISSUE: In order for a valid contract to be formed, must an offer be so definite as to its material terms, or require such definite terms in the acceptance, that the promises and performances to be rendered by each party are reasonably certain?

HOLDING AND DECISION: (Heiple, J.) Yes. In order for a valid contract to be formed, an offer must be so definite as to its material terms, or require such definite terms in the acceptance, that the promises and performances to be rendered by each party are reasonably certain. Here, the parties manifested an intent to enter a contract, but failed to provide sufficiently detailed terms to effect that intent. Although a contract may be enforced even though some contract terms may be missing or unresolved, if the essential terms are so uncertain that there is no basis for deciding whether the agreement has been made or broken, then there is. no contract. The pertinent language of the agreement lacks the definite and certain essential terms required for the formation of an enforceable contract and it does not provide the court with a means of determining the intent of the parties. It is not the role of the court to decide which stories should be included in the anthology. Here, a major source of controversy between the parties was the length of the proposed book, and the agreement shed no light on the minimum or maximum number of stories or pages to be published. The agreement was also silent as to which party would decide which stories would be included in the book. The absence of these and other critical terms reflected the absence of mutual assent, or meeting of the minds. The trial court incorrectly supplied minimum compliance terms to the agreement to find that there was an enforceable contract, because there was no standard set by the parties to guide the court in doing so. Reversed.

ANALYSIS

Neither the common law nor the Uniform Commercial Code (UCC) will imply terms where the parties were silent after a conscious or overt attempt at agreement. Furthermore, at common law, an attempt to leave a present term open to be agreed upon later leads to the failure of the contract. However, the UCC is more flexible when the parties leave the price open for later determination as long as the other essential elements are clearly defined.

Quicknotes

DECLARATORY JUDGMENT An adjudication by the courts which grants not relief but is binding over the legal status of the parties involved in the dispute.

Continued on next page.

MATERIAL TERMS OF CONTRACT A fact without the existence of which a contract would not have been entered.

OFFER A proposed promise to undertake performance of an action, or to refrain from acting, that is to become binding upon acceptance by the offeree.

■══■

Akers v. J. B. Sedberry, Inc.

Employee (P) v. Employer (D)

Tenn. Ct. App., 39 Tenn. App. 633, 286 S.W.2d 617 (1955).

NATURE OF CASE: Action for damages for breach of contract.

FACT SUMMARY: J. B. Sedberry's (D) president had not responded to an offer of resignation by Akers (P), an employee under contract, during the conversation in which it took place, but she later sent him a telegram attempting to accept his offer.

🏛 RULE OF LAW
Ordinarily, an offer made by one to another in a face-to-face conversation is deemed to continue only to the close of the conversation and cannot be accepted thereafter.

FACTS: Both Akers (P) and Whitsitt (P) had five-year employment contracts with J. B. Sedberry, Inc. (Sedberry) (D). During a face-to-face conversation with Sedberry's (D) president and primary stockholder, Mrs. Sedberry, the two men said that to show their good faith they would offer to resign on a 90-day notice, provided they were paid according to their contracts for that period. Mrs. Sedberry said nothing about accepting the offer but proceeded to discuss business matters (including friction between the new manager and the two employees). However, four days later, Mrs. Sedberry sent telegrams attempting to accept the offer of resignation. She contended that she had not wanted to respond to the offer until she had a chance to talk with her manager. Akers (P) and Whitsitt (P) brought suits to recover damages for breach of contract. Sedberry (D) appealed judgments awarding both the requested recovery.

ISSUE: Does an offer made in a face-to-face conversation continue only until the end of the conversation?

HOLDING AND DECISION: (Felts, J.) Yes. Ordinarily, an offer made by one to another in a face-to-face conversation is deemed to continue only to the close of their conversation and cannot be accepted thereafter. This is the natural consequence of the rule that an offer must be accepted within the time fixed by the terms of the offer itself or, if no time is fixed, within a reasonable time. What is a reasonable time is a question of fact, depending on the nature of the contract proposed, the usages of business, and other circumstances of the case. In the case at hand, Mrs. Sedberry did not accept the offer made by the time the conversation in which it was made ended. Furthermore, by her conduct, she led the others to believe she had rejected it. Thus, her later attempt to accept it was futile. Affirmed.

▶ ANALYSIS

According to Restatement, Second, Contracts § 41(3), "unless otherwise indicated by the language or the circumstances, . . . an offer sent by mail is seasonably accepted if an acceptance is mailed any time before midnight on the day on which the offer is received." The ability to accept all other offers terminates at the time specified or at the end of a reasonable time. § 41(1).

Quicknotes

ACCEPTANCE Assent to the specified terms of an offer, resulting in the formation of a binding agreement.

OFFER A proposed promise to undertake performance of an action, or to refrain from acting, that is to become binding upon acceptance by the offeree.

Ardente v. Horan

Buyer (P) v. Seller (D)

R.I. Sup. Ct., 117 R.I. 254, 366 A.2d 162 (1976).

NATURE OF CASE: Action to specifically enforce an agreement.

FACT SUMMARY: Ardente (P) asserted that he had accepted the Horans' (D) offer to sell their home and that a contract had thus been formed, but the Horans (D) insisted he had made only a counteroffer.

> ## 🏛 RULE OF LAW
> An acceptance which is equivocal or upon condition or with a limitation is a counteroffer and requires acceptance by the original offeror before a contractual relationship can exist.

FACTS: The Horans (D) offered their home for sale, whereupon Ardente (P) made a $250,000 bid that was communicated to them through their attorney. The attorney advised Ardente (P) that the bid was acceptable to the Horans (D) and prepared a purchase and sale agreement that was forwarded for Ardente's (P) signature to his attorney. Ardente (P) executed the agreement after investigating certain title conditions. His attorney sent it to the Horans (D) along with a $20,000 check and a letter from Ardente's (P) attorney stating his client's concern that certain items remain with the real estate as they would be difficult to replace (dining room set and tapestry in dining room, fireplace fixtures, and sun parlor furniture). It stated, "I would appreciate your confirming that these items are a part of the transaction." The Horans (D) refused to include the items and did not sign the agreement, which their attorney returned along with the check. Ardente (P) filed an action for specific performance, arguing that a contract had been formed. In granting summary judgment for the Horans (D), the court held the aforementioned letter was a conditional acceptance amounting to a counteroffer which was not accepted by the Horans (D).

ISSUE: Is a conditional acceptance treated as a counteroffer which must itself be accepted?

HOLDING AND DECISION: (Doris, J.) Yes. To be effective, an acceptance must be definite and unequivocal. An acceptance which is equivocal or upon condition or with a limitation is a counteroffer and requires acceptance by the original offeror before a contract arises. However, an acceptance may be valid despite conditional language if the acceptance is clearly independent of the condition. Ardente's (P) acceptance was not clearly independent of the condition and thus operated as a counteroffer that was not accepted by the Horans (D). Thus, no contract was formed. Affirmed.

▶ ANALYSIS

Restatement, Second, Contracts § 39, Comment (b) indicates that an offeree can state he is holding the offer under advisement but if the offeror desires to close the bargain immediately, he makes a counteroffer. In this way, the original offer remains open for its original term, but the counteroffer is nonetheless introduced. Thus, the counteroffer does not kill the original offer.

■▬■

Quicknotes

ACCEPTANCE Assent to the specified terms of an offer, resulting in the formation of a binding agreement.

COUNTEROFFER A statement by the offeree which has the legal effect of rejecting the offer and of proposing a new offer to the offeror.

SPECIFIC PERFORMANCE An equitable remedy whereby the court requires the parties to perform their obligations pursuant to a contract.

■▬■

Petterson v. Pattberg

Mortgagee (P) v. Mortgagor (D)

N.Y. Ct. App., 248 N.Y. 86, 161 N.E. 428 (1928).

NATURE OF CASE: Action for breach of contract.

FACT SUMMARY: Pattberg (D) offered to discount the mortgage on J. Petterson's estate on the condition that it was paid on a certain date. Pattberg (D) then sold the mortgage before Petterson (P), as executor of the estate, had paid him.

🏛 RULE OF LAW
An offer to enter into a unilateral contract may be withdrawn at any time prior to performance of the act requested to be done.

FACTS: Pattberg (D) held a mortgage on property belonging to J. Petterson's estate. Petterson (P) was executor of that estate. Pattberg (D) offered to discount the amount of the mortgage on the condition that it was paid on a certain date. Before that date, Petterson (P) went to Pattberg's (D) home and offered to pay him the amount of the mortgage. Pattberg (D) told Petterson (P) that he had already sold the mortgage to a third person.

ISSUE: Can an offer to enter into a unilateral contract be withdrawn prior to performance of the act requested to be done?

HOLDING AND DECISION: (Kellogg, J.) Yes. An offer to enter into a unilateral contract may be withdrawn at any time prior to performance of the act requested to be done. Here, Pattberg's (D) offer proposed to Petterson (P) the making of a unilateral contract, the gift of a promise (to discount the mortgage) in exchange for the performance of an act (payment by a certain date). Pattberg (D) was free to revoke his offer any time before Petterson (P) accepted by performing the act. He revoked the offer by informing Petterson (P) that he had sold the mortgage. An offer to sell property may be withdrawn before acceptance without any formal notice to the person to whom the offer is made. It is sufficient if that person has actual knowledge that the person who made the offer has done some act inconsistent with the continuance of the offer, such as selling the property to a third person. Reversed and complaint dismissed.

DISSENT: (Lehman, J.) Until the act requested was performed, Pattberg (D) had the right to revoke the offer. However, he could not revoke it after Petterson (P) had offered to make the payment.

▶ ANALYSIS

Other facts in *Petterson* which do not appear in the opinion may have influenced the court. The trial record shows that Pattberg (D) was prevented from testifying as to a letter sent to J. Petterson (P), in which the offer was revoked. The record also suggests that Petterson (P) knew of the sale of the mortgage. Note, 1928, 14 *Cornell L.Q.* 81. The Restatement of Contracts, Second, provides, "Where an offer invites an offeree to accept by rendering performance, an option contract is created when the offeree begins performance." Actual performance is necessary. Preparations to perform, though they may be essential to performance, are not enough. However, they may constitute justifiable reliance sufficient to make the offeror's promise binding under § 90.

Quicknotes

ACCEPTANCE Assent to the specified terms of an offer, resulting in the formation of a binding agreement.

MORTGAGE An interest in land created by a written instrument providing security for the payment of a debt or the performance of a duty.

OFFER A proposed promise to undertake performance of an action, or to refrain from acting, that is to become binding upon acceptance by the offeree.

REVOCATION The cancellation or withdrawal of some authority conferred or an instrument drafted, such as the withdrawal of a revocable contract offer prior to the offeree's acceptance.

UNILATERAL CONTRACT An agreement pursuant to which a party agrees to act, or to forbear from acting, in exchange for performance on the part of the other party.

Marchiondo v. Scheck

Offeree (P) v. Offeror (D)

N.M. Sup. Ct., 78 N.M. 440, 432 P.2d 405 (1967).

NATURE OF CASE: Action to recover real estate commission.

FACT SUMMARY: Scheck (D) offered to sell realty to a specified prospective buyer and agreed to pay Marchiondo (P) a broker's commission. Later, Scheck (D) revoked the offer. Shortly after the revocation and within the time limit set by the offer, Marchiondo (P) obtained the offeree's acceptance.

🏛 RULE OF LAW
Where an offer invites an offeree to accept by rendering a performance, an option contract so created is conditional on the offeree's completion of performance in accordance with the terms of the offer.

FACTS: Scheck (D) offered to sell real estate to a specified prospective buyer and agreed to pay Marchiondo (P) a percentage of the sales price as a commission. The offer set a six-day time limit for acceptance, and Marchiondo (P) received Scheck's (D) revocation of the offer on the sixth day. Later that day, Marchiondo (P) obtained the offeree's acceptance.

ISSUE: Does partial performance by the offeree of an offer of a unilateral contract result in a binding contract which is conditional upon the offeree's full performance?

HOLDING AND DECISION: (Wood, J., App. Ct.) Yes. Where an offer invites an offeree to accept by rendering a performance, an option contract is created when the offeree begins to partially perform. The offeror's duty of performance under an option contract so created is conditional on the offeree's completion of performance in accordance with the terms of the offer. In such a case, the offeree's part performance furnishes the acceptance and consideration for a binding contract conditional upon the offeree's full performance. Hence, here, Scheck's (D) right to revoke his offer depends upon whether Marchiondo (P) had partially performed before he received Scheck's (D) revocation. What constitutes partial performance will vary from case to case since what can be done toward performance is determined by what is authorized to be done. Hence, it is a question of fact to be determined at the trial. This case is remanded to the trial court so that it can make a finding on the issue of Marchiondo's (P) partial performance prior to the revocation.

▌ *ANALYSIS*

In many cases involving real estate brokers, it has been held that the owner is no longer privileged to revoke after the broker has taken substantial steps toward rendering performance by advertising the property, soliciting prospective sellers, showing the property, or otherwise. Where notice of revocation is given when the broker's services have proceeded to the point where success is probable, the court may be convinced it was given for the purpose of avoiding payment of the commission while at the same time enjoying the benefit of the services. Such a revocation is in bad faith, and the broker may be held entitled to the commission on the ground that the owner has wrongfully prevented fulfillment of the condition precedent to the right to payment.

Quicknotes

ACCEPTANCE Assent to the specified terms of an offer, resulting in the formation of a binding agreement.

OPTION CONTRACT A contract pursuant to which a seller agrees that property will be available for the buyer to purchase at a specified price and within a certain time period.

PARTIAL PERFORMANCE Partial performance of a contract, promise or obligation.

Davis v. Jacoby

Offeree (P) v. Nephews (D)

Cal. Sup. Ct., 1 Cal. 2d 370, 34 P.2d 1026 (1934).

NATURE OF CASE: Action for specific performance of an alleged contract to make a will.

FACT SUMMARY: Whitehead invited the Davises (P) to help him with his business affairs and to look after his sick wife; the Davises (P) accepted by letter, but before they could move down, Whitehead killed himself.

> ## 🏛 RULE OF LAW
> In case of doubt, it is presumed that an offer invites the formation of a bilateral rather than a unilateral contract.

FACTS: Mr. Whitehead, whose health, as well as his business, was ailing, invited by means of a series of letters his wife's niece, Mrs. Davis (P), and her husband (P), to settle their affairs in Canada and to come and stay with him and his wife. The two families were very close and the Whiteheads regarded Mrs. Davis (P) as their daughter. In one letter, Mr. Whitehead stated that if Mr. Davis (P) could help him with his failing business, and if Mrs. Davis (P) would look after his sick wife, Mrs. Davis (P) "will inherit everything." This letter further asked, "Will you let me hear from you as soon as possible." The Davises (P) immediately dispatched a letter in which they accepted Mr. Whitehead's offer, and started to pack their belongings. Mr. Whitehead again wrote a letter in which he acknowledged receipt of the Davises' (P) acceptance. Before the Davises (P) could leave, Mr. Whitehead committed suicide. The Davises (P) nonetheless came down and tended after Mrs. Whitehead until her death. It was not until that point that the Davises (P) realized that Mr. Whitehead had failed to make a will in their favor and had instead left all his property to some distant nephews (D). In an action brought by the Davises (P) for specific enforcement of the alleged contract to make a will, the trial court ruled that Mr. Whitehead's offer was one to enter into a unilateral contract and since they had not performed prior to his death, the Davises' (P) acceptance by letter was ineffective.

ISSUE: Will an ambiguous offer be interpreted as inviting the formation of a bilateral, rather than a unilateral, contract?

HOLDING AND DECISION: (Per curiam) Yes. In case of doubt, it is presumed that an offer invites the formation of a bilateral contract by an acceptance amounting in effect to a promise by the offeree to perform what the offer requests, rather than the formation of one or more unilateral contracts by actual performance on the part of the offeree. A bilateral contract is favored since it immediately and fully protects the expectations of both parties. Mr. Whitehead's offer was one to enter into a bilateral contract since the facts suggest that he wanted only a promise to perform and not performance. The parties, being very close, were not dealing at arm's length. Mr. Whitehead was looking to the Davises (P) for assurance and peace of mind. He had asked for a reply. When an offer has indicated the mode and means of acceptance, an acceptance in accordance with that mode or means is binding on the offeror. Finally, since the offer contemplated a service which could not be fully performed until after his death—caring for Mrs. Whitehead—he had to rely on the Davises' (P) promise. Consequently, specific performance should be granted. Reversed.

▶ ANALYSIS

U.C.C. § 2-206(1) provides: "Unless otherwise unambiguously indicated by the language or circumstances, (a) an offer to make a contract shall be construed as inviting acceptance in any manner . . . reasonable in the circumstances; (b) an order or other offer to buy goods for prompt or current shipment shall be construed as inviting acceptance either by a prompt promise to ship or by the prompt or current shipment of . . . goods."

Quicknotes

ACCEPTANCE Assent to the specified terms of an offer, resulting in the formation of a binding agreement.

OFFER A proposed promise to undertake performance of an action, or to refrain from acting, that is to become binding upon acceptance by the offeree.

SPECIFIC PERFORMANCE An equitable remedy whereby the court requires the parties to perform their obligations pursuant to a contract.

Houston Dairy, Inc. v. John Hancock Mutual Life Insurance Co.

Borrower (P) v. Lender (D)

643 F.2d 1185 (5th Cir. 1981).

NATURE OF CASE: Appeal from award of liquidated damages in action for breach of loan agreement.

FACT SUMMARY: John Hancock Mutual Life Insurance Co. (D) agreed to loan Houston Dairy, Inc. (P) money if a commitment letter was signed and a deposit forwarded within seven days, but Houston Dairy (P) took 18 days and later asked for its deposit back when it found more favorable loan terms elsewhere.

> **RULE OF LAW**
> A purported "acceptance" by an offeree after the time for acceptance designated by the offeror has expired constitutes a counteroffer, which must be separately accepted in a communication by the original offeror to the original offeree.

FACTS: John Hancock Mutual Life Insurance Co. (John Hancock or Hancock) (D) agreed to loan Houston Dairy, Inc. (P) $800,000 at 9 1/4 percent interest, provided Houston Dairy (P) signed and returned a commitment letter, as well as forwarded a $16,000 deposit, within seven days. Houston Dairy (P) in fact took 18 days to send the signed letter and deposit (in the form of a cashier's check). As the lawyers for Houston Dairy (P) and John Hancock (D) conferred on how the loan would be closed and how their fees would be computed, John Hancock (D) deposited the check. However, a few days later, Houston Dairy (P) found a similar loan at a lower rate of interest and asked for its $16,000 deposit back from John Hancock (D). When John Hancock (D) refused, Houston Dairy (P) sued in federal district court, alleging that Hancock's (D) offer for the loan had expired after seven days and that its forwarding of the letter and deposit constituted a counteroffer, which had not been accepted in a communication from John Hancock (D). The district court disagreed, holding that John Hancock (D) had waived the seven-day limitation and had accepted Houston Dairy's (P) counteroffer and that it was entitled to retain the $16,000 deposit as liquidated damages. Houston Dairy (P) appealed.

ISSUE: Does a purported "acceptance" by an offeree after the time for acceptance designated by the offeror has expired constitute a counteroffer, which must be separately accepted in a communication by the original offeror to the original offeree in order to be binding?

HOLDING AND DECISION: (Ainsworth, J.) Yes. A purported "acceptance" by an offeree after the time designated by the offeror has expired constitutes a counteroffer, which must be separately accepted in a communication by the original offeror to the original offeree in order to be binding. It is fundamental that a contract is formed only upon acceptance of an offer. Just as basic is the principle that an offeror is free to limit acceptance to a fixed time period. Consequently, once an offeror's time period has terminated, a contract may be formed only by formal acceptance of the counteroffer and not by any theory that the offeror waived the expired time limitation. Here, John Hancock's (D) offer expired at the end of seven days. Thus, Houston Dairy's (P) action in signing the commitment letter and returning it with a deposit constituted a counteroffer. However, that counteroffer was not accepted by John Hancock (D); Hancock (D) merely deposited the money and was silent with regard to Houston Dairy (P) as to whether it had accepted Houston Dairy's (P) counteroffer. Nothing in the previous dealings between the parties or the way Hancock (D) dealt with Houston Dairy (P) after the counteroffer suggested or implied that John Hancock (D) could accept the counteroffer through silence and retention of funds. Further, the parties' attorneys had no knowledge of acceptance of the counteroffer which could be charged to Houston Dairy (P), because they were concerned only with their fees and the manner in which the loan would close. Reversed.

> **ANALYSIS**
>
> This case exemplifies the hoary maxim, "The offeror is the master of his offer." The offeror is free to establish any time duration she likes with regard to acceptance of the offer. And when no time for acceptance is specified, courts will imply a "reasonable" time. See, e.g., *Textron Inc v. Froelich*, 223 Pa. Super. 506, 302 A.2d 426 (1973). Further, although silence generally does not constitute an acceptance, Restatement of Contracts § 72 specifies certain circumstances in which inaction may in fact constitute an acceptance, despite the general rule (e.g., offeree accepts services with knowledge the offeror expects to be paid for them, where the offeror has led the offeree to believe silence implies acceptance, or where the previous dealings between the parties have allowed silence as a mode of acceptance).

Quicknotes

COUNTEROFFER A statement by the offeree which has the legal effect of rejecting the offer and of proposing a new offer to the offeror.

Cole-McIntyre-Norfleet Co. v. Holloway

Buyer (D) v. Seller (P)

Tenn. Sup. Ct., 141 Tenn. 679, 214 S.W. 817 (1919).

NATURE OF CASE: Appeal from judgment in a breach of contract action.

FACT SUMMARY: Cole-McIntyre-Norfleet Co. (D) delayed in notifying Holloway (P) of its acceptance or rejection of a contract for delivery of perishable goods.

🏛 RULE OF LAW
Delay in notification amounts to acceptance of an offer when the subject goods of the contract will become unmarketable by delay.

FACTS: On March 16, 1917, a representative of Cole-McIntyre-Norfleet Co. (Cole) (D) received from Holloway (P) an order for goods, which included a number of barrels of meal. Holloway (P), upon receipt of the meal, would resell it at his store. The contract stated that it would not be binding until it was accepted by Cole's (D) main office. For many months, Holloway (P) thought he had entered into a valid contract. Additionally, Cole (D) never notified Holloway (P) of any rejection of the offer despite weekly visits. On May 26, 1917, Holloway (P) demanded delivery of the goods, and Cole (D) refused, claiming it had not accepted Holloway's (P) offer. Holloway (P) was unable to enjoy the benefits of increased prices in the goods for his resale. Holloway (P) sued Cole (D) for breach of contract and the trial court found Cole's (D) delay in notifying Holloway (P) amounted to an acceptance. The appellate court affirmed, and Cole (D) appealed.

ISSUE: Does delay in notification amount to acceptance of an offer when the subject goods of the contract will become unmarketable by delay?

HOLDING AND DECISION: (Lansden, C.J.) Yes. Delay in notification amounts to acceptance of an offer when the subject goods of the contract will become unmarketable by delay. The goods consisted of perishable meal, so time was of the essence. Cole (D) had a number of opportunities to notify Holloway (P) of acceptance or rejection either on its own or through the representative, who had continual contact with Holloway (P). Cole (D) was the offeree in this situation and simply waited to test the market as to whether or not it would deliver the goods, stranding Holloway (P). Such actions are unacceptable. Therefore, Cole's (D) unreasonable delay amounted to an acceptance of Holloway's (P) offer. Writ denied.

▶ ANALYSIS

This case highlights the importance of communicating acceptance. The other primary elements in contract formation are offer and consideration. In these cases, the offeror should specifically dictate what constitutes official acceptance in order to avoid potential conflicts.

━━■

Quicknotes

ACCEPTANCE Assent to the specified terms of an offer, resulting in the formation of a binding agreement.

OFFER A proposed promise to undertake performance of an action, or to refrain from acting, that is to become binding upon acceptance by the offeree.

REJECTION The refusal to accept the terms of an offer.

━━■

Seaview Assn. of Fire Island, N.Y., Inc. v. Williams

Homeowners' association (P) v. Buyer (D)

N.Y. Ct. App., 69 N.Y.2d 987, 517 N.Y.S.2d 709, 510 N.E.2d 793 (1987).

NATURE OF CASE: Appeal from judgment for plaintiff in action to recover homeowners' association fees.

FACT SUMMARY: Seaview (P) brought an action against Williams (D) to collect homeowners' association fees from Williams (D) when Williams (D) bought homes within the Seaview (P) community, even though Williams (D) claimed not to be a member of the association.

🏛 RULE OF LAW
Where there is knowledge that a private community homeowners' association provides facilities and services for the benefit of the community residents, the purchase of property there may manifest acceptance of conditions of ownership, including payment for the facilities and services offered.

FACTS: Seaview Assn. of Fire Island, N.Y., Inc. (Seaview) (P) was a homeowners' association that provides facilities and services to an unincorporated community on Fire Island, generally used as a summer resort. Williams (D) was a full-time resident of Fire Island. He originally owned property outside the Seaview (P) community, but over the years bought seven homes within the Seaview (P) community. Seaview (P) provided numerous services and facilities to the residents of the community for which the residents were required to pay annual assessments. Williams (D) claimed he was not a member of the association, as he did not use the facilities, and therefore refused to pay the assessments. Seaview (P) sued Williams (D) to collect back-assessment payments for the years 1976 through 1984. The trial court found, and the appellate court affirmed, that because Williams (D) bought the seven homes within Seaview (P) with full knowledge of the association requirements, he impliedly accepted the association requirements, and thus had to pay the back fees. Williams (D) appealed.

ISSUE: Where there is knowledge that a private community homeowners' association provides facilities and services for the benefit of the community residents, does the purchase of property there manifest acceptance of conditions of ownership, including payment for the facilities and services offered?

HOLDING AND DECISION: (Memorandum Opinion) Yes. Where there is knowledge that a private community homeowners' association provides facilities and services for the benefit of the community residents, the purchase of property there may manifest acceptance of conditions of ownership, including payment for the facilities and services offered. In this case, Williams (D) bought not one, but seven homes within the Seaview (P) community, with the full knowledge of the association requirements. It did not matter that Williams (D) did not utilize the facilities. When he bought the homes with the notice and knowledge of the association requirements, Williams (D) impliedly accepted the association requirements. As a result, Williams (D) owes the full back payments, and not simply payment proportionate to Williams' (D) use of the facilities. Affirmed.

▶ ANALYSIS

This case highlights the idea of fair play as an alternative to consent in contract cases. Fair play dictates that when parties voluntarily enjoy benefits from collective agreements, obligations will attach to the parties for the benefit of the community. Fair play notions can be applied to entire agreements, thereby obligating an individual enjoying the benefits of collective agreement, as well as to conditions of agreements, requiring parties to agreements to meet certain implied conditions to fairly meet the parties' original intent.

Quicknotes

COLLECTIVE AGREEMENTS Negotiations between an employer and employee that are mediated by a specified third party.

CONSENT A voluntary and willful agreement by an individual possessing sufficient mental capacity to undertake an action suggested by another.

IMPLIED CONDITION A condition that is not expressly stated in the terms of an agreement, but which is inferred from the parties' conduct or the type of dealings involved.

NOTION OF FAIR PLAY Equitable notion that persons must deal with each other fairly and justly.

ProCD, Inc. v. Zeidenberg

Software manufacturer (P) v. Purchaser (D)

86 F.3d 1477 (7th Cir. 1996).

NATURE OF CASE: Appeal from an order in favor of defendant in a case alleging breach of the terms of a shrinkwrap or end-user license.

FACT SUMMARY: When Zeidenberg (D), a customer, bought and then resold the data compiled on its CD-ROM software disk, ProCD, Inc. (P) sued for breach of contract.

> 🏛 **RULE OF LAW**
> A buyer accepts goods when, after an opportunity to inspect, he fails to make an effective rejection.

FACTS: ProCD (P) compiled information from over 3,000 telephone directories into a computer database which it sold on CD-ROM disks. Every box containing the disks declared that the software came with restrictions stated in an enclosed license. This license, which was encoded on the CD-ROM disks as well as printed in the manual, and which appeared on a user's screen every time the software ran, limited use of the application program and listings to noncommercial purposes. Zeidenberg bought a ProCD (P) software package but decided to ignore the license and to resell the information in the database. Zeidenberg (D) also made the information from ProCD's (P) database available over the Internet for a price, through his corporation. ProCD (P) sued for breach of contract. The district court found that placing the package of software on the shelf was an "offer" which the customer "accepted" by paying the asking price and leaving the store with the goods. A contract includes only those terms which the parties have agreed to and one cannot agree to secret terms. Thus, the district court held that buyers of computer software need not obey the terms of shrinkwrap licenses. Such licenses were found to be ineffectual because their terms did not appear on the outsides of the packages. ProCD (P) appealed.

ISSUE: Does a buyer accept goods when, after an opportunity to inspect, he fails to make an effective rejection?

HOLDING AND DECISION: (Easterbrook, J.) Yes. A buyer accepts goods when, after an opportunity to inspect, he fails to make an effective rejection under § 2-602 of the Uniform Commercial Code. A vendor, as master of the offer, may invite acceptance by conduct, and may propose limitations on the kind of conduct that constitutes acceptance. ProCD (P) proposed a contract that a buyer would accept by using the software after having an opportunity to read the license at leisure. Zeidenberg (D) did this, since he had no choice when the software splashed the license across his computer screen and would not let him proceed without indicating acceptance. The license was an ordinary contract accompanying the sale of products and was therefore governed by the common law of contracts and the Uniform Commercial Code. Transactions in which the exchange of money precedes the communication of detailed terms are common—buying insurance or buying a plane ticket being two common examples. ProCD (P) extended an opportunity to reject if a buyer should find the license terms unsatisfactory. Zeidenberg (D) inspected the package, tried out the software, learned of the license, and did not reject the goods. Reversed and remanded.

▶ **ANALYSIS**

The sale of information contained in computer databases presented new challenges to courts. Some courts found that the sale of software was the sale of services, rather than of goods. This case treated the sale of software as a sale of goods governed by Article 2 of the Uniform Commercial Code.

▬▬

Quicknotes

CD-ROM Compact disc—read only memory.

INSPECTION OF GOODS The examination of goods, which are the subject matter of a contract for sale, for the purpose of determining whether they are satisfactory.

REJECTION The refusal to accept the terms of an offer.

SHRINKWRAP LICENSE Terms of restriction packaged inside a product.

U.C.C. § 2-602 Provides that a rejection after an opportunity to inspect may be effective unless the buyer manifests acceptance in the manner invited by the offeror.

▬▬

Empire Machinery Co. v. Litton Business Telephone Systems

Buyer-offeror (P) v. Seller-offeree (D)

Ariz. Ct. App., 115 Ariz. 568, 566 P.2d 1044 (1977).

NATURE OF CASE: Appeal from summary judgment denying damages for breach of contract.

FACT SUMMARY: In response to a breach of contract action brought by Empire Machinery Co. (Empire) (P), Litton (D) claimed that it never accepted Empire's (P) offer to purchase a telephone system.

🏛 RULE OF LAW
Where a buyer-offeror makes an offer to purchase by means of a form supplied by the seller-offeree, the buyer-offeror has the power to waive any specified manner of acceptance in such a form, and thus the offer can be deemed accepted and ripened into a contract if the seller-offeree takes actions that are directed toward the contractual obligation.

FACTS: Litton (D), the seller-offeree, submitted a "sales agreement" to Empire Machinery Co. (Empire) (P), the buyer-offeror, for the installation of a telephone system. Empire (P) signed the agreement which included a clause that stated the "agreement shall become effective only upon approval, acceptance and execution by the Litton (D) home office." Subsequent to Empire's (P) signing of this agreement: (1) Litton (D) wrote Mountain Bell Telephone Co. concerning its contractual relationship with Empire (P) and that it was installing the new telephone system; (2) Empire (P) at Litton's (D) request purchased $12,000 worth of telephone installation equipment; (3) Litton (D) cashed a check for $8,546 that Empire (P) had given to Litton (D) as a down payment; and (4) Litton (D) requested that Mountain Bell Telephone give Empire (P) a new telephone number. Six months after Empire (P) had signed the "sales agreement," Litton (D) refunded Empire's (P) down payment and informed Empire (P) that it would be unable to install the new telephone system. Empire (P) then sued Litton (D) for breach of contract. The trial court found that Litton (D) had never accepted Empire's (P) offer to purchase in the manner specifically described in the sales agreement. Therefore, the trial court granted a summary judgment in favor of Litton (D). Empire (P) appealed.

ISSUE: Can the conduct of an offeree constitute a valid acceptance, even though the offer by its terms indicates that acceptance can only be made in a particular manner?

HOLDING AND DECISION: (Jacobson, J.) Yes. Where a buyer-offeror makes an offer to purchase by means of a form supplied by the seller-offeree, the buyer-offeror has the power to waive any specified manner of acceptance in such a form, and thus the offer can be deemed accepted and ripened into a contract if the seller-offeree takes actions that are directed towards fulfilling the contractual obligations. Here, the fact that Litton (D) notified Mountain Bell Telephone of its contractual relationship with Empire (P), cashed Empire's (P) check, and requested Mountain Bell Telephone to issue Empire (P) a telephone number demonstrated conduct that constituted sufficient evidence that Litton (D) accepted Empire's (P) offer to purchase. This evidence coupled with the fact that Empire (P) had the power to waive the clause in the "sales agreement," which required Litton's (D) home office approval before Litton (D) could accept, is sufficient evidence for a trier of fact to find that Litton (D) accepted Empire's (P) offer to purchase. Reversed and remanded.

▶ ANALYSIS

The court held that the submission of the "sales agreement" by Litton (D) to Empire (P) was not an offer. This decision was based on Corbin, *Contracts* § 88 (1963), which states: When one party solicits and receives an order or other expression of agreement from another, clearly specifying that there is to be no contract until ratification or assent by some officer or representative of the solicitor, the solicitation is not itself an offer; it is a request for an offer. The order that is given upon such request is an offer, not an acceptance.

■▬■

Quicknotes

ACCEPTANCE Assent to the specified terms of an offer, resulting in the formation of a binding agreement.

OFFER A proposed promise to undertake performance of an action, or to refrain from acting, that is to become binding upon acceptance by the offeree.

SOLICITATION Contact initiated by an attorney for the purpose of obtaining employment.

■▬■

Power Paragon, Inc. v. Precision Technology USA, Inc.

Manufacturer (P) v. Manufacturer (D)

605 F. Supp. 2d 722 (E.D. Va. 2008).

NATURE OF CASE: Motion to dismiss for improper venue in action for breach of contract and unjust enrichment.

FACT SUMMARY: Power Paragon, Inc. (P) contended that a forum selection clause in Precision Technology USA, Inc.'s (Precision's) (D) purchase order did not become part of their contract for delivery, installation, and support of a product manufactured by Power Paragon (P) because the purchase order materially altered Power Paragon's (P) offer. Precision (D) contended that the forum selection provision in its purchase order was controlling.

🏛 RULE OF LAW
An offer expires according to its express term, so that once expired it cannot be accepted.

FACTS: In response to an email solicitation from Precision Technology USA, Inc. (Precision) (D), Power Paragon, Inc.'s (P) parent company, L-3 Communications Corp. (L-3), sent to Precision (D) a proposal on December 20, 2005, for delivery, installation, and support of a product manufactured by Power Paragon (P). Discussions between the parties ensued, and, on March 1, 2006, L-3 sent Precision (D) a letter that included pricing details. On March 10, 2006, in response, Precision (D) sent a purchase order that established the contract price and the price for support. The purchase order contained a forum selection clause that specified that venue would be in the applicable state or federal court in Roanoke, Virginia—which is in the Western District of Virginia. The product was eventually shipped to its intended destination. Based upon the agreed upon payment terms, Power Paragon (P) was to be paid for the product in seven monthly payments, but Precision (D) made only the first three, and Precision (D) also refused to pay Power Paragon's (P) invoices for support. Power Paragon (P) brought suit against Precision (D) in federal court in the Eastern District for Virginia for breach of contract and unjust enrichment. Precision (D) moved to dismiss the case for improper venue, contending that the forum selection clause in its purchase order was controlling. Power Paragon (P) contended that the terms of its December 20, 2005 letter, requiring arbitration of disputes, were controlling. The district court considered the motion.

ISSUE: Does an offer expire according to its express term, so that once expired, it cannot be accepted?

HOLDING AND DECISION: (Jackson, J.) Yes. An offer expires according to its express term, so that once expired it cannot be accepted. The determination of which

forum selection provision controls must be decided under the Uniform Commercial Code's (UCC's) "battle of the forms" provisions. Power Paragon (P) asserts that its December 20, 2005 proposal was the offer and that Precision's (D) March 10, 2006 purchase order constituted the acceptance of that offer. Under UCC § 2-207, an accepting merchant's additional terms that are different from the offering merchant's terms become part of the contract unless they materially alter the offeror's terms. Thus, Power Paragon (P) argues that because Precision's (D) venue and choice of law provisions were in direct conflict with Power Paragon's (P) arbitration provision, the two terms were "knocked out" under § 2-207. Power Paragon (P) argues that the additional forum selection term also materially altered its arbitration term. However, Power Paragon's (P) analysis fails to take into account the effect that the actual timing of contract formation had on the terms of its offer, which expressly provided that it would remain open for only 45 days. State law provides that an offer remains open for a reasonable time or for such time as the parties treat the offer as continuing. Therefore, Power Paragon's (P) offer expired after February 3, 2006, and Precision (D) could not accept it after that date—it was as if the offer had never been made. Under UCC § 2-206, an order between merchants for the sale of goods is treated as an offer, which can be accepted by prompt shipment of conforming or nonconforming goods. Accordingly, Precision's (D) purchase order constituted the offer, and Power Paragon's (P) shipment constituted the acceptance of that offer, along with the offer's forum selection provisions. As such, Precision's (D) choice of venue governs the case. Therefore, although the motion to dismiss for improper venue is denied, the case is transferred to the correct venue under the parties' contract, i.e., to the district court in the Western District of Virginia.

▌ *ANALYSIS*

As this case illustrates, under the UCC's battle of the forms provisions, a crucial determination is which form constitutes the offer and which form constitutes the acceptance. If Power Paragon's (P) offer of December 20, 2005, had not limited how long it would stay open, arguably, Precision's (D) purchase order of March 10, 2006, would have constituted the offer's acceptance—contrary to the actual result in the case. Under UCC § 2-207, in such instance, if the purchase order's acceptance did not expressly limit acceptance to its own terms, there would be a contract

Continued on next page.

notwithstanding that the purchase order contained terms that were in addition to or different from those in Power Paragon's (P) proposal. At this point, as Power Paragon (P) suggested in its arguments to the court, if Precision's (D) terms could not coexist with Power Paragon's (P) terms, both terms would be "knocked out" of the contract and UCC gap-fillers would step in. Here, because arbitration and judicial resolution of disputes cannot co-exist, those terms would have been "knocked out." In addition, Precision's (D) venue selection terms arguably would have been considered outside the contract because they materially altered Power Paragon's (P) arbitration terms.

■═■

Quicknotes

FORUM SHOPPING Refers to a situation in which one party to an action seeks to have the matter heard and determined by a court or in a jurisdiction that will provide it with the most favorable result.

■═■

Ionics, Inc. v. Elmwood Sensors, Inc.

Buyer (P) v. Seller (D)

110 F.3d 184 (1st Cir. 1997).

NATURE OF CASE: Breach of contract suit.

FACT SUMMARY: Ionics (P) sued Elmwood (D) to recover costs incurred as the result of fires allegedly caused by defective thermostats it purchased from Elmwood (D).

RULE OF LAW
Where the terms in two forms are contradictory, each party is assumed to object to the other party's conflicting clause.

FACTS: Ionics, Inc. (P) purchased thermostats from Elmwood Sensors, Inc. (Elmwood) (D) for installation in water dispensers which it manufactured. Ionics' (P) order included language stating that the contract would be governed exclusively by the terms included on the purchase order and that all remedies available under state law would be available to Ionics (P). Elmwood (D) sent Ionics (P) an Acknowledgement stating that the contract was governed exclusively by the terms in the Acknowledgment, including a limitation on Elmwood's (D) liability. Several of the dispensers later caused fires which allegedly resulted from the defects in the sensors. Ionics (P) brought suit to recover costs incurred as a result of the fires. The district court denied Elwood's (D) motion for summary judgment.

ISSUE: Where the terms in two forms are contradictory, is each party assumed to object to the other party's conflicting clause?

HOLDING AND DECISION: (Torruella, C.J.) Yes. Where the terms in two forms are contradictory, each party is assumed to object to the other party's conflicting clause. This case involves a "battle of the forms." The issue to be resolved is whether the language of Uniform Commercial Code (UCC) § 2-207(1) or (3) applies. Mere acceptance of the goods by the buyer is insufficient to infer consent to the seller's terms under the language of § 2-207(1), nor do such terms become a part of the contract under subsection (2) because notification of the objection has been given by the conflicting forms. Section 2-207(3) prevails and the terms of the particular contract consists of those on which the writings of the parties agree. Affirmed and remanded.

ANALYSIS

The court here expressly overrules its holding in *Roto-Lith, Ltd. v. F.P. Bartlett & Co.*, 297 F.2d 497 (1st Cir. 1962), which held that § 2-207(1) applied. The purpose of § 2-207 was to modify the harshness of the "mirror image rule," which provided that a response that did not precisely "mirror"

the terms of an offer constituted a rejection and counter-offer. Moreover, it would give the power to the sender of the last form to dictate the terms of the agreement and essentially rewrite the contract.

Quicknotes

ACCEPTANCE Assent to the specified terms of an offer, resulting in the formation of a binding agreement.

COUNTEROFFER A statement by the offeree which has the legal effect of rejecting the offer and of proposing a new offer to the offeror.

OFFER A proposed promise to undertake performance of an action, or to refrain from acting, that is to become binding upon acceptance by the offeree.

Sun Printing & Publishing Assn. v. Remington Paper & Power Co., Inc.

Buyer (P) v. Seller (D)

N.Y. Ct. App., 235 N.Y. 338, 139 N.E. 470 (1923).

NATURE OF CASE: Appeal from appellate court reversal of judgment invalidating contract.

FACT SUMMARY: Sun (P) brought an action against Remington (D) to collect damages resulting from Remington's (D) refusal to deliver rolls of paper to Sun (P).

🏛 RULE OF LAW
A contract will be deemed invalid due to incompleteness if the agreement does not establish the length of time the terms of the agreement, such as the price, shall apply.

FACTS: Sun Printing & Publishing Assn. (Sun) (P) and Remington Paper & Power Co., Inc. (Remington) (D) entered into an agreement for Remington (D) to sell Sun (P) 16,000 tons of paper between September, 1919, and December, 1920—1,000 tons per month. For the first four months of the agreement, which was drafted by Remington (D), the price and the length of time that price would apply were clearly established. The remaining time in the contract called for the price to be determined by the parties, but not to exceed the price charged by the Canadian Export Paper Company. The length of time that price would apply was to be determined by the parties as well. Remington (D) delivered the paper to Sun (P) for the first four months, but then refused to deliver any more, claiming the contract was incomplete, as no price or length of time for a price had been established in the contract. Sun (P) demanded delivery for the remaining months and then sued Remington (D) for damages resulting from its failure to deliver. The trial court found in favor of Remington (D), stating that the contract was incomplete as it did not specify the length of time any agreed-upon price would be in effect. However, the appellate court reversed, noting that the parties intended to make a binding contract and with the rule of reason, the court could fashion terms in the light of fair dealing. Remington (D) appealed.

ISSUE: Is a contract invalid due to incompleteness if the agreement does not establish the length of time the terms of the agreement, such as the price, shall apply?

HOLDING AND DECISION: (Cardozo, J.) Yes. A contract will be deemed invalid due to incompleteness if the agreement does not establish the length of time the terms of the agreement, such as the price, shall apply. Here, the contract, after the first four months, did not specify the price or the length of time that price shall apply to the parties. Both elements are essential to the contract. If only the price were left open, it could be reasoned that Sun (P) was the holder of an option. However, because the length of time that price would apply was left open, the contract was incomplete. Despite the definiteness of the maximum placed by the Canadian Export Paper Company, no one knew if that price would change, or when. Remington (D) would be left on a day-to-day whim of the market, never assured of its position. Because of this, the agreement with respect to time is as essential as the agreement with respect to price. The court cannot take that active a role in determining what the parties intended when such terms are left out of the agreement. Therefore, while the time was undetermined, the agreement was invalid. Reversed.

DISSENT: (Crane, J.) The rules of reason and fair dealing should govern this case, and a fair contract should be fashioned. The parties intended for the sale of 16,000 tons of paper. Remington (D) drew up the contract and was aware of the overall purpose of the agreement. As to the vagueness in price, the parties allowed for the maximum established by the Canadian Export Paper Company. As for the vagueness in time, the court should fashion a fair interpretation of what the parties originally intended, from the facts available. This would not be an overinterpretation by the court, but rather an assertion of the principle of fair dealing.

▶ ANALYSIS

This case highlights the issue of the formulation of contracts in the context of negotiations. Generally, when negotiations are in progress, agreements by the parties on specific points in the contract, before the contract is agreed upon as a final whole, are not intended to have legal consequences until the whole contract takes effect.

Quicknotes

FAIR DEALING An implied warranty that the parties will deal honestly in the satisfaction of their obligations and without an intent to defraud.

Arnold Palmer Golf Co. v. Fuqua Industries, Inc.

Golf-supplies marketer (P) v. Golf-supplies manufacturer (D)

541 F.2d 584 (6th Cir. 1976).

NATURE OF CASE: Suit for breach of contract.

FACT SUMMARY: Arnold Palmer Golf Co. (P) and Fuqua Industries, Inc. (D) negotiated and drafted a six-page "memorandum of intent" outlining their planned business relationship. The manufacturer then unilaterally terminated the transaction.

🏛 RULE OF LAW
A trial court cannot grant summary judgment in a contract dispute where the writing itself and extrinsic evidence support conflicting inferences on whether the parties intended to be bound by the writing.

FACTS: Arnold Palmer Golf Co. (Palmer) (P), a golf-supplies marketer, sought to expand its golf-supplies design and marketing business by affiliating with Fuqua Industries, Inc. (Fuqua) (D), a golf-supplies manufacturer. The two companies held several meetings throughout 1969 to discuss a business relationship. In late 1969, the discussions resulted in a negotiated, mutually reviewed six-page "memorandum of intent." The memorandum provided that a "general understanding ha[d] been reached" between the companies about their planned affiliation. The document stated that the transaction depended on counsel for both sides drafting a "definitive agreement," and that the companies' obligations were conditioned on the drafting of that definitive agreement and on the approval of Fuqua's (D) board of directors. The memorandum also, however, described many specific areas of the parties' relationship in unqualified terms. Representatives for both companies signed the memorandum. In January 1970, Fuqua's (D) president informed the news media that the two companies "ha[d] agreed to cooperate in an enterprise. . . ." In February 1970, Fuqua (D) unilaterally terminated the transaction. Palmer (P) sued for breach of contract. The trial court granted Fuqua's (D) motion for summary judgment, reasoning that the parties' "memorandum of intent" was not a contract because they did not intend to be bound by it. Palmer (P) appealed.

ISSUE: Can a trial court grant summary judgment in a contract dispute where the writing itself and extrinsic evidence support conflicting inferences on whether the parties intended to be bound by the writing?

HOLDING AND DECISION: (McCree, J.) No. A trial court cannot grant summary judgment in a contract dispute where the writing itself and extrinsic evidence support conflicting inferences on whether the parties intended to be bound by the writing. In this case, a trier of fact must decide whether the parties intended to be bound by the

"memorandum of intent" because, at this stage of the proceedings, evidence supports reasonable inferences for both parties' interpretations. The memorandum's requirement of a later "definitive agreement" suggests that the parties did not intend to be bound by the writing. On the other hand, the whole document, in addition to the circumstances under which it was adopted, is relevant to determining the parties' intent. The memorandum's unqualified statement of many terms in the planned transaction justifies an inference that the parties did intend to be bound, and so does the public statement by Fuqua's (D) president. The provision requiring a "definitive agreement" can be read either as requiring a memorialization of an agreement that had already been entered or as evincing intent not to be bound. Given the fact-issues on the question of the parties' intent, the case cannot be decided on summary judgment. Reversed and remanded.

▶ ANALYSIS

On the substantive issues of contract law in *Arnold Palmer*, one should note at least two key practice points. First, a writing such as the "memorandum of intent" in this case should unambiguously state whether the parties intend to be bound by the writing. Second, the writing should not then implicitly contradict its own express statements about the parties' intent. Here, for example, any express statement that the parties did not intend to be bound—which is a reasonable construction of the memorandum's tenth and eleventh paragraphs—was implicitly undermined by the document's own unqualified statements of several important terms in the parties' planned business relationship.

◼▬◼

Quicknotes

EXTRINSIC EVIDENCE Evidence that is not contained within the text of a document or contract but which is derived from the parties' statements or the circumstances under which the agreement was made.

SUMMARY JUDGMENT Judgment rendered by a court in response to a motion by one of the parties, claiming that the lack of a question of material fact in respect to an issue warrants disposition of the issue without consideration by the jury.

◼▬◼

Copeland v. Baskin Robbins U.S.A.

Purchaser (P) v. Seller (D)

Cal. Ct. App., 96 Cal. App. 4th 1251, 117 Cal Rptr. 2d 875 (2002).

NATURE OF CASE: Appeal from summary judgment for defendant in action for breach of contract.

FACT SUMMARY: Copeland (P) brought a breach of contract action against Baskin Robbins U.S.A. (D) on the theory that an enforceable contract was formed by the parties' agreement to negotiate a mutual purchase arrangement.

> 🏛 **RULE OF LAW**
> A contract to negotiate an agreement can be formed and breached like any other contract.

FACTS: Baskin Robbins U.S.A. (D) publicly announced its intentions to close one of its manufacturing plants, and Copeland (P) expressed an interest in acquiring it, provided Baskin Robbins (D) would agree to purchase ice cream he manufactured at the plant. The parties reached a tentative agreement that Copeland (P) would purchase the plant and Baskin Robbins (D) would purchase seven million gallons of ice cream from Copeland (P) over a three-year period. This duel purchasing arrangement is known as "co-packing" and was considered critical to Copeland (P). The agreement was confirmed in letters between the parties, and Copeland (P) submitted a $3,000 deposit to Baskin Robbins (D). Negotiations broke down, however, over the additional terms for the purchase of the ice cream, including the price, flavor, quality control standards, trademark protection and who would bear the loss from spoilage. Baskin Robbins (D) returned Copeland's (P) deposit and informed Copeland (P) that it would continue negotiations on the sale of the plant and the lease of the plant's assets, but not on the part of the agreement for purchase of the ice cream. Copeland (P) sued, alleging Baskin Robbins (D) breached the contract by refusing to reach agreement on the terms for the co-packing agreement, or, alternatively, that it failed to negotiate in good faith. The trial court granted Baskin Robbins' (D) motion for summary judgment, finding that the essential elements of the co-packing deal were never agreed upon, and, consequently, there was no enforceable contract. The state's intermediate appellate court granted review.

ISSUE: Can a contract to negotiate an agreement be formed and breached like any other contract?

HOLDING AND DECISION: (Johnson, J.) Yes. A contract to negotiate an agreement can be formed and breached like any other contract. It is still a general rule that, where the essential elements of a promise are reserved for future agreement, no legal obligation arises until that future agreement is reached. However, persons are free to enter into contracts for anything that does not involve illegal or immoral subject matter, and a valid contract to negotiate the remaining terms of a contract can be entered into by the parties. This is distinguishable from an unenforceable "agreement to agree" for two reasons. First, a contract to negotiate terms of an agreement is not of the same substance as a mere "agreement to agree" in that such a contract is discharged as long as the parties negotiate in good faith. Second, performance is ascertainable in that sufficient terms of the negotiation can be articulated creating the required substantive elements of the contract. In this instance, where the negotiations concern the sale of goods, the correspondence between the parties sufficiently identified the subject matter as more than just an "idea," and binds the parties to complete the negotiations. Consequently, the covenant of good faith and fair dealing applies. Sound public policy reasons exist for protecting parties from bad faith practices during business negotiations. Negotiations today are extremely complex and are often reached on a piecemeal basis through a series of communications. These slow forming contracts are time consuming and costly, and the parties' investments should be protected from bad faith dealing. However, here, damages lie only on the basis of reliance theory because expectation damages are not ascertainable. Here, Copeland (P) cannot recover because there is no way to know what the ultimate terms of the agreement would have been if there had ever been an agreement. Therefore, summary judgment is appropriate, but on grounds that differ from those on which the trial court granted summary judgment. Affirmed.

> ▌ *ANALYSIS*
>
> This decision attempts to reach an equitable result by recognizing the complexity and cost associated with modern business negotiations while balancing available damages should a party succeed on this theory of breach. As noted, the court of appeals affirmed the trial court's grant of summary judgment to Baskin Robbins (D). The court of appeals found that the proper measure of damages for breach of a contract to negotiate would be reliance damages, or those damages incurred by the plaintiff's reliance on the defendant to negotiate in good faith. This measure of damages would encompass the plaintiff's out-of-pocket costs in conducting the negotiations and potentially lost opportunity costs. Expectation damages in a situation such as the one at bar cannot be recovered as there is no adequate way of predicting the terms of the

Continued on next page.

final agreement or if such a final agreement would have been reached. In this instance, Copeland (P) disavowed reliance damages, so there were no remaining genuine issues of material fact. Accordingly, summary judgment was still appropriate, but not based on a failure of the parties to form a contract.

■══■

Quicknotes

EXPECTATION DAMAGES Damages awarded in actions for non-performance of a contract, which are calculated by subtracting the injured party's actual dollar position as a result of the breach from that party's expected dollar position had the breach not occurred.

■══■

Chomicky v. Buttolph

Buyer (P) v. Seller (D)

Vt. Sup. Ct., 147 Vt. 128, 513 A.2d 1174 (1986).

NATURE OF CASE: Appeal challenging lower court's decision to order specific performance for the sale of land.

FACT SUMMARY: Chomicky (P) sued Buttolph (D) for specific performance for the sale of land, claiming that an oral contract that they had allegedly concluded over the phone was binding.

RULE OF LAW
Contracts for the sale of land, and any proposed changes and modifications to such contracts, must be in writing to be enforceable.

FACTS: Buttolph (D) owned a parcel of lakeside property and wanted to sell a portion of the property. Chomicky (P) and Buttolph (D) discussed the sale and drew up a purchase and sale agreement reflecting the terms of their agreement. The contract was made contingent on Chomicky (P) obtaining a subdivision permit from the Planning Commission. While the petition was pending, the parties discussed an alternative to the contract, in the event that the permit was denied, whereby Buttolph (D) would grant Chomicky (P) a right-of-way in lieu of outright ownership. On October 1, 1985, Buttolph (D) called Chomicky (P) and said that the right-of-way alternative they had discussed would be acceptable, but the parties made no formal, written form of this alternative. On October 12, 1985, the Commission rejected Chomicky's (P) petition, and Chomicky (P) requested that the right-of-way alternative take effect. Buttolph (D) refused, and Chomicky (P) sued for specific performance based on the oral agreement regarding the alternative. The lower court found in favor of Chomicky (P), and Buttolph (D) appealed.

ISSUE: Must contracts for the sale of land, and any proposed changes and modifications to such contract, be in writing to be enforceable?

HOLDING AND DECISION: (Hill, J.) Yes. Contracts for the sale of land, and any proposed changes and modifications to such contract, must be in writing to be enforceable. The requirement of a writing for a contract to sell land, or for any modification to that contract, ensures that such contracts or interests therein are not entered into improvidently. Here, while the parties entered into a written contract contingent on the approval of a subdivision permit, they did not formalize the alleged modification of the contract in a writing, and therefore the modification violated the Statute of Frauds. Furthermore, Chomicky (P) may not rely on the doctrine of part performance, as Chomicky (P) did not show evidence supporting a valid claim that he substantially and irretrievably changed his position in reliance on the oral agreement. Reversed.

▶ **ANALYSIS**

With the exception of three states, all jurisdictions have general statutes of frauds. Each state's specific statute, however, can vary in its wording, so one must take care to examine the specific requirements of each state's statute when dealing with this issue. In addition to contracts for the sale of land, other contracts generally covered by the Statute of Frauds include agreements not to be performed within one year or within the lifetime of the promisor, promises to pay another's debts, and promises made upon consideration of marriage. Land contracts, however, remain the most frequently litigated agreement under modern statutes of frauds.

■━■

Quicknotes

PART PERFORMANCE Partial performance of a contract, promise or obligation.

RELIANCE Dependence on a fact that causes a party to act or refrain from acting.

RIGHT-OF-WAY The right of a party to pass over the property of another.

SPECIFIC PERFORMANCE An equitable remedy whereby the court requires the parties to perform their obligations pursuant to a contract.

STATUTE OF FRAUDS A statute that requires specified types of contracts to be in writing in order to be binding.

■━■

Radke v. Brenon

Buyer (P) v. Seller (D)

Minn. Sup. Ct., 271 Minn. 35, 134 N.W.2d 887 (1965).

NATURE OF CASE: Appeal challenging lower court's decision to order specific performance for the sale of land.

FACT SUMMARY: Radke (P) sued Brenon (D) for specific performance for the sale of land, claiming that under the circumstances, a letter written by Brenon (D) to Radke (P) offering the land was a memorandum sufficient to satisfy the Statute of Frauds.

🏛 **RULE OF LAW**
Under Minnesota law, memoranda regarding the sale of land are sufficient under the Statute of Frauds when the memoranda express the consideration; are inscribed by the party by whom the sale is to be made or by his lawful agent authorized in writing, and state expressly or by necessary implication the parties to the contract, the lands involved, and the general terms and conditions upon which the sale will be made.

FACTS: After Brenon (D) acquired a parcel of lakeside property, he decided to sell portions of the property to Radke (P) and his other neighbors. Brenon (D) sent an official letter, with his name typed on it, offering to sell each parcel of land for $212 to each of his neighbors. Radke (P) expressed interest in the purchase. Sometime later, two neighbors declined the offering, so the sale price increased to $262. On May 7, 1961, Radke (P) accepted the new offer and agreed to buy the land. Some delays in the delivery of abstracts occurred, but on August 14, Radke (P) wrote a check to Brenon (D) for $262 to complete the sale, but withheld payment until the delivery of the deed occurred. On August 16, Brenon (D) wrote Radke (P) that the offer to sell was revoked. Radke (P) sued Brenon (D) for specific performance of the sale and the trial court ruled in favor of Radke (P). Brenon (D) appealed.

ISSUE: Under Minnesota law, are memoranda regarding the sale of land sufficient under the Statute of Frauds when the memoranda express the consideration; are inscribed by the party by whom the sale is to be made or by his lawful agent authorized in writing; and state expressly or by necessary implication the parties to the contract, the lands involved, and the general terms and conditions upon which the sale will be made?

HOLDING AND DECISION: (Rogosheske, J.) Yes. Under Minnesota law, memoranda regarding the sale of land are sufficient under the Statute of Frauds when the memoranda express the consideration; are inscribed by the party by whom the sale is to be made or by his lawful agent authorized in writing; and state expressly or by necessary implication the parties to the contract, the lands involved, and the general terms and conditions upon which the sale will be made. While the Statute of Frauds requires a writing for the sale of land, courts must also look to the intention of the statute to avoid fraud in the sale of land by both parties. Here, Brenon's (D) letter was sufficient to satisfy the statute. The expressed consideration requirement is satisfied, despite the subsequent change from $212 to $262, because the letter included the price and there was no dispute that the price represented an equal share each neighbor would pay for his parcel. The subscription requirement is satisfied because Brenon's (D) typewritten name was tantamount to a signature and, although his wife jointly owned the property and did not sign the letter, Brenon (D) did not raise that issue at trial and cannot originate it on appeal. Furthermore, Radke's (P) name was included in the letter and Brenon's (D) name was at the bottom. The land to be sold was positively delineated. By the parties' conversations before and after the receipt of the letter, no confusion existed as to the property sold or the terms of the contract. Each case regarding the sufficiency of a memorandum is to be decided on a case-by-case basis. Here, the letter was sufficient. Affirmed.

📝 **ANALYSIS**

When analyzing a state's Statute of Frauds, three primary issues will arise. First, you must ask whether the writing falls within the state's statute. Second, you must examine the specific conditions under which the statute is satisfied. Third, you must examine the legal ramifications if the statute is not satisfied.

Quicknotes

CONSIDERATION Value given by one party in exchange for performance, or a promise to perform, by another party.

MEMORANDUM A brief written note outlining the terms of a transaction or an agreement.

STATUTE OF FRAUDS A statute that requires specified types of contracts to be in writing in order to be binding.

Powell v. City of Newton

Property owner (P) v. Municipality (D)

N.C. Sup. Ct., 703 N.E.2d 723 (2010).

NATURE OF CASE: Appeal from affirmance of order requiring specific performance of an agreement settling an action for trespass.

FACT SUMMARY: Powell (P) contended that a settlement agreement with the City of Newton ("the City") (D) that he agreed to in open court and orally ratified violated the statute of frauds because it lacked his signature, so that it was error to order specific performance of the agreement. The City contended that Powell's (P) in-court statements combined with email correspondence between counsels for the parties constituted the requisite signature under the statute of frauds.

🏛 RULE OF LAW
The doctrine of judicial estoppel renders enforceable a settlement agreement reached in open court and orally ratified by the parties before a judge, but never memorialized by a signed writing, that otherwise would be unenforceable as a violation of the statute of frauds.

FACTS: Powell (P) brought suit against the City of Newton ("the City") (D) for trespass and wrongful cutting of his trees as the result of the City's (D) preparing land adjacent to Powell's (D) for use as a park. The City (D) in turn brought third-party complaints against the contractors it had hired to do the work that resulted in the trespass. All the parties reached a settlement under which Powell (P) agreed to quitclaim his interest in the disputed land for a total of $40,000. In court, Powell (P) orally affirmed his assent to the agreement, which was subject to the city council's approval. The attorneys for the parties used email to exchange a draft document that memorialized the agreement, and the City (D) delivered the $40,000 to Powell's (P) attorney. Powell (P) subsequently refused to execute the agreement and consummate the settlement. The City (D) moved for an order requiring Powell's (P) specific performance to execute the agreement. Powell (P) countered that the settlement agreement, as a contract for the sale of land, was void under the statute of frauds because it was not in writing and was not signed by him—"the party to be charged." The trial court ruled that Powell (P) had voluntarily entered into a valid and binding settlement of all issues and that the City (D) was entitled to specific performance. The state's intermediate appellate court affirmed, finding that Powell's (P) statements in open court and the subsequent email correspondence between the attorneys constituted the

signature required to satisfy the statute of frauds. The state's highest court granted review.

ISSUE: Does the doctrine of judicial estoppel render enforceable a settlement agreement reached in open court and orally ratified by the parties before a judge, but never memorialized by a signed writing, that otherwise would be unenforceable as a violation of the statute of frauds?

HOLDING AND DECISION: (Edmunds, J.) Yes. The doctrine of judicial estoppel renders enforceable a settlement agreement reached in open court and orally ratified by the parties before a judge, but never memorialized by a signed writing, that otherwise would be unenforceable as a violation of the statute of frauds. Here there was a contract for the sale of real property. Although the attorneys used email to exchange drafts and correspondence regarding this contract, their understanding was that Powell's (P) signature would be his physical signature, as expressly reflected in an email sent by the City's (D) attorney requesting that Powell (P) execute the final version of the agreement. Because the parties intended for Powell's (P) physical signature to appear on the contract, and because he never signed that document, the writing is not signed. Therefore, the document does not satisfy the signature requirement of the statute of frauds, and the court below erred as to this issue. Notwithstanding that the statute of frauds is not satisfied, the doctrine of judicial estoppel operates to override the statute of frauds and make the agreement enforceable. Here, Powell's (P) statements in open court provide a compelling basis for invoking the doctrine of judicial estoppel, which is designed to protect the integrity of the judicial process by prohibiting parties from deliberately changing positions according to the exigencies of the moment. In other words, the doctrine prevents a party from acting in a way that is inconsistent with its earlier position before the court. Typically, there are three factors that are considered in deciding whether the doctrine should be applied. These are whether: (1) the party's subsequent position is clearly inconsistent with its earlier position; (2) judicial acceptance of a party's position might threaten judicial integrity because a court has previously accepted that party's earlier inconsistent position; and (3) the party seeking to assert an inconsistent position would derive an unfair advantage or impose an unfair detriment on the opposing party as a result. Here, as to the first factor, Powell's (P) subsequent refusal to execute the agreement was plainly inconsistent

Continued on next page.

with his statements to the court. As to the second factor, any conclusion that Powell (P) had not reached an agreement or that the matter had not been resolved would be inconsistent both with his own words and with the actions of the trial court. Moreover, failure to estop him from asserting a contradictory position would indicate either that he misled the first court into believing he had agreed to the settlement or that he misled the second court into believing he had not agreed to the settlement. As to the third factor, failure to estop Powell (P) from reversing his position after he agreed to the settlement in court would give him unfair power to extract additional concessions from the city and other defendants in any further settlement negotiations. For these reasons, invocation of the doctrine of judicial estoppel is appropriate. Modified and affirmed.

▌ ANALYSIS

Here, the court reversed the lower court's holding that the agreement was signed electronically because the email exchange between the attorneys that followed the in-court agreement satisfied the requirements of the Uniform Electronic Transactions Act. The court based its reversal on the grounds that the provisions of the Electronic Transactions Act apply only to "transactions between parties each of which has agreed to conduct transactions by electronic means. Whether the parties agree to conduct a transaction by electronic means is determined from the context and surrounding circumstances, including the parties' conduct." Here, the court concluded, based on the parties' email exchanges, that the parties intended Powell (P) to sign a physical copy of the contract. Thus, based on these circumstances, the court concluded that there was no signature, electronic or otherwise, notwithstanding that the parties otherwise conducted transactions relating to the agreement by electronic means.

■═■

Quicknotes

JUDICIAL ESTOPPEL Doctrine pursuant to which a party is prohibited from asserting a position in a subsequent action contrary to that taken in a prior proceeding.

SPECIFIC PERFORMANCE An equitable remedy whereby the court requires the parties to perform their obligations pursuant to a contract.

■═■

The Justification Principle

Quick Reference Rules of Law

Congregation Kadimah Toras-Moshe v. DeLeo

Promisee (P) v. Estate administrator (D)

Mass. Sup. Jud. Ct., 405 Mass. 365, 540 N.E.2d 691 (1989).

NATURE OF CASE: Appeal from dismissal of action for damages for breach of contract.

FACT SUMMARY: Congregation Kadimah Toras-Moshe (P) sought to enforce a decedent's oral promise to donate money to it.

> 🏛 **RULE OF LAW**
> An oral promise to donate money is unenforceable.

FACTS: During the course of a terminal illness, a decedent promised to donate $25,000 to Congregation Kadimah Toras-Moshe (P). The decedent did not complete the gift before his death. When DeLeo (D) the estate's administrator, refused to give over the money, the Congregation (P) sued, having already incorporated the sum into its budget. The trial court dismissed, and the state judicial supreme court granted review.

ISSUE: Is an oral promise to donate money enforceable?

HOLDING AND DECISION: (Liacos, C.J.) No. An oral promise to donate money is unenforceable. A gratuitous promise to do or give something to another, without any benefit accruing to the promisor, lacks the element of consideration, and therefore no contract has been entered. Justifiable detrimental reliance may constitute consideration. Here, however, the mere incorporation of the $25,000 into the Congregation's (P) budget was insufficient to create an estoppel. As there was no consideration or basis for an estoppel here, the promise was unenforceable. Affirmed.

> ▌ *ANALYSIS*
>
> In a sense, an attempt to enforce an oral promise after the promissor's death would be very much like attempting to enforce an oral will, a situation wide open to fraudulent claims. This approach is rejected in almost all jurisdictions. Due to serious proof problems with oral wills, virtually all states require wills to be written and witnessed.

Quicknotes

CONSIDERATION Value given by one party in exchange for performance, or a promise to perform, by another party.

DECEDENT A person who is deceased.

DETRIMENTAL RELIANCE Action by one party, resulting in loss, that is based on the conduct or promises of another.

GRATUITOUS PROMISE Promise made to someone who has not received consideration for it, which makes the promise unenforceable as a legal contract.

Schnell v. Nell

Testator's husband (D) v. Will beneficiary (P)

Ind. Sup. Ct., 17 Ind. 29, 79 Am. Dec. 453 (1861).

NATURE OF CASE: Action for breach of contract.

FACT SUMMARY: Out of consideration for his deceased wife, Schnell (D) agreed to pay Nell (P) $200 in return for Nell's (P) payment of one cent and agreement to forbear all claims against the wife's estate.

🏛 RULE OF LAW
A contract will be vitiated for lack of consideration where the consideration given by one party is only nominal and is intended to be so.

FACTS: Theresa Schnell's will left $200 to Nell (P). The will was declared a nullity since Theresa, at the time of her death, held no property in her own name. Nonetheless, Theresa's husband, Zacharias Schnell (D), agreed to give Nell (P) $200 out of the love and respect he had for his wife. In return, Nell (P) agreed to pay Schnell (D) the sum of one cent and also agreed to forbear any claim he might have against Theresa's estate. When Schnell (D) refused to honor his promise, Nell (P) sued for breach.

ISSUE: Will a consideration of one cent, which is intended to be merely nominal, support a contract?

HOLDING AND DECISION: (Perkins, J.) No. The general proposition that inadequacy of consideration will not vitiate a contract does not apply where consideration offered by one party is plainly intended to be nominal. Since Schnell (D) was not bound to honor his promise on a tender of one cent, it is necessary to determine if there was any other sufficient consideration. A moral consideration will not support a promise, nor will forbearance of a legally groundless claim. Honor of a deceased wife for her past services is inadequate since the consideration is past and also because veneration in memory of a deceased person is not a legal consideration for a promise to pay any third person money. Schnell's (D) promise is, therefore, unenforceable. Reversed, per curiam.

▶ ANALYSIS

The holding here represents an exception to the general rule that where an action is at law for breach of contract, a court will not examine the fairness of the bargained-for exchanges. However, where the action is in equity for specific performance of the contract, the general rule is reversed: Before relief will be granted, there must be a showing that the agreed exchanges were substantially equal in value.

Quicknotes

CONSIDERATION Value given by one party in exchange for performance, or a promise to perform, by another party.

MORAL CONSIDERATION An inducement to enter a contract that is not enforceable at law, but is made based on a moral obligation, and may be enforceable in order to prevent unjust enrichment on the part of the promisor.

NOMINAL Small; trivial; with reference to name only.

SPECIFIC PERFORMANCE An equitable remedy whereby the court requires the parties to perform their obligations pursuant to a contract.

Hamer v. Sidway

[Parties not identified.]

N.Y. Ct. App., 124 N.Y. 538, 27 N.E. 256 (1891).

NATURE OF CASE: Action on appeal to recover upon a contract which is supported by forbearance of a right as consideration.

FACT SUMMARY: William Story, Sr., (D) promised to pay $5,000 to William Story 2d (P) if he would forbear in the use of liquor, tobacco, swearing, or playing cards or billiards for money until he became twenty-one years of age.

RULE OF LAW
Forbearance is valuable consideration.

FACTS: William Story, Sr. (Story Sr.) (D) agreed with his nephew William Story, 2d (Story 2d) (P) that if Story 2d (P) would refrain from drinking liquor, using tobacco, swearing, and playing cards or billiards for money until he became twenty-one years of age, Story Sr. would pay him $5,000. Upon becoming twenty-one years of age, Story 2d (P) received a letter from Story Sr. (D) stating he had earned the $5,000 and it would be kept at interest for him. Twelve years later, Story Sr. (D) died and this action was brought by the assignees of Story 2d (P) against the executor (D) of the estate of Story Sr. (D). Judgment was entered in favor of Story 2d (P) at the trial at Special Term and was reversed at General Term of the Supreme Court. The assignee of Story 2d (P) appealed.

ISSUE: Is forbearance on the part of a promisee sufficient consideration to support a contract?

HOLDING AND DECISION: (Parker, J.) Yes. Valuable consideration may consist either of some right, interest, profit, or benefit accruing to the one party, or some forbearance, detriment, loss, or responsibility given, suffered, or undertaken by the other. Reversed.

> **ANALYSIS**

The surrendering or forgoing of a legal right constitutes a sufficient consideration for a contract if the minds of the parties meet on the relinquishment of the right as a consideration. Consideration may be forbearance to sue on a claim, extension of time, or any other giving up of a legal right in consideration of a promise.

Quicknotes

CONSIDERATION Value given by one party in exchange for performance, or a promise to perform, by another party.

FORBEARANCE Refraining from doing something that one has the legal right to do.

Batsakis v. Demotsis

Lender (P) v. Borrower (D)

Tex. Ct. Civ. App., 226 S.W.2d 673 (1949).

NATURE OF CASE: Action to recover on a promissory note.

FACT SUMMARY: Batsakis (P) loaned Demotsis (D) 500,000 drachmae (which, at the time, had a total value of $25 in American money) in return for Demotsis' (D) promise to repay $2,000 in American money.

🏛 RULE OF LAW

Mere inadequacy of consideration will not void a contract.

FACTS: During World War II, Batsakis (P), a Greek resident, loaned Demotsis (D), also a Greek resident, the sum of 500,000 drachmae which at the time had a distressed value of only $25 in American money. In return, Demotsis (D), eager to return to the United States, signed an instrument in which she promised to repay Batsakis (P) $2,000 of American money. When Demotsis (D) refused to repay, claiming that the instrument was void at the outset for lack of adequate consideration, Batsakis (P) brought an action to collect on the note and recovered a judgment for $750 (which, at the time, after the war, reflected the rising value of drachmae), plus interest. Batsakis (P) appealed on the ground that he was entitled to recover the stated sum of the note—$2,000—plus interest.

ISSUE: Will mere inadequacy of consideration void a contract?

HOLDING AND DECISION: (McGill, J.) No. Only where the consideration for a contract has no value whatsoever will the contract be voided. A plea of want of consideration amounts to a contention that the instrument never became a valid obligation in the first instance. As a result, mere inadequacy of consideration is not enough. Here, the trial court obviously placed a value on the consideration—the drachmae—by deeming them to be worth $750. Thus, the trial court felt that there was consideration of value for the original transaction. Furthermore, the 500,000 drachmae was exactly what Demotsis (D) bargained for. It may not have been a good bargain, but she nonetheless agreed to repay Batsakis (P) $2,000. Accordingly, Batsakis (P) is entitled to recover $2,000, and not just $750, plus interest. As modified, affirmed.

▌ ANALYSIS

Official comment (e) to the Restatement of Contracts, Second, § 81, states, "gross inadequacy of consideration may be relevant in the application of other rules, (such as) . . . lack of capacity, fraud, duress, undue influence or mistake." Section 234 provides for the avoidance of a contract which, at the time it is made, contains an unconscionable term. The official comment (c) to this section states that "gross disparity in the values exchanged . . . may be sufficient ground, without more, for denying specific performance."

Quicknotes

PROMISSORY NOTE A written promise to tender a stated amount of money at a designated time and to a designated person.

UNCONSCIONABLE A situation in which a contract, or a particular contract term, is unenforceable if the court determines that such term(s) are unduly oppressive or unfair to one party to the contract.

Newman & Snell's State Bank v. Hunter

Lender (P) v. Debtor (D)

Mich. Sup. Ct., 243 Mich. 331, 220 N.W. 665, 59 A.L.R. 311 (1928).

NATURE OF CASE: Appeal from lower court's determination that a valid contract existed and consideration for the contract was sufficient.

FACT SUMMARY: Newman (P) sued Hunter (D) to collect on a note Hunter (D) had pledged to Newman (P) in exchange for Hunter's (D) deceased, insolvent husband's note to Newman (P) and the husband's stock in his insolvent company.

> ### 🏛 RULE OF LAW
> In order for a contract to be valid, valuable consideration must be exchanged between the parties.

FACTS: On March 1, 1926, Hunter (D) gave Newman (P) a note in exchange for her deceased husband's note to Newman (P) and her deceased husband's stock in his company, which Newman (P) held. Hunter (D) also paid Newman (P) the earned interest on the deceased's note. When Hunter's (D) husband died, he was insolvent and could not pay off his debts, nor provide for his wife's allowance. Additionally, the company was insolvent, though still operational. Hunter (D) sought to invalidate the note for want of consideration and Newman (P) brought suit. The trial court ruled in favor of Newman (P) and Hunter (D) appealed.

ISSUE: In order for a contract to be valid, must valuable consideration be exchanged between the parties?

HOLDING AND DECISION: (Fellows, J.) Yes. In order for a contract to be valid, valuable consideration must be exchanged between the parties. Here, no valuable consideration was exchanged between the parties. Hunter (D) provided the note to Newman (P) in exchange for her insolvent, deceased husband's note, which was a worthless piece of paper. Hunter (D) received nothing of value for this exchange, and as there were no assets in her husband's estate, Newman's (P) waiving of its right as a creditor of the husband's estate to administer the assets was of no value as well. Additionally, because the company was insolvent, the stock had no value. Besides, according to the facts, Newman (P) never surrendered the stock to Hunter (D) and still had it in its possession. For these reasons, no valuable consideration was given to Hunter (D) in exchange for the agreement, and therefore the agreement is invalid. Reversed.

▶ ANALYSIS

This case highlights the relationship between contract law and social injustice. It can be argued that the concept of consideration can be utilized to protect the social responsibilities people have toward one another. The idea of valuable consideration can be used, as above, to make certain just results emerge from litigation.

◼━◼

Quicknotes

VALUABLE CONSIDERATION Value given by one party in exchange for performance, or a promise to perform, by another party.

◼━◼

Dyer v. National By-Products, Inc.

Employee (P) v. Employer (D)

Iowa. Sup. Ct., 380 N.W.2d 732 (1986).

NATURE OF CASE: Appeal for summary judgment dismissing a breach of contract action.

FACT SUMMARY: Dyer (P) sued National By-Products, Inc. (D) for breach of a settlement agreement regarding a job-related accident.

🏛 RULE OF LAW
Settlement of an unfounded claim asserted in good faith constitutes valuable consideration for settlement agreements.

FACTS: Dyer (P) was employed as a foreman for National By-Products, Inc. (National) (D). On October 29, 1981, Dyer (P) lost his right foot in a job-related accident. Dyer (P) returned to work as a foreman for National (D) on August 16, 1982 after a fully paid leave of absence. On March 11, 1983, National (D) indefinitely laid off Dyer (P). Dyer (P) sued National (D) for breach of a settlement agreement alleging that in exchange for Dyer (P) foregoing a lawsuit against National (D), National (D) agreed to employ Dyer (P) for life. National (D) denied making such a deal since Dyer (P) was barred from a civil lawsuit by Workers' Compensation. National (D) maintained that even if a settlement agreement existed, Dyer's (P) forbearance of an invalid claim did not constitute valuable consideration for the agreement. The trial court granted summary judgment, and Dyer (P) appealed.

ISSUE: Does settlement of an unfounded claim asserted in good faith constitute valuable consideration for a settlement agreement?

HOLDING AND DECISION: (Schultz, J.) Yes. Settlement of an unfounded claim asserted in good faith constitutes valuable consideration for a settlement agreement. It is in the best interests of the legal system to encourage settlement and negotiation. Thus, circumstances may arise where forbearance of an invalid claim can constitute sufficient consideration. So long as the forbearing party has a good faith belief that he is forbearing the pursuit of a legitimate claim, such forbearance will be valid consideration. Summary judgment was inappropriate in the instant case because a material question of fact existed as to whether or not Dyer (P) had a good faith belief that his civil claim was valid. Reversed and remanded.

▌ *ANALYSIS*

This case highlights the significance of valuable consideration in the context of contractual obligations. Often, the issue of consideration can be manipulated to rectify social justice concerns. When one party has more power than another, valuable consideration in contractual obligations can be used to level the playing field.

Quicknotes

FORBEARANCE Refraining from doing something that one has the legal right to do.

VALUABLE CONSIDERATION Value given by one party in exchange for performance, or a promise to perform, by another party.

Lake Land Employment Group of Akron v. Columber

Former employer (P) v. Former employee (D)

Ohio Sup. Ct., 101 Ohio St. 3d 242, 804 N.E.2d 27 (2004).

NATURE OF CASE: Suit for breach of covenant not to compete.

FACT SUMMARY: After Columber's (D) job ended, he started a company that competed with his former employer, Lake Land Employment Group of Akron (Lake Land) (P), in violation of his noncompetition agreement. Columber (D) resisted Lake Land's (P) suit by arguing that the agreement was void for lack of consideration.

🏛 RULE OF LAW
Continued employment alone satisfies the contractual requirement of consideration in a covenant not to compete entered into by an at-will employee who is already employed by the employer.

FACTS: Columber (D) was an at-will employee of Lake Land Employment Group of Akron (Lake Land) (D) from 1988 to 2001. Lake Land (P) asked him to sign a covenant not to compete in 1991, and Columber (D) signed the agreement. The noncompetition agreement prohibited Columber (D) from being employed by a competitor of Lake Land (P) within a 50-mile radius of Akron, Ohio, for three years after his employment with Lake Land (P) ended. Columber (D) started a business similar to Lake Land's (P) after he stopped working for Lake Land (P). Lake Land (P) sued. Columber (D) answered by pleading that the noncompetition agreement was void for lack of consideration. The trial judge granted Columber's (D) motion for summary judgment, agreeing that no consideration supported the agreement because nothing material to Columber's (D) employment relationship changed after he signed the agreement. The court of appeals affirmed, but it also asked the Ohio Supreme Court to resolve a conflict between its rationale and the rationale used in a similar case by another of the state's intermediate appellate courts. The Ohio Supreme Court accepted jurisdiction over the case.

ISSUE: Does continued employment alone satisfy the contractual requirement of consideration in a covenant not to compete entered into by an at-will employee who is already employed by the employer?

HOLDING AND DECISION: (Moyer, C.J.) Yes. Continued employment alone satisfies the contractual requirement of consideration in a covenant not to compete entered into by an at-will employee who is already employed by the employer. Although disfavored, covenants not to compete are appropriate where they impose reasonable temporal and geographic limitations. States are split

on the particular issue in this appeal, but, consistent with Ohio law, an at-will employer's forbearance from discharging an employee is sufficient consideration to support a noncompetition agreement. In Ohio, consideration can take either of two forms: a detriment to the promisee or a benefit to the promisor. Since at-will employment is an essentially contractual relationship, either side in the relationship can propose different terms for the relationship at any time. Viewed in this context, a request for an at-will employee to sign a noncompetition agreement is in effect a proposal to renegotiate the employment relationship. When the employee agrees to such different terms, the consideration lies in the employer's forbearance from ending the employer's employment. Reversed and remanded.

DISSENT: (Resnick, J.) No consideration supports the agreement here because, contrary to the majority's creative euphemisms, nothing changed in the underlying employment relationship in this case. Lake Land (P) gave up nothing: after the agreement was executed, the company had the same right to fire Columber (D), for any reason or no reason at all, whenever it wanted. Likewise, Columber (D) received nothing, either. Any "forbearance" by the employer in such circumstances consists solely in not firing the employee until after he signs the agreement.

▶ ANALYSIS

Judge Resnick's dissent has much merit; compared to her arguments, the majority's rationale reads as an exercise in legal fiction. The potential weakness in Judge Resnick's own reasoning, though, appears in her statement: "[t]he only actual 'forbearance,' 'proposal,' or 'promise' made by the employer in this situation is declining to fire the employee until he executes the noncompetition agreement." Her reasonably reductive definition of "forbearance" focuses on the precise instant at which the employee signs the agreement. That reductive sense of "forbearance" could be substantially more vital, though, if specific facts showed that an at-will employer was indeed ready to fire an employee unless he signed a noncompetition agreement.

Quicknotes

AT-WILL EMPLOYMENT The rule that an employment relationship is subject to termination at any time, or for any cause, by an employee or an employer in the absence of a specific agreement otherwise.

Continued on next page.

CONSIDERATION Value given by one party in exchange for performance, or a promise to perform, by another party.

FORBEARANCE Refraining from doing something that one has the legal right to do.

■━■

Wood v. Lucy, Lady Duff-Gordon

Marketer (P) v. Designer (D)

N.Y. Ct. App., 222 N.Y. 88, 118 N.E. 214 (1917).

NATURE OF CASE: Action for damages for breach of a contract for an exclusive right.

FACT SUMMARY: Wood (P), in a complicated agreement, received the exclusive right for one year, renewable on a year-to-year basis if not terminated by 90 days' notice, to endorse designs with Lucy's (D) name and to market all her fashion designs for which she would receive one half of the profits derived. Lucy (D) broke the contract by placing her endorsement on designs without Wood's (P) knowledge.

🏛 RULE OF LAW
While an express promise may be lacking, the whole writing may be instinct with an obligation—an implied promise—imperfectly expressed so as to form a valid contract.

FACTS: Lucy (D), a famous-name fashion designer, contracted with Wood (P) that for her granting to him an exclusive right to endorse designs with her name and to market and license all of her designs, they were to split the profits derived by Wood (P) in half. The exclusive right was for a period of one year, renewable on a year-to-year basis, and terminable upon 90 days' notice. Lucy (D) placed her endorsement on fabrics, dresses, and millinery without Wood's (P) knowledge and in violation of the contract. Lucy (D) claims that the agreement lacked the elements of a contract as Wood (P) allegedly is not bound to do anything.

ISSUE: If a promise may be implied from the writing even though it is imperfectly expressed, is there a valid contract?

HOLDING AND DECISION: (Cardozo, J.) Yes. While the contract did not precisely state that Wood (P) had promised to use reasonable efforts to place Lucy's (D) endorsement and market her designs, such a promise can be implied. The implication arises from the circumstances. Lucy (D) gave an exclusive privilege and the acceptance of the exclusive agency was an acceptance of its duties. Lucy's (D) sole compensation was to be one-half the profits resulting from Wood's (P) efforts. Unless he gave his efforts, she could never receive anything. Without an implied promise, the transaction could not have had such business efficacy as they must have intended it to have. Wood's (P) promise to make monthly accountings and to acquire patents and copyrights as necessary showed the intention of the parties that the promise has value by showing that Wood (P) had some duties. The promise to pay Lucy (D) half the profits and make monthly account-

ings was a promise to use reasonable efforts to bring profits and revenues into existence. Reversed.

▶ ANALYSIS

A bilateral contract can be express, implied in fact, or a little of each. The finding of an implied promise for the purpose of finding sufficient consideration to support an express promise is an important technique of the courts in order to uphold agreements which seem to be illusory and to avoid problems of mutuality of obligation. This case is the leading case on the subject. It is codified in UCC § 2-306(2) where an agreement for exclusive dealing in goods imposes, unless otherwise agreed, an obligation to use best efforts by both parties.

Quicknotes

ILLUSORY PROMISE A promise that is not legally enforceable because performance of the obligation by the promisor is completely within his discretion.

IMPLIED PROMISE A promise inferred by law from a document as a whole and the circumstances surrounding its implementation.

Levine v. Blumenthal

Lessor (P) v. Lessee (D)

N.J. Sup. Ct., 117 N.J.L. 23, 186 A. 457 (1936).

NATURE OF CASE: Appeal from judgment denying enforcement of a contract for lack of consideration.

FACT SUMMARY: Levine (P) sued Blumenthal (D) to recover rents not paid on a commercial lease when Blumenthal (D) paid less rents than specified in the contract in the final year and did not pay the last month's rent at all.

🏛 RULE OF LAW
A promise to do what the promisor is already legally bound to do is invalid consideration and does not support a contract.

FACTS: Levine (P) entered into a two-year lease with Blumenthal (D) whereby Levine (P) would rent commercial space to Blumenthal (D) for two years at a rent of $175 per month the first year and $200 per month the second year. Before the expiration of the first year, Blumenthal (D) could not pay the $25 increase in the rent. Blumenthal (D) claimed that Levine (P) accepted this agreement, but Levine (P) claimed that he accepted the agreement on account and expected full payment by the end. Regardless, Blumenthal (D) paid $175 per month for eleven months in the second year, did not renew the lease, and did not pay the last month's rent. Levine (P) sued Blumenthal (D) for the $25 per month balance for the eleven months and for the full $200 for the last month's rent. The trial court ruled in favor of Levine (P), and Blumenthal (D) appealed.

ISSUE: Does a promise to do what the promisor is already legally bound to do constitute sufficient consideration to support a contract?

HOLDING AND DECISION: (Heher, J.) No. A promise to do what the promisor is already legally bound to do is invalid consideration and will not support a contract. Here, Blumenthal (P) was already legally obligated to pay the $200-a-month rent to Levine (P) for the second year pursuant to the original contract. The alleged new contract, whereby Blumenthal (D) would pay less rent, was not supported by consideration because Blumenthal (D) was already obligated to pay the rent to Levine (P). The change in the economy does not allow Blumenthal (D) to escape his obligations to Levine (P) or provide the grounds for valid consideration. Affirmed.

▌ ANALYSIS

The Uniform Commercial Code (UCC) states that modifications in contracts for the sale of goods do not require specific consideration. The present case was not governed by the UCC As a result, new and independent consideration was required to impose the obligation of a contract on this new agreement that might be considered a modification.

Quicknotes

VALID CONSIDERATION Value given by one party in exchange for performance, or a promise to perform, by another party.

Gross Valentino Printing Co. v. Clarke

Printer (P) v. Publisher (D)

III. App. Ct., 120 III. App. 3d 907, 458 N.E.2d 1027 (1983).

NATURE OF CASE: Appeal from summary judgment and award of damages on a breach of contract claim.

FACT SUMMARY: (P) sued Clarke (D) on a breach of contract claim after the parties had entered into an agreement for the printing of magazines at a certain price, which was later modified to an increased price.

> ### RULE OF LAW
> Under Uniform Commercial Code (UCC) § 2-209, a modification of an existing contract within the UCC needs no consideration to be binding.

FACTS: In July, 1979, Clarke (D), the publisher of a magazine, contacted Gross Valentino Printing Co. (Gross) (P), a printer, to print his magazines. Gross (P) sent Clarke (D) a letter, including a price quotation of $6,695, and Clarke (D) accepted the terms. As discussions for the layout proceeded, Gross (P) told Clarke (D) in a phone conversation that the job would cost more than originally planned. Clarke (D) made no objection to Gross (P), despite Clarke's (D) concerns regarding the increase. On August 15, 1979, Gross (P) sent Clarke (D) a letter specifying the work and indicating the increased price. Clarke (D) made no objection to the increase until a later date. By October 28, 1979, Gross (P) had delivered the entire shipment, but Clarke (D) made only a partial payment, stating he would not accept the increased price. Gross (P) sued Clarke (D) for breach of contract and Clarke (D) asserted the affirmative defenses of lack of consideration, fraud, and business compulsion. Gross (P) moved for summary judgment and the trial court granted the motion, awarding him $5,116. Clarke (D) appealed.

ISSUE: Under UCC § 2-209, does a modification of an existing contract within the UCC need consideration to be binding?

HOLDING AND DECISION: (Goldberg, J.) No. Under UCC § 2-209, a modification of an existing contract within the UCC needs no consideration to be binding. Consequently, Clarke's (D) affirmative defense of lack of consideration was properly dismissed by summary judgment. This contract falls under the UCC, as the agreement was for the acquisition of magazines, rather than for the printing services. Clarke (D) accepted the original terms of the contract and did not object to the modification in price until well after Gross's (P) completion of the job. Gross (P) notified Clarke (D) of the modification and Clarke (D) did not object. Such a modification of an existing contract under the UCC needs no consideration to be binding

and, therefore, Clarke's (D) lack of consideration defense was properly dismissed. Additionally, Clarke's (D) other defenses were properly dismissed as well. With respect to the fraud defense, Clarke (D) did not allege sufficient facts to sustain a false statement of material fact by Gross (P), which Gross (P) knew or believed was false, made with the intent to induce Clarke (D) to act, upon which Clarke (D) justifiably relied, resulting in damage to Clarke (D). With respect to the business compulsion defense, Clarke (D) did not allege sufficient facts to sustain a wrongful act by Gross (P) to make a contract under circumstances that deprived Clarke (D) of the exercise of free will. Affirmed.

▌ANALYSIS

Even though modifications of contracts for the sale of goods need no consideration under the UCC, the modifications must still satisfy the standard of "good faith" under UCC § 1-203. UCC § 1-203 states that "every contract or duty within this Act imposes an obligation of good faith in its performance or enforcement." As a result, modifications that are not fair and equitable will most likely not be binding on the parties to a contract for the sale of goods under the UCC.

■▬■

Quicknotes

AFFIRMATIVE DEFENSE A manner of defending oneself against a claim not by denying the truth of the charge but by the introduction of some evidence challenging the plaintiff's right to bring the claim.

FRAUD A false representation of facts with the intent that another will rely on the misrepresentation to his detriment.

MODIFICATION A change to the terms of a contract without altering its general purpose.

■▬■

Angel v. Murray

Taxpayer (P) v. City (D)

R.I. Sup. Ct., 113 R.I. 482, 322 A.2d 630 (1974).

NATURE OF CASE: Action for breach of contract.

FACT SUMMARY: Maher (D) asked for $10,000 more per year to collect refuse even though his contract with the city to provide this service had not yet expired.

🏛 RULE OF LAW
Where unanticipated circumstances or conditions have occurred, the parties to a contract may voluntarily increase the amount of compensation due even if no additional consideration is given.

FACTS: Maher (D) entered into a five-year contract with the city to provide it refuse collection services. A totally unanticipated growth in construction increased the number of units from which Maher (D) had to collect refuse by 20–25 percent. Maher (D) requested an additional $10,000 per year for the remainder of the contract because of this unexpected increase. The city council discussed the matter at a public meeting and agreed to give Maher (D) $10,000 for that year, and an additional $10,000 was given him the following year. Apparently, Angel (P), a taxpayer, and others (P) brought a civil action against Maher (D) and Murray (D), the City Treasurer, to compel Maher (D) to repay the $20,000 in additional compensation received by him. Angel (P) alleged that there was no new consideration to support the modification since Maher (D) was already under a duty to collect the refuse.

ISSUE: May a contract be voluntarily modified by the parties without new consideration where unexpected situations or conditions have arisen?

HOLDING AND DECISION: (Roberts, C.J.) Yes. The preexisting duty rule has, in the past, been used to hold such contracts invalid for lack of consideration. A modification of a contract is itself a contract which must be supported by consideration. We find that where the parties voluntarily agree to modify an existing contract, without coercion or duress, because of unanticipated conditions or circumstances, the modification is valid. There is no reason to prevent the parties from modifying their contractual agreements. The new contract is valid. Judgment for Maher (D). Reversed and remanded.

▶ *ANALYSIS*

Some courts have gone through elaborate attempts to avoid the preexisting duty rule by first finding a rescission and then a new contract. *Linz v. Schuck*, 106 Md. (1907). Many jurisdictions no longer temper application of the preexisting duty rule along the lines mentioned in *Angel*. Modifications made before the contract is fully executed

on either side will be upheld if equitable and free from coercion. Restatement, Second, Contracts § 89D(a).

■=■

Quicknotes

CONSIDERATION Value given by one party in exchange for performance, or a promise to perform, by another party.

MODIFICATION A change to the terms of a contract without altering its general purpose.

PREEXISTING DUTY RULE A common law doctrine that renders unenforceable a promise to perform a duty, which the promisor is already legally obligated to perform, for lack of consideration.

RESCISSION The canceling of an agreement and the return of the parties to their positions prior to the formation of the contract.

■=■

Devecmon v. Shaw

Employee (P) v. Employer's estate (D)

Md. Ct. App., 69 Md. 199, 14 A. 464 (1888).

NATURE OF CASE: Action against estate to recover on promise by deceased.

FACT SUMMARY: At his employer's request, and in return for his promise of repayment, an employee expended his own funds in making a nonbusiness trip to Europe.

🏛 RULE OF LAW
Sufficient consideration is present where the performing party, in reliance on the other party's promise of repayment, has done something in a manner which he otherwise would not have been compelled to do.

FACTS: Devecmon (P) served in his uncle's employ as a clerk. At his uncle's request, and upon a promise from the uncle for reimbursement, Devecmon (P) made a non-business trip to Europe. The expenses of the trip were paid by Devecmon (P). After his uncle's death, Devecmon (P) sued his uncle's estate (D) to recover the expenses. The uncle's executors (D) claimed that Devecmon (P) was not entitled to reimbursement since he had provided no consideration for the promise to repay from the uncle.

ISSUE: Does an act which benefits the performing party constitute sufficient consideration if, by the act, that party had obligated himself to do something he otherwise would not have done?

HOLDING AND DECISION: (Bryan, J.) Yes. Consideration is sufficient if it involves some detriment to the promisor. Where an act is in exchange for a promise of repayment, all that need be shown is that the performing party was induced by the other party to spend his money in a certain way, rather than in some other fashion. It is unnecessary here for Devecmon (P) to prove that, but for the promise he would not have made the trip. Nor is it important that Devecmon (P) may himself have benefitted from the trip. It was a burden which was incurred at the request of his uncle. Devecmon (P) may therefore recover on his uncle's promise of repayment. Any other rule would permit persons who have relied on express promises to spend beyond their means to their great injury. Judgment reversed and new trial ordered.

▶ ANALYSIS

The legal detriment test for sufficiency of consideration is the majority rule. Under it, a plaintiff who can show that by his requested-for act the other party has received a benefit, but who cannot also prove that he himself has incurred a legal detriment, will not recover. The minority rule, adopted by the Restatement, holds that either a showing of legal detriment suffered by the plaintiff or a legal benefit conferred on the other party is sufficient for recovery. The distinction between the two approaches seldom arises since legal benefit is almost invariably accompanied by some legal detriment.

Quicknotes

CONSIDERATION Value given by one party in exchange for performance, or a promise to perform, by another party.

DETRIMENT A loss or injury sustained by an individual personally or to his interest in property.

EXPRESS PROMISE The expression of an intention to act, or to forbear from acting, granting a right to the promisee to expect and enforce its performance.

RELIANCE Dependence on a fact that causes a party to act or refrain from acting.

Garwood Packaging Co. v. Allen & Co., Inc.

Company (P) v. Investment firm (D)

378 F.3d 698 (7th Cir. 2004).

NATURE OF CASE: Appeal from grant of summary judgment to defendants in action for promissory estoppel.

FACT SUMMARY: Garwood Packaging, Inc. (P), which was desperately seeking investors so it could avoid bankruptcy, contended that a statement by Martin (D), a vice-president of Allen & Co., Inc. (Allen) (D), to see that a potential investment deal went through "come hell or high water" constituted a promise, and that based on that "promise," Allen (D) was liable for damages under a theory of promissory estoppel based on its withdrawal from the deal.

RULE OF LAW

Where a plaintiff cannot reasonably understand a statement to be a legally enforceable promise, the plaintiff cannot bring an action for promissory estoppel on the basis of that statement.

FACTS: Garwood Packaging, Inc. (GPI) (P) was broke, and it engaged an investment company, Allen & Co., Inc. (Allen) (D) and Allen's (D) vice-president, Martin (D), to search for investors. After an initial search turned up nothing, Martin (D) told GPI (P) that Allen (D) would consider investing $2 million of its own money in GPI (P) if another investor could be found who would make a comparable investment. Martin (D) found Hobart Corp., which would make an investment in return for equity in GPI (P). However, negotiations with Hobart were difficult, as there were sticking points regarding the amount of equity Hobart would receive and the obtaining of releases from GPI's (P) creditors, which included the Internal Revenue Service (IRS). Martin (D) told GPI (P) that he would see that the deal went through "come hell or high water" and repeatedly confirmed Allen's (D) unconditional commitment to the deal. Eventually, however, the deal collapsed, Allen (D) pulled out, and GPI (P) was forced to declare bankruptcy. GPI (P) (and its principals) brought suit against Allen (D) and Martin (D), claiming that Martin's (D) unequivocal promise to see the deal through to completion bound Allen (D) by the doctrine of promissory estoppel. In reliance on Martin's (D) statement, GPI's (P) principals moved their residences from one state to another to be close to Hobart's plant, forgave their loans to GPI (P), and incurred other costs. The district court granted Allen (D) and Martin (D) summary judgment, and the court of appeals granted review.

ISSUE: Where a plaintiff cannot reasonably understand a statement to be a legally enforceable promise, can the plaintiff bring an action for promissory estoppel on the basis of that statement?

HOLDING AND DECISION: (Posner, J.) No. Where a plaintiff cannot reasonably understand a statement to be a legally enforceable promise, the plaintiff cannot bring an action for promissory estoppel on the basis of that statement. The key issue is whether Martin's (D) statements and reassurances constituted actual promises, and whether they were likely to be understood as such. Here, GPI's (P) principals were sophisticated businessmen. Unless blinded by optimism or desperation, they had to know that Martin (D) could not mean literally that the deal would go through no matter what—especially given Hobart's demands and that the IRS would not give a release until GPI's (P) debts were paid in full. GPI (P) and its principals were also aware that other creditors, too, would not readily provide releases. Thus, although Martin's (D) promises were definite, they could not have been reasonably understood by GPI (P) to be promises rather than expressions of optimism and determination. Accordingly, acts undertaken in reliance on Martin's (D) promises were gambles that the deal would actually go through. Here, the statements could not reasonably have been understood as legally enforceable promises, and, therefore, there can be no promissory estoppel. Ordinarily, the question of whether a plaintiff has reasonably understood a statement to be a promise is a question of fact left for a factfinder, and so this question ordinarily cannot be resolved in summary judgment proceedings. Where, however, that question can be answered in only one way, there is no need to submit it to a jury. That is the case here—the only answer is that GPI (P) and its principals could not reasonably have understood Martin's (D) statements to be legally enforceable promises. Affirmed.

ANALYSIS

The doctrine of promissory estoppel allows reliance to be substituted for consideration as the basis for making a promise enforceable. The most persuasive reason for the requirement of consideration in the law of contracts is that in a system in which oral contracts are enforceable the requirement provides some evidence that there really was a promise that was intended to be relied on as a real commitment. However, a difference between breach of contract and promissory estoppel as grounds for legal relief is that while the promise relied on to trigger an estoppel must be definite in the sense of being clearly a

Continued on next page.

promise and not just a statement of intentions, its terms need not be as clear as a contractual promise would have to be in order to be enforceable. One possible explanation for this difference between breach of contract and promissory estoppel is that promissory estoppel only provides for damages as justice requires and does not attempt to provide the plaintiff damages based upon the benefit of the bargain. The usual measure of damages under a theory of promissory estoppel is the loss incurred by the promisee in reasonable reliance on the promise, or "reliance damages," which are relatively easy to determine, whereas the determination of expectation or benefit of the bargain damages available in a contract action requires more detailed proof of the terms of the contract. However, where the promise giving rise to an estoppel is clear, the plaintiff will usually be awarded its value, which would be the equivalent of the expectation measure of damages in an ordinary breach of contract case.

■■■

Quicknotes

PROMISSORY ESTOPPEL A promise that is enforceable if the promisor should reasonably expect that it will induce action or forbearance on the part of the promisee, and does in fact cause such action or forbearance, and it is the only means of avoiding injustice.

■■■

Feinberg v. Pfeiffer Co.

Employee (P) v. Employer (D)

Mo. Ct. App., 322 S.W.2d 163 (1959).

NATURE OF CASE: Appeal from award of damages.

FACT SUMMARY: Feinberg (P), an employee of the Pfeiffer Co. (D), retired after Pfeiffer (D) promised to pay her $200 per month for life upon her retirement, but subsequently the payments were terminated.

🏛 RULE OF LAW
Under the doctrine of promissory estoppel, as stated in § 90 of the Restatement of the Law of Contracts, "a promise which the promisor should reasonably expect to induce action or forbearance of a definite and substantial character on the part of the promisee and which does induce such action or forbearance is binding if injustice can be avoided only by enforcement of the promise," and it is not necessary that such a promise be given for consideration to be enforceable.

FACTS: Feinberg (P) was an employee of the Pfeiffer Co. (D). In 1947, the Board of Directors of the Pfeiffer (D), in recognition of Feinberg's (P) many years of "long and faithful service," adopted a resolution approving payment to Feinberg (P) of $200 per month for life after her retirement. Thereafter, Feinberg (P) retired and received $200 per month for several years. Subsequently, though, Feinberg (P) was notified that she would receive only $100. When she refused to accept this reduced amount, all further payments were terminated. Thereupon, Feinberg (P) brought an action against Pfeiffer (D) for breach of contract. Although the trial court found that there was no consideration for a contract (i.e., past services are not valid consideration for a promise), it did hold that Feinberg (P) was entitled to damages because she justifiably relied on Pfeiffer's (D) promise. Thereupon, Pfeiffer (D) brought this appeal.

ISSUE: Is a promise per se invalid if it is given without consideration?

HOLDING AND DECISION: (Doerner, Comm.) No. Under the doctrine of promissory estoppel, as stated in § 90 of the Restatement of the Law of Contracts, "a promise which the promisor should reasonably expect to induce action or forbearance of a definite and substantial character on the part of the promisee and which does induce such action or forbearance is binding if injustice can be avoided only by enforcement of the promise," and such a promise can be enforced even if it was given for no consideration. Of course, even though some cases have considered "promissory estoppel" as a "species of consideration," consideration is not required because an action based upon promissory estoppel is not equivalent to a breach of contract action. Here, Feinberg (P) has no breach of contract action because Pfeiffer's (D) promise was not supported by sufficient consideration (as found by the trial court). Feinberg (P), though, does have an action under the doctrine of promissory estoppel. She justifiably relied on Pfeiffer's (D) promise by retiring from a lucrative position. Furthermore, it is irrelevant that when the payments were terminated Feinberg (P) was unable to work because of illness. Since Feinberg (P) relied, by her retirement, on Pfeiffer's (D) promise, injustice would result by not enforcing this promise regardless of her subsequent illness. Affirmative judgment recommended.

▶ ANALYSIS

This case illustrates the generally recognized doctrine of promissory estoppel. This doctrine is an exception to the general rule that a promise cannot be enforced without valuable consideration. Under promissory estoppel, "substantial detrimental reliance" on a promise takes the place of consideration. Note that the Restatement, Second, dispenses with the requirement that reliance must be "substantial" and only requires that it is reasonable. Furthermore, the Restatement, Second, suggests that a court need not enforce the whole promise relied on but may limit the remedy to such relief "as justice requires."

Quicknotes

CONSIDERATION Value given by one party in exchange for performance, or a promise to perform, by another party.

PROMISSORY ESTOPPEL A promise that is enforceable if the promisor should reasonably expect that it will induce action or forbearance on the part of the promisee, and does in fact cause such action or forbearance, and it is the only means of avoiding injustice.

Drennan v. Star Paving Co.

General contractor (P) v. Subcontractor (D)

Cal. Sup. Ct., 51 Cal. 2d 409, 333 P.2d 757 (1958).

NATURE OF CASE: Appeal of an award of damages for breach of contract.

FACT SUMMARY: Drennan (P) sued Star Paving Co. (D) to recover damages when Star (D) could not perform the paving work at the price quoted in its subcontracting bid.

RULE OF LAW
Reasonable reliance on a promise binds an offeror even if there is no other consideration.

FACTS: In formulating a bid to the Lancaster School District, Drennan (P), a general contractor, solicited bids for subcontracting work. Star Paving Co. (Star) (D) submitted the lowest paving bid, and Drennan (P) used that bid in formulating its bid to the school district. Using Star's (D) subcontracting bid of $7,131.60, Drennan (P) was awarded the general contract. Star (D) then told Drennan (P) that it made a mistake and could not do the work for less than $15,000. Star (D) refused to do the work, and Drennan (P) found a substitute company that did the work for $10,948.60. Drennan (P) sued Star (D) for the difference, claiming that Drennan (P) had reasonably relied on Star's (D) offer. Star (D) claimed that it had made a revocable offer. The trial court ruled in favor of Drennan (P) on the grounds of promissory estoppel, and Star (D) appealed.

ISSUE: Does reasonable reliance on a promise bind the offeror if there no other consideration?

HOLDING AND DECISION: (Traynor, J.) Yes. Reasonable reliance on a promise binds the offeror even if there is no other consideration. Section 90 of the Restatement of Contracts provides that when a promise is made that induces action or forbearance of the promisee, the promissor is bound if injustice would result from nonenforcement. In the case of a unilateral offer, the offeror is bound to the promise if it produces reasonable reliance. Star (D) made a promise to Drennan (P) of a certain price. Star's (D) bid was the lowest, and Drennan (P) reasonably relied on it in formulating its bid and winning the contract. As a result, Drennan (P) was obligated to do the work at the price quoted and even had to put up a bond. Star (D) should have known such a result would occur if Star's (D) bid was accepted. The absence of consideration is not fatal to Star's (D) initial promise, as Drennan (P) substantially changed its position in reliance on Star (D). Injustice can only be avoided by the enforcement of Star's (D) subcontracting promise. Affirmed.

► ANALYSIS

Such reasonable reliance cases are often called firm offers. Firm offers can sometimes be implied promises to hold an offer open and have received criticism on the grounds that one party (the subcontractor) is bound while the other party (the general contractor) is not. Nonetheless, the modern trend is to enforce such promises.

Quicknotes

CONSIDERATION Value given by one party in exchange for performance, or a promise to perform, by another party.

FIRM OFFER Under the Uniform Commercial Code, refers to a signed, written offer to enter into a contract for the sale of goods that is irrevocable for a specified period of time, or if no time is stated then for a reasonable time period not exceeding three months.

PROMISSORY ESTOPPEL A promise that is enforceable if the promisor should reasonably expect that it will induce action or forbearance on the part of the promisee, and does in fact cause such action or forbearance, and it is the only means of avoiding injustice.

RELIANCE Dependence on a fact that causes a party to act or refrain from acting.

REVOCABLE OFFER An offer that may be retracted by the promisor without the assent of the offeree.

Southern California Acoustics Co., Inc. v. C.V. Holder, Inc.

Subcontractor (P) v. General contractor (D)

Cal. Sup. Ct., 71 Cal. 2d 719, 456 P.2d 975 (1969).

NATURE OF CASE: Appeal from dismissal of an action for breach of contract.

FACT SUMMARY: Southern California Acoustics Co. (Southern) (P), an acoustic subscontactor, sued C.V. Holder, Inc. (C.V.) (D), a general contractor, to recover damages sustained in replacing Southern (P) after C.V. (D) claimed that Southern (P) was listed by mistake.

RULE OF LAW
Silence in the face of an offer is not an acceptance unless it is understood as acceptance due to relationship between the parties and previous course of dealings.

FACTS: In formulating its bid to the Los Angeles School District, C.V. Holder, Inc. (C.V.) (D), a general contractor, solicited bids for subcontracting jobs. Southern California Acoustics Co., Inc. (Southern) (P), an acoustics company, submitted its bid to C.V. (D) for use in its general contracting bid. C.V. (D) won the contract and listed Southern (P) as a subcontractor. A local trade paper listed Southern (P) as the subcontractor. Reading the trade paper and thinking it would be the subcontractor, Southern (P) held off on accepting other work for another month. However, C.V. (D) never officially told Southern (P) it had the contract. Soon thereafter, C.V. (D) substituted another subcontractor, as Southern (P) was listed by mistake. Southern (P) filed an action to prevent the substitution and then, upon that failure, sued for damages. C.V. (D) demurred. The trial court sustained the demurrer and dismissed the action. Southern (P) appealed.

ISSUE: Is silence in the face of an offer an acceptance if there is no relationship between the parties of a previous course of dealing pursuant to which silence would be understood as acceptance?

HOLDING AND DECISION: (Traynor, C.J.) No. Silence in the face of an offer is not an acceptance unless it is understood as acceptance due to the relationship between the parties and previous course of dealings. Without a prior relationship and course of dealings, silence does not constitute acceptance of an offer. In the present case, C.V. (D) never informed Southern (P) that its bid was accepted. Simply because Southern (P) read in a paper that it had been included as the subcontractor did not amount to an acceptance. There were no prior dealings or relationship between C.V. (D) and Southern (P) to suggest to Southern (P) that C.V.'s (D) silence constituted acceptance of its offer bid. Therefore, the demurrer was proper with respect to these allegations.

ANALYSIS

This case highlights the inequity subcontractors face when dealing with general contractors. The subcontractor is bound by its firm offer to the general contractor, but the general contractor is not bound until an official expression of acceptance is communicated to the subcontractor. This inequity has lately been criticized by legal scholars.

Quicknotes

ACCEPTANCE Assent to the specified terms of an offer, resulting in the formation of a binding agreement.

COURSE OF DEALING Previous conduct between two parties to a contact which may be relied upon to interpret their actions.

OFFER A proposed promise to undertake performance of an action, or to refrain from acting, that is to become binding upon acceptance by the offeree.

Sparks v. Gustafson

Executor (D) v. Friend of decedent (P)

Alaska Sup. Ct., 750 P.2d 338 (1988).

NATURE OF CASE: Appeal from judgment awarding compensation for services in breach of oral agreement action.

FACT SUMMARY: Gustafson (P) sued Sparks (D) on a breach of contract claim for the sale of a building and an unjust enrichment claim on the maintenance of the building after Gustafson (P) had maintained Sparks's (D) building, but had received no compensation.

🏛 RULE OF LAW

Unjust enrichment exists where the defendant has received a benefit from the plaintiff, which the plaintiff has not provided gratuitously, and it would be inequitable for the defendant to retain the benefit without compensating the plaintiff for its value.

FACTS: Sparks (D) was the executor of his father's estate. Gustafson (P) was a friend of the decedent and, during the decedent's life, managed a building for the decedent free of charge. Decedent died on March 1, 1981, and Gustafson (P) continued to manage the building with Sparks's (D) knowledge. The building operated at a loss under Gustafson's (P) management and Gustafson (P) paid numerous expenses for the building out of his own account. In February, 1982, Sparks (D) signed a purchase agreement for Gustafson (P) to buy the building, indicating that the deed would be delivered once the details of the purchase had been worked out. No details were ever agreed upon. Sparks (D) ultimately sold the building to a third party, and Gustafson (P) ceased to manage the building at that time. In July, 1983, Gustafson (P) sued Sparks (D), claiming breach of an oral agreement to sell Gustafson (P) the building and asserting an equitable lien on the property for the time and money Gustafson (P) had put into the building. Sparks (D) filed an answer and a counterclaim demanding an accounting of all moneys collected and expended on the building. The trial court found no breach of an oral contract and concluded that Gustafson (P) did not have an equitable lien on the property, but did find that Sparks (D) was unjustly enriched by Gustafson's (P) services and improvements in the amount of $65,706 during his two years of managing the building after the decedent's death. Sparks (D) appealed.

ISSUE: Does unjust enrichment exist where the defendant has received a benefit from the plaintiff, which the plaintiff has not provided gratuitously, and it would be inequitable for the defendant to retain the benefit without compensating the plaintiff for its value?

HOLDING AND DECISION: (Matthews, J.) Yes. Unjust enrichment exists where the defendant has received a benefit from the plaintiff, which the plaintiff has not provided gratuitously, and it would be inequitable for the defendant to retain the benefit without compensating the plaintiff for its value. Here, Sparks (D) unjustly benefited from Gustafson's (P) services during his two years of managing the building after the decedent's death. During the decedent's life, Gustafson (P) volunteered his services to his friend, the decedent. After his death, however, Gustafson's (P) actions went far beyond what any reasonable person would consider to be rendered by a friend gratuitously. As a result, Sparks (D) was unjustly enriched by Gustafson's (P) actions. Affirmed.

▌ ANALYSIS

The theory of unjust enrichment is often described as quasi-contractual recovery. The idea is to restore to the injured party any benefit he conferred upon the other party, so as to restore the status quo. Under modern authority, with some limitations, the party in breach of the contract can maintain an action in quasi-contract, even though the party in breach might not be able to sue on the contract.

■▬■

Quicknotes

QUASI-CONTRACT An implied contract created by law to prevent unjust enrichment.

UNJUST ENRICHMENT The unlawful acquisition of money or property of another for which both law and equity require restitution to be made.

■▬■

Mills v. Wyman

Nurse-caretaker (P) v. Parent (D)

Mass. Sup. Jud. Ct., 20 Mass. (3 Pick.) 207 (1825).

NATURE OF CASE: Action on appeal to recover upon alleged promise.

FACT SUMMARY: Mills (P) took care of Wyman's (D) son without being requested to do so and for so doing was promised compensation for expenses arising out of the rendered care by Wyman (D). Wyman (D) later refused to compensate Mills (P).

🏛 RULE OF LAW
A moral obligation is insufficient as consideration for a promise.

FACTS: Mills (P) nursed and cared for Levi Wyman, the son of Wyman (D). Upon learning of Mills's (P) acts of kindness toward his son, Wyman (D) promised to repay Mills (P) his expenses incurred in caring for Levi Wyman. Later, Wyman (D) refused to compensate Mills (P) for his expenses. Mills (P) filed an action in the Court of Common Pleas where the Wyman (D) was successful in obtaining a non suit against Mills (P). Mills (P) appealed.

ISSUE: Is a moral obligation sufficient consideration for a promise?

HOLDING AND DECISION: (Parker, C.J.) No. It is said a moral obligation is sufficient consideration to support an express promise. However, the universality of the rule cannot be supported. Therefore, there must be some other preexisting obligation which will suffice as consideration. Affirmed.

▶ ANALYSIS

In cases such as this one, the nearly universal holding is that the existing moral obligation is not a sufficient basis for the enforcement of an express promise to render the performance that it requires. The general statement is that it is not sufficient consideration for the express promise. The difficulties and differences of opinion involved in the determination of what is a moral obligation are probably much greater than those involved in determining the existence of a legal obligation. This tends to explain the attitude of the majority of courts on the subject and justifies the generally stated rule.

■═■

Quicknotes

CONSIDERATION Value given by one party in exchange for performance, or a promise to perform, by another party.

EXPRESS PROMISE The expression of an intention to act, or to forbear from acting, granting a right to the promisee to expect and enforce its performance.

■═■

Webb v. McGowin

Good Samaritan (P) v. Estate (D)

Ala. Ct. App., 27 Ala. App. 82, 168 So. 196 (1935).

NATURE OF CASE: Action on appeal to collect on a promise.

FACT SUMMARY: Webb (P) saved the now deceased J. McGowin from grave bodily injury or death by placing himself in grave danger and subsequently suffering grave bodily harm. J. McGowin, in return, promised Webb (P) compensation. McGowin's executors (D) now refuse to pay the promised compensation.

🏛 RULE OF LAW
A moral obligation is a sufficient consideration to support a subsequent promise to pay where the promisor has received a material benefit.

FACTS: Webb (P), while in the scope of his duties for the W.T. Smith Lumber Co., was clearing the floor, which required him to drop a 75-lb. pine block from the upper floor of the mill to the ground. Just as Webb (P) was releasing the block, he noticed J. McGowin below and directly under where the block would have fallen. In order to divert the fall of the block, Webb (P) fell with it, breaking an arm and leg and ripping his heel off. The fall left Webb (P) badly crippled and incapable of either mental or physical labor. In return for Webb's (P) act, J. McGowin promised to pay Webb (P) $15 every two weeks for the rest of Webb's (P) life. J. McGowin paid the promised payments until his death eight years later. Shortly after J. McGowin's death, the payments were stopped and Webb (P) brought an action against N. McGowin (D) and J.F. McGowin (D) as executors of J. McGowin's estate for payments due him. The executors (D) of the estate were successful in obtaining a nonsuit against Webb (P) in the lower court. Webb (P) appealed.

ISSUE: Was the moral obligation to compensate as promised sufficient consideration?

HOLDING AND DECISION: (Bricken, J.) Yes. It is well settled that a moral obligation is a sufficient consideration to support a subsequent promise to pay where the promisor has received a material benefit, although there was no original duty or liability resting on the promisor. Reversed and remanded.

CONCURRENCE: (Samford, J.) The strict letter of the rule as stated by the judges would perhaps bar the plaintiff from recovery. As Chief Justice Marshall stated in *Hoffman v. Porter*, 2 Brock. 156, however, "... [the] law ought [not] to be separated from justice, where it is most doubtful."

▶ ANALYSIS

In most cases where the moral obligation is asserted, the court feels that the promise ought not be enforced; instead of going into the uncertain field of morality, the court chooses to rely upon the rule that moral obligation is not a sufficient consideration. On the other hand, in cases where the promise is one which would have been kept by most citizens, and the court feels that enforcement is just, a few courts will enforce the promise using the *Webb v. McGowin* rule. In general, the *Webb v. McGowin* rule is the minority rule and the *Mills v. Wyman* rule, Mass. Sup. Jud. Ct., 20 Mass. (3 Pick.) 207 (1825), is the majority rule.

Quicknotes

MATERIAL BENEFIT An advantage gained by entering into a contract that is essential to the performance of the agreement and without which the contract would not have been entered into.

MORAL OBLIGATION A duty that is not enforceable at law, but is consistent with ethical notions of justice.

Quick Reference Rules of Law

A.Z. v. B.Z.

Former husband (P) v. Former wife (D)

Mass. Sup. Jud. Ct., 725 N.E.2d 1051 (2000).

NATURE OF CASE: Appeal from grant of permanent injunction prohibiting the use of frozen preembryos.

FACT SUMMARY: B.Z. (D), the former wife of A.Z. (P), contended that pursuant to a consent form between the couple and an in vitro fertilization clinic, she should be allowed to use a vial of frozen preembryos for possible conception. A.Z. (P) opposed such use on the grounds that if conception were successful, he would be forced to become a parent over his present objection.

🏛 **RULE OF LAW**
An agreement permitting the use of frozen preembryos for possible conception is not enforceable against a party to the agreement where that party no longer wishes to become a parent.

FACTS: When A.Z. (P) and B.Z. (D) were married, they underwent in vitro fertilization (IVF) treatments over a period of several years that involved the freezing of preembryos. At each treatment, both A.Z. (P) and B.Z. (D) signed consent forms as to the ultimate disposition of the preembryos. Although A.Z. (P) signed the forms, B.Z. (D) was the one who indicated that if the couple was to separate, the preembryos should be returned to her for implantation. As a result of one of the treatments, B.Z. (D), the wife, conceived and gave birth to twins. During that treatment, more preembryos were formed than were necessary for immediate implantation, and two vials of preembryos were frozen for possible future implantation. Four years later, without A.Z.'s (P) knowledge, B.Z. (D) used one of the vials to attempt conception. Relations between A.Z. (P) and B.Z. (D) deteriorated around this time. B.Z. (D) sought a protective order against A.Z. (P), and they eventually separated and divorced. At the time of divorce, one vial of preembryos remained at the clinic. A.Z. (P) filed a motion for a permanent injunction to prohibit B.Z. (D) from using this vial for attempted conception. B.Z. (D) contended that the consent form governing the vial should be given effect. The trial court ruled that the agreement at issue was unenforceable because of "change in circumstances" that occurred in the four years after the couple signed it. The trial court said that "no agreement should be enforced in equity when intervening events have changed the circumstances such that the agreement which was originally signed did not contemplate the actual situation now facing the parties." In the absence of a binding agreement, the trial court determined that the best solution was to balance B.Z.'s (D) interest in procreation against A.Z.'s (P) interest in avoiding procreation. The court

ultimately determined that A.Z.'s (P) interest in avoiding procreation outweighed B.Z.'s (D) interest in having additional children and granted the permanent injunction in favor of A.Z. (P). The state's highest court transferred the case to itself on its own motion.

ISSUE: Is an agreement permitting the use of frozen preembryos for possible conception enforceable against a party to the agreement where that party no longer wishes to become a parent?

HOLDING AND DECISION: (Cowin, J.) No. An agreement permitting the use of frozen preembryos for possible conception is not enforceable against a party to the agreement where that party no longer wishes to become a parent. First, it is doubtful that the consent form represented the intent of the husband and the wife regarding the disposition of the preembryos in the case of a dispute between them. In any event, there are independent policy reasons the form should not be enforced in circumstances such as those presented by this case. Even if the agreement had been unambiguous about the disposition of the pre-embryos, such an agreement would not be enforceable to compel one of the donors to become a parent against his or her will. It is well-established that courts will not enforce contracts that violate public policy, and, as a matter of public policy, forced procreation is not an area amenable to judicial enforcement. In a case such as the one at bar, freedom of contract is outweighed by public policy against compelling an individual to become a parent over his or her contemporaneous objection. This policy is derived from other manifestations by the state legislature, as well as judicial precedent, that individuals shall not be compelled to enter into intimate family relationships, and that the law shall not be used as a mechanism for forcing such relationships when they are not desired. This policy is grounded in the notion that respect for liberty and privacy requires that individuals be accorded the freedom to decide whether to enter into a family relationship. Here, enforcing the consent form against A.Z. (P) would compel him to become a parent against his present wishes. Public policy prohibits enforcement of the consent form. Affirmed.

▶ **ANALYSIS**

Few courts have addressed the issue presented by this case, and not all that have follow the reasoning of the court in this case. Some of those courts have held that agreements between donors regarding the disposition of preembryos should be presumed valid and should be

Continued on next page.

enforced, on the grounds that such agreements minimize misunderstanding, maximize procreative liberty, and provide needed certainty to IVF programs. See, e.g., *Kass v. Kass,* 91 N.Y.2d 554 (N.Y. 1998).

∎▬∎

Quicknotes

PERMANENT INJUNCTION A remedy imposed by the court ordering a party to cease the conduct of a specific activity until the final disposition of the cause of action.

∎▬∎

Kass v. Kass

Former wife (P) v. Former husband (D)

N.Y. Ct. App., 696 N.E.2d 174 (1998).

NATURE OF CASE: Appeal from order enforcing an agreement controlling the disposition of frozen preembryos. [The complete procedural posture of the case is not presented in the casebook extract.]

FACT SUMMARY: In an attempt to conceive a child during their marriage, Maureen Kass (P) and Steven Kass (D) participated in in vitro fertilization (IVF) procedures and had five preembryos frozen. At the time, Maureen (P) and Steven (D) entered into a consent agreement that in the event they could not agree regarding the disposition of the preembryos, the preembryos would be donated to the IVF program. Shortly thereafter, Maureen (P) initiated divorce proceedings and sought custody of the preembryos; Steven (D) objected and sought specific performance of the consent agreement.

> ### RULE OF LAW
> An agreement between progenitors, or gamete donors, regarding disposition of their pre-zygotes generally is presumed valid and binding, and to be enforced in any dispute between them.

FACTS: In an attempt to conceive a child during their marriage, Maureen Kass (P) and Steven Kass (D) participated in in vitro fertilization (IVF) procedures for around five years. They failed to conceive. As part of the final procedure, they had five preembryos (also known as "pre-zygotes") frozen. At the time, in May 1993, Maureen (P) and Steven (D) entered into a consent agreement that in the event they could not agree regarding the disposition of the preembryos, the preembryos would be donated to the IVF program for scientific research. Barely three weeks after signing the consent, and knowing that divorce was imminent, Maureen (P) and Steven (D) drew up and signed an "uncontested divorce" agreement that provided that the preembryos would be disposed of in the manner specified in the consent, and that neither Maureen (P) nor Steven (D) or anyone else would lay claim to custody of the pre-zygotes. Contrary to this agreement, three weeks later Maureen (P) informed the IVF program of her opposition to destruction or release of the preembryos. A month after that, she commenced a matrimonial action, requesting sole custody of the preembryos so she could undergo another implantation procedure. She argued that implantation of the preembryos was her only chance for genetic motherhood. Steven (D) opposed Maureen's (P) further attempts to become pregnant with the pre-zygotes, and he counterclaimed for specific performance of the parties' consent agreement. He objected to the burdens of unwanted fatherhood. The state's intermediate appellate court ordered

enforcement of the consent agreement, and the state's highest court granted review. [The complete procedural posture of the case is not presented in the casebook extract.]

ISSUE: Is an agreement between progenitors, or gamete donors, regarding disposition of their pre-zygotes generally presumed valid and binding, and to be enforced in any dispute between them?

HOLDING AND DECISION: (Kaye, C.J.) Yes. An agreement between progenitors, or gamete donors, regarding disposition of their pre-zygotes generally is presumed valid and binding, and to be enforced in any dispute between them. Currently, the state does not have statutes touching on the disposition of stored embryos. There are also not many cases in the country dealing with the issue presented by this case. One jurisdiction has ruled that in the absence of a written agreement between the parties—which should be presumed valid and implemented—courts should balance the parties' competing interests. Another approach is to regard the progenitors as holding a "bundle of rights" in relation to the preembryos that can be exercised through joint disposition agreements. Yet another view is that no embryo should be implanted, destroyed or used in research over the objection of an individual with decision-making authority. Because the disposition of pre-zygotes does not implicate a woman's right of privacy or bodily integrity in the area of reproductive choice, and because pre-zygotes are not recognized as "persons" for constitutional purposes, the issue comes down to who had dispositional authority over them. Here, the parties have answered that question. Agreements between progenitors, or gamete donors, regarding disposition of their pre-zygotes should generally be presumed valid and binding, and enforced in any dispute between them. Indeed, such agreements should be encouraged, as advance directives in this area or reproductive choice can avoid costly litigation, both in hard costs as well as intangible costs. Written agreements also provide the certainty needed for effective operation of IVF programs. Especially given that the freezing of preembryos provides time for minds and circumstances to change, it is particularly important that courts honor the parties' expressions of choice made before disputes arise. Advance agreements as to disposition would have little purpose if they were enforceable only in the event the parties continued to agree. Thus, to the extent possible, it should be the progenitors—not the State and not the courts—who by their prior directive make this

Continued on next page.

deeply personal life choice. Here, the consent signed by Maureen (P) and Steven (D) make clear their intent regarding disposition of the preembryos; they unambiguously directed that in the present circumstances, the prezygotes be donated for research to the IVF program. It is also clear that they intended that the disposition of the preembryos would be their joint decision. Accordingly, the law will give effect to their intention. Affirmed.

▶ *ANALYSIS*

Although the subject of the dispute in this case was novel, the court applied common-law principles governing contract interpretation to reach its holding. One of the principles the court applied is that whether an agreement is ambiguous is a question of law for the courts and ambiguity is determined by looking within the four corners of the document, not to outside sources. Here, the court, after thoroughly examining the consent agreement, determined that the contract was not ambiguous, and that the parties' intent was clear from the consent itself. Moreover, had the court found parts of the contract to be ambiguous, it could have looked to the parties' "uncontested divorce" agreement, executed just a weeks after the consent agreement was executed, to resolve any ambiguities. While extrinsic evidence cannot be used to create an ambiguity in an agreement, it can be used to resolve any ambiguity. Here, the uncontested divorce agreement would have reaffirmed the earlier understanding that neither party would alone lay claim to possession of the pre-zygotes.

■≡■

Quicknotes

EXTRINSIC EVIDENCE Evidence that is not contained within the text of a document or contract, but which is derived from the parties' statements or the circumstances under which the agreement was made.

SPECIFIC PERFORMANCE An equitable remedy whereby the court requires the parties to perform their obligations pursuant to a contract.

■≡■

Stambovsky v. Ackley

Buyer (P) v. Seller (D)

N.Y. App. Div., 169 A.D.2d 254, 572 N.Y.S.2d 672 (1991).

NATURE OF CASE: Appeal from dismissal of an action for rescission of a contract.

FACT SUMMARY: Stambovsky (P) sought to rescind a contract to purchase a house upon discovering that it was allegedly haunted.

🏛 RULE OF LAW
Nondisclosure by the seller of facts solely within its knowledge and undiscoverable by a prudent buyer constitutes a basis for rescission of the contract.

FACTS: Stambovsky (P) contracted to purchase a house from Ackley (D). Stambovsky (P) properly examined the house and found that it was acceptable for purchase. Stambovsky (P) did not know that Ackley (D) had publicized the house as being haunted. When Stambovsky (P) discovered that the house was allegedly haunted, he sought to rescind the contract. The trial court granted Ackley's (D) motion to dismiss the complaint, and Stambovsky (P) appealed.

ISSUE: Does nondisclosure by the seller of facts solely within its knowledge and undiscoverable by a prudent buyer constitute a basis for rescission?

HOLDING AND DECISION: (Rubin, J.) Yes. Nondisclosure by the seller of facts solely within its knowledge and undiscoverable by a prudent buyer constitutes grounds for rescission. The principle of caveat emptor disallows the recovery of money damages. However, equity allows rescission of contracts where the seller conceals material facts. Stambovsky (P) had no way of discovering the presence of ghosts in the house. Ackley's (D) nondisclosure was an active concealment that could never be discovered with proper examination. Therefore, the complaint should not have been dismissed and the cause of action should be reinstated. Reversed.

DISSENT: (Smith, J.) New York's policy of caveat emptor clearly provides that the seller of real property was under no duty to speak. Ackley's (D) silence, without some deceptive act, does not amount to fraudulent concealment.

▌ ANALYSIS

The majority stretches credibility in finding that the house's reputation was not discoverable by a prudent investigation. However, they were more concerned with protecting the expectations of the buyer. Still, courts must take care when adjudicating mistake cases so as to not confuse mistakes with mere regrets.

Quicknotes

CAVEAT EMPTOR Let the buyer beware; doctrine that a buyer purchases something at his own risk.

FRAUDULENT CONCEALMENT The concealing of a material fact which a party is under an obligation to disclose.

MATERIAL FACT A fact without the existence of which a contract would not have been entered.

MISTAKE An act or failure to perform due to a lack of knowledge or a misconception as to a law or fact.

SCI Minnesota Funeral Services, Inc. v. Washburn-McReavy Funeral Corp.

Cemetery association seller (P) v. Subsequent purchaser of cemetery association (D)

Minn. Sup. Ct., 795 N.W.2d 855 (2011).

NATURE OF CASE: Appeal from affirmance of judgment denying reformation or rescission of a stock sale agreement.

FACT SUMMARY: SCI Minnesota Funeral Services, Inc. (SCI) (P), which sold Crystal Lake Association (Crystal Lake) to Corinthian Enterprises (Corinthian) (P) through a stock sale, and Corinthian (P), which in turn sold Crystal Lake to Washburn-McReavy Funeral Corp. (Washburn) (D) through a share purchase agreement, contended that both agreements should be reformed or rescinded based on mutual mistake or lack of mutual assent, as neither SCI (P) nor Corinthian (P) knew that two vacant lots were transferred in the stock sale.

RULE OF LAW
(1) Rescission is not available to rescind a stock sale agreement transferring a corporation's stock where the parties are mistaken about the extent of the corporation's assets, even where the intent of the transaction is to transfer the assets.
(2) Reformation is not available to reform a stock sale agreement transferring a corporation's stock where the parties are mistaken about the extent of the corporation's assets, but the seller is deemed to have constructive knowledge of all its assets and has the opportunity to exclude assets from the sale that it does not want included in the transaction.

FACTS: SCI Minnesota Funeral Services, Inc. (SCI) (P), sold Crystal Lake Association (Crystal Lake) to Corinthian Enterprises (Corinthian) (P) through a stock sale. Neither party knew or intended that the sale would transfer two vacant lots in addition to three cemetery properties, as they did not know about the existence of the lots. The consideration for the sale was $1 million, which reflected the value of the cemeteries. The lots were worth $2 million. Subsequently, Corinthian (P) sold and assigned Crystal Lake to Washburn-McReavy Funeral Corp. (Washburn) (D) through a share purchase agreement. There was no language in either agreement that expressly excluded or included the vacant lots from the sale, or that limited the sale to the three cemeteries owned by Crystal Lake. Under the terms of the agreements, SCI (P) could have removed the vacant lots from the assets of Crystal Lake prior to the transaction, but it failed to do so. However, SCI (P) kept paying the taxes on the lots after the transaction. A few years later, Washburn (D) learned that it owned one of the

lots when SCI (P) asked it for a quitclaim deed to the lot. SCI (P) and Corinthian (D) sued Washburn (D), requesting reformation or rescission of both agreements. Each party moved for summary judgment, and the trial court granted summary judgment to Washburn (D). The state's intermediate appellate court affirmed, and the state's highest court granted review.

ISSUE:
(1) Is rescission available to rescind a stock sale agreement transferring a corporation's stock where the parties are mistaken about the extent of the corporation's assets, even where the intent of the transaction is to transfer the assets?
(2) Is reformation available to reform a stock sale agreement transferring a corporation's stock where the parties are mistaken about the extent of the corporation's assets, but the seller is deemed to have constructive knowledge of all its assets and has the opportunity to exclude assets from the sale that it does not want included in the transaction?

HOLDING AND DECISION: (Gildea, C.J.)
(1) No. Rescission is not available to rescind a stock sale agreement transferring a corporation's stock where the parties are mistaken about the extent of the corporation's assets, even where the intent of the transaction is to transfer the assets. Rescission is an equitable remedy generally available if both parties to an agreement were mistaken with respect to material facts. Here, SCI (P) and Corinthian (P) claim both mutual mistake and lack of mutual assent. The trial court concluded that the subject matter of their agreement was SCI's (P) stock in Crystal Lakes, whereas SCI (P) and Corinthian (P) argue that the true subject matter of the transaction was the underlying assets—the cemeteries. Here, the subject matter of the transaction was the stock. Because the parties knew that a stock transaction would transfer everything that was not specifically excluded, as the trial court concluded, there was no mutual mistake. Even if there was a mistake as to the value of the transaction (here, $1 million versus $3 million), the court will not look behind the form of the transaction when the mistake is one of value. Moreover, there is no sound reason to depart from this holding to look beyond the form of the transfer (here, stock) to the subject of the transfer (here, assets). Accordingly, rescission is inapplicable. Affirmed as to this issue.

Continued on next page.

(2) No. Reformation is not available to reform a stock sale agreement transferring a corporation's stock where the parties are mistaken about the extent of the corporation's assets, but the seller is deemed to have constructive knowledge of all its assets and has the opportunity to exclude assets from the sale that it does not want included in the transaction. To prevail on a reformation claim, a party must show by clear and convincing evidence that: (1) there was a valid agreement between the parties expressing their real intentions; (2) the written instrument failed to express the real intentions of the parties; and (3) that failure was due to a mutual mistake of the parties, or a unilateral mistake accompanied by fraud or inequitable conduct by the other party. Here, SCI (P) and Corinthian (P) have not met their burden of proof. As to the second element, under the stock sale agreement, SCI (P) could have excluded the vacant lots, but it did not do so. Under state law, when a business sells all of its stock, it is selling all of its assets and liabilities unless any assets or liabilities are expressly excluded. Therefore, as a matter of law, it cannot be shown that the agreement did not reflect the parties' true intention. Also, as to the third element necessary for reformation, SCI (P) and Corinthian (P) have failed, as a matter of law, to prove that the stock sale agreement failed to express their true intentions as a result of mutual mistake. Because SCI (P) had the opportunity to exclude property that was not utilized in the operation of Crystal Lake's cemetery business, SCI (P) bore the risk of any mistake here. The mistake was SCI's (P) alone, because it alone failed to remove the lots from the transaction. Under general corporate law principles, a corporation is charged with constructive knowledge of all material facts known by its agents acquired while acting in the scope of their corporate authority. Even if those SCI (P) employees who negotiated the agreement at issue were unaware of the lots, some of SCI's (P) employees must have, at least at some point, been aware of the existence of the lots, as some employees must have purchased the lot, and other employees paid the taxes thereon. Therefore, SCI (P) is deemed to have known of the lots' existence and could have removed them from the sale. A court cannot reform a contract based on a unilateral mistake unless there was some evidence of fraud or inequitable conduct—and neither type of conduct was involved here. Accordingly, SCI (P) and Corinthian (P) have failed to prove the elements necessary for reformation. Affirmed as to this issue.

▶ *ANALYSIS*

Reformation is an equitable remedy that is available when a party seeks to alter or amend language in a contract so that the contract reflects the parties' true intent when they entered into the contract. Rescission is a different equitable remedy that seeks to void the entire contract. In a rescission case, courts look not only at the parties' true intent, but also focus on the form or subject matter of the transaction that is sought to be undone. In keeping with these analytic principles, the court in this case declined to look at the form or subject matter of the transaction when it ruled on the plaintiffs' reformation claim.

Quicknotes

MUTUAL ASSENT A requirement of a valid contract that the parties possess a mutuality of assent as manifested by the terms of the agreement and not by a hidden intent.

MUTUAL MISTAKE A mistake by both parties to a contract, who are in agreement as to what the contract terms should be, but the agreement as written fails to reflect that common intent; such contracts are voidable or subject to reformation.

REFORMATION OF CONTRACT An equitable remedy whereby the written terms of an agreement are altered in order to reflect the true intent of the parties; reformation requires a demonstration by clear and convincing evidence of mutual mistake by the parties to the contract.

RESCISSION The canceling of an agreement and the return of the parties to their positions prior to the formation of the contract.

UNILATERAL MISTAKE A mistake or misunderstanding as to the terms of a contract made by one party which is generally not a basis for relief by rescission or reformation.

Williams v. Walker-Thomas Furniture Co.

Buyer (D) v. Seller (P)

350 F.2d 445 (D.C. Cir. 1965).

NATURE OF CASE: Action in replevin.

FACT SUMMARY: Williams (D) made a series of purchases, on credit, from Walker-Thomas Furniture Co. (P), but defaulted on her payments.

▣ RULE OF LAW

Where, in light of the general commercial background of a particular case, it appears that gross inequality of bargaining power between the parties has led to the formation of a contract on terms to which one party has had no meaningful choice, a court should refuse to enforce such a contract on the ground that it is unconscionable.

FACTS: Beginning about 1957, Walker-Thomas Furniture Co. (Walker-Thomas) (P), a retail furniture company, began using a standard form contract for all credit transactions which contained, inter alia, a clause by which the company (P) reserved the right, upon default by a purchaser, to repossess all items contemporaneously being purchased by the buyer at the time of the repossession. This clause was accompanied by one which stated that all credit purchases made from Walker-Thomas (P) were to be handled through one account, with each installment payment spread pro rata over all items purchased (even where purchased separately and at different times), until all items were paid for. Williams (D) began purchasing items from Walker-Thomas (D) in 1957. In 1962, she bought a stereo set there. When she defaulted on a payment soon thereafter, Walker-Thomas (D) filed this action to replevy (i.e., repossess) all items she had purchased (and was still paying for) since 1957. From judgment for Walker-Thomas (P), this appeal followed.

ISSUE: May a court refuse to enforce an unreasonable contract, even though no evidence of fraud can be produced?

HOLDING AND DECISION: (Wright, J.) Yes. Where, in light of the general commercial background of a particular case, it appears that gross inequality of bargaining power between the parties has led to the formation of a contract on terms to which one party has had no meaningful choice, a court should refuse to enforce such a contract on the ground that it is unconscionable. It is true that the common law, operating by the caveat emptor rationale, refused to look into the essential fairness of a contract absent evidence of out and out fraud. The Uniform Commercial Code (UCC), however, notably § 2-302, as adopted in this jurisdiction, has accepted the rule that courts should seek to prevent overreaching in contracts of adhesion such

as the one at bar. Williams (D) and others come from a socioeconomic class to whom credit is difficult to obtain. To permit Walker-Thomas (P) to exploit this condition with provisions such as those pointed out above is clearly unconscionable. Judgment reversed, and the trial court is ordered to undertake an examination of these provisions in light of this opinion.

DISSENT: (Danaher, J.) The court ignores many policy considerations in its decision today. For one, the high risk of granting credit to the poor for companies like Walker-Thomas (D) is not even addressed. A more cautious approach is warranted.

▶ ANALYSIS

This case points up the major application which the UCC § 2-302 concept of unconscionability has had to date: adhesion (i.e., form) contracts. Note that the general common-law rule regarding such contracts remains the general rule today. That rule is that a person who signs a contract will be held responsible for any clauses or conditions which a reasonable man making a reasonable inspection would have discovered. The UCC rule merely qualifies this to say that, where one party to a form contract has no real choice over whether to accept the terms because of his relative economic position, then the fact he knows of the terms will not be enough to constitute a "meeting of the minds" on his part necessary to form a valid contract.

▬▭▬

Quicknotes

ADHESION CONTRACT A contract that is not negotiated by the parties and is usually prepared by the dominant party on a "take it or leave it" basis.

CAVEAT EMPTOR Let the buyer beware; doctrine that a buyer purchases something at his own risk.

FRAUD A false representation of facts with the intent that another will rely on the misrepresentation to his detriment.

REPLEVIN An action to recover personal property wrongfully taken.

UNCONSCIONABLE A situation in which a contract, or a particular contract term, is unenforceable if the court determines that such term(s) are unduly oppressive or unfair to one party to the contract.

▬▭▬

Toker v. Westerman

Seller (P) v. Buyer (D)

N.J. Union Cty. Dist. Ct., 113 N.J. Super. 452, 274 A.2d 78 (1970).

NATURE OF CASE: Action for breach of install-ment sales contract.

FACT SUMMARY: Westerman (D) alleged that he had been so grossly overcharged for a refrigerator-freezer that the contract was unconscionable.

> ### 🏛 RULE OF LAW
> A flagrantly excessive purchase price for goods may be deemed unconscionable.

FACTS: Westerman (D) was sold a refrigerator-freezer by a door-to-door salesman working for People's Food (P). The price of the unit was $900 and, with credit life insur-ance, taxes, and interest, Westerman (D) was obligated to pay a total of $1,229 under an installment sales contract. After paying more than $650 of the price, Westerman (D) refused to pay the balance. People's Food (P) assigned its rights to Toker (P), and suit was brought for breach of contract. Westerman (D) alleged that the purchase price for the unit was unconscionable. Evidence introduced at trial established that the unit was a stripped-down model which could be purchased for $350 to $400.

ISSUE: Is a flagrantly excessive purchase price sufficient grounds for finding that a contract is unconscionable?

HOLDING AND DECISION: (McKenzie, J.) Yes. A flagrantly excessive purchase price is grounds for finding that a contract is unconscionable. Here, the price was approximately 2.5 times the true value of the refrigerator-freezer. It was sold door-to-door, requiring less overhead than a normal retail outlet. Under the Uniform Commer-cial Code, "unconscionability" is defined as a situation in which there is inequality so strong, gross, and manifest that it must be impossible to justify. We find that where a purchase price is so excessive as to be shocking to the court, unconscionability may be found. Since People's Food (P) has already received $650 on the freezer contract, we find that it has been adequately compensated. Judgment for defendants.

▌ ANALYSIS

Generally, inadequacy of consideration, standing alone, is deemed to be insufficient grounds for finding a contract unconscionable. Most modern courts now view sharp commercial practices plus inadequate consideration in consumer situations as sufficient grounds for finding unconscionability if the price charged is deemed to be truly excessive. *American Home Improvement, Inc. v. MacI-ver,* 105 N.H. 435 (1964).

Quicknotes

CONSIDERATION Value given by one party in exchange for performance, or a promise to perform, by another party.

INSTALLMENT CONTRACT A contract pursuant to which the parties are to render performance or payment in periodic intervals.

UNCONSCIONABLE A situation in which a contract, or a particular contract term, is unenforceable if the court determines that such term(s) are unduly oppressive or unfair to one party to the contract.

Frostifresh Corp. v. Reynoso

Seller (P) v. Buyer (D)

N.Y. Nassau Cty. Dist. Ct., 52 Misc. 2d 26, 274 N.Y.S.2d 757 (1966).

NATURE OF CASE: Action to collect on a retail installment contract.

FACT SUMMARY: Frostifresh Corp. (P) sued Reynoso (D) to collect on a contract for the sale of a refrigerator.

🏛 RULE OF LAW
Courts have the power under § 2-302 of the Uniform Commercial Code to refuse to enforce provisions of a contract in order to prevent an unconscionable result.

FACTS: Frostifresh Corp. (P) and Reynoso (D) entered into a contract for the sale of a refrigerator-freezer. The negotiations were conducted entirely in Spanish, as Reynoso (D) did not speak English very well. Using distracting and deluding tactics, Frostifresh (P) convinced Reynoso (D) to enter into the retail installment contract, despite Reynoso's (D) objections that he could not afford it. The contract was entirely in English and was neither translated nor explained to Reynoso (D). The contract specified a price of $900 and a credit charge of $245.88, totaling $1,145.88. Frostifresh (P) admitted the appliance cost only $348. Reynoso (D), however, never raised the defense of fraud. The court, on its own, raised the issue of unconscionability.

ISSUE: Do courts have the power under § 2-302 of the Uniform Commercial Code to refuse to enforce provisions of a contract in order to prevent an unconscionable result?

HOLDING AND DECISION: (Donovan, J.) Yes. Courts have the power under § 2-302 of the Uniform Commercial Code to refuse to enforce provisions of a contract in order to prevent an unconscionable result. Here, the service charge almost equaled the cost of the appliance. The terms of the contract and the price of the appliance are unconscionable and will therefore be modified to reflect a just result. The service charge equaled the cost of the appliance. Reynoso (D) never received an explanation or translation of the contract. Because, under the Uniform Commercial Code, courts have the power to police contracts in order to prevent oppression and unfair surprise, this court will police this contract and modify it to reflect a just result. Reynoso (D) is still in possession of the appliance and will therefore be required to reimburse Frostifresh (P) its costs of $348 for the appliance.

▶ ANALYSIS

This case once again highlights the issues involving the relative bargaining power of the parties to a contract.

Pursuant to the Uniform Commercial Code, courts on their own accord can police contracts in order to protect just results. For example, with respect to unconscionable contracts, courts will often look to potential illegality, substantive unfairness, and public policy in determining whether or not a contract is unconscionable.

■══■

Quicknotes

FRAUD A false representation of facts with the intent that another will rely on the misrepresentation to his detriment.

INSTALLMENT CONTRACT A contract pursuant to which the parties are to render performance or payment in periodic intervals.

UNCONSCIONABLE A situation in which a contract, or a particular contract term, is unenforceable if the court determines that such term(s) are unduly oppressive or unfair to one party to the contract.

■══■

Frostifresh Corp. v. Reynoso

Seller (P) v. Buyer (D)

N.Y. App. Term, 54 Misc. 2d 119, 281 N.Y.S.2d 964 (1967).

NATURE OF CASE: Appeal from decision by the trial court to modify the amount retailer could collect on a contract.

FACT SUMMARY: Frostifresh Corp. (P) sued Reynoso (D) to collect on a contract for the sale of a refrigerator.

🏛 RULE OF LAW
Courts have the power under § 2-302 of the Uniform Commercial Code to refuse to enforce provisions of a contract in order to prevent an unconscionable result.

FACTS: Frostifresh Corp. (P) and Reynoso (D) entered into a contract for the sale of a refrigerator-freezer. The negotiations were conducted entirely in Spanish, as Reynoso (D) did not speak English very well. Using distracting and deluding tactics, Frostifresh (P) convinced Reynoso (D) to enter into the retail installment contract, despite Reynoso's (D) objections that he could not afford it. The contract was entirely in English and was neither translated nor explained to Reynoso (D). The contract specified a price of $900 and a credit charge of $245.88, totaling $1,145.88. Frostifresh (P) admitted the appliance cost only $348. Reynoso (D) never raised the defense of fraud. The court, on its own, raised the issue of unconscionability. The court ruled that, because Reynoso (D) did not return the appliance, he must reimburse Frostifresh (P) for the refrigerator. However, the court modified the amount Frostifresh (P) could collect under the contract to $348, the cost of the appliance to Frostifresh (P), on the grounds that the terms of the contract were unconscionable. Frostifresh (P) appealed.

ISSUE: Do courts have the power under § 2-302 of the Uniform Commercial Code to refuse to enforce provisions of a contract in order to prevent an unconscionable result?

HOLDING AND DECISION: (Per curiam) Yes. Courts have the power under § 2-302 of the Uniform Commercial Code to refuse to enforce provisions of a contract in order to prevent an unconscionable result. Here, the trial court determined that the price of the appliance was unconscionable and modified it to reflect a just result. This determination was correct. However, the trial court erred when it modified the amount solely to represent the cost of the appliance to Frostifresh (P). Frostifresh (P) should recover the net cost of the appliance, plus a reasonable profit, in addition to trucking and service charges necessarily incurred and reasonable finance charges. Reversed and remanded to determine the proper costs.

▶ ANALYSIS

This case once again highlights the issues involving the relative bargaining power of the parties to a contract. In this appellate ruling, the court is demonstrating the importance of a just result, by finding a way to make certain each of the parties receives a fair deal. The Uniform Commercial Code allows for such intervention in order to protect fairness and justice.

Quicknotes

FRAUD A false representation of facts with the intent that another will rely on the misrepresentation to his detriment.

INSTALLMENT CONTRACT A contract pursuant to which the parties are to render performance or payment in periodic intervals.

UNCONSCIONABLE A situation in which a contract, or a particular contract term, is unenforceable if the court determines that such term(s) are unduly oppressive or unfair to one party to the contract.

Carnival Cruise Lines, Inc. v. Shute

Cruise ship owner (D) v. Injured passenger (P)

499 U.S. 585 (1991).

NATURE OF CASE: Appeal from reversal of grant of defendant's motion for summary judgment in personal injury action.

FACT SUMMARY: After Mrs. Shute (P), a Washington resident, was injured on a Carnival Cruise Lines (D) ship, she filed suit in Washington, notwithstanding a forum selection clause printed on her ticket that required adjudication of disputes in Florida.

RULE OF LAW

A forum selection clause in a commercial passage contract is enforceable if it is fundamentally fair.

FACTS: The Shutes (P), Washington state residents, purchased tickets on a Carnival Cruise from a Washington travel agent. Carnival Cruise Lines, Inc.'s (Carnival's) (D) principal place of business was in Florida. The Shutes (P) received the cruise ticket in the mail. The tickets called attention to the terms of the contract printed on the back of the tickets. The contract terms included a forum selection clause requiring all litigation to be brought in Florida. Mrs. Shute (P) was injured while the ship was off the coast of Mexico. She brought suit against Carnival (D) in Washington federal court. The district court dismissed for lack of personal jurisdiction. The court of appeals reversed. It held that the forum selection clause was unenforceable because it was not freely bargained for. Carnival (D) appealed, and the Supreme Court granted certiorari.

ISSUE: Is a forum selection clause in a commercial passage contract enforceable if it is fundamentally fair?

HOLDING AND DECISION: (Blackmun, J.) Yes. A forum selection clause in a commercial passage contract is enforceable if it is fundamentally fair. In any event, it is not unenforceable simply because it was not freely bargained for. The realities of form passage contracts must be accounted for. It would be entirely unreasonable to assume that a cruise passenger would or could negotiate the terms of a forum clause in a routine commercial cruise ticket form. Nevertheless, including a reasonable forum clause in such a form contract well may be permissible for several reasons. Because it is not unlikely that a mishap in a cruise could subject a cruise line to litigation in several different fora, the line has a special interest in limiting such fora. Moreover, a clause establishing ex ante the dispute resolution forum has the salutary effect of dispelling confusion as to where suits may be brought and defended, thereby sparing litigants time and expense and conserving judicial resources. Furthermore, it is likely that passengers purchasing tickets containing a forum clause like the one here at issue benefit in the form of reduced fares reflecting the savings that the cruise line enjoys by limiting the fora in which it may be sued. In this case, the Shutes (P) admit that they were on notice that the forum selection clause was a term of the contract. Also rejected is the court of appeals' conclusion that the clause here at issue should not be enforced on grounds of inconvenience because the Shutes (P) are physically and financially incapable of pursuing this litigation in Florida. Not only did the district court not make findings regarding such impediments faced by the Shutes (P), but in any event they have not satisfied the heavy burden of proof required to set aside the otherwise valid clause on grounds of inconvenience, especially given that the Shutes do not deny they were on notice of the forum clause. Reversed.

DISSENT: (Stevens, J.) First, only the most meticulous passenger would be likely to become aware of the forum selection clause, and then only after they purchased and received the ticket. Most passengers who even read the clause would then probably accept the risk of filing suit in Florida, rather than having to cancel their trip at the last minute without a refund. A cruise line can thus reduce its litigation costs and liability insurance by essentially forcing this choice on its passengers: this is unfair and renders the provision unreasonable. A clause limiting or preventing a passenger's right to trial is fundamentally unfair and contrary to public policy and should not be enforced.

ANALYSIS

The dissent argued that the forum selection clause used by Carnival (D) was null and void under the terms of the Limitation of Vessel Owner's Liability Act, Chapter 46, U.S.C. App. § 183c. The relevant provision prohibited any vessel owner from limiting its liability or lessening the right of any claimant "to a trial by court of competent jurisdiction. . . ." The majority, on the other hand, concluded that this provision did not address forum selection clauses. Congress subsequently overruled this decision by inserting the word "any" before "court" in the sentence quoted above.

Quicknotes

CERTIORARI A discretionary writ issued by a superior court to an inferior court in order to review the lower court's decisions; the Supreme Court's writ ordering such review.

FORUM SELECTION CLAUSE Provision contained in a contract setting forth the particular forum in which the parties would resolve a matter if a dispute were to arise.

SUMMARY JUDGMENT Judgment rendered by a court in response to a motion by one of the parties, claiming that the lack of a question of material fact in respect to an issue warrants disposition of the issue without consideration by the jury.

Nagrampa v. MailCoups, Inc.

Franchisee (P) v. Franchisor (D)

469 F.3d 1257 (9th Cir. 2006).

NATURE OF CASE: Appeal from judgment in action challenging an arbitration clause in a franchise agreement as unconscionable. [The complete procedural posture of the case is not presented in the casebook extract.]

FACT SUMMARY: Nagrampa (P), a franchisee of MailCoups, Inc. (D), contended that an arbitration provision in the franchise agreement between the parties was unconscionable because it was adhesive, oppressive, one-sided, and lacked mutuality, among other things.

> 🏛 **RULE OF LAW**
> An arbitration clause in a franchise agreement is unconscionable where, procedurally, it is adhesive and oppressive, even if minimally so, and where, substantively, it strongly exhibits a lack of mutuality.

FACTS: Nagrampa (P), who lived in California, entered into a franchise agreement with MailCoups, Inc. (D) to operate a direct mail coupon advertising franchise. She had experience working in direct mail marketing but had never before been a franchisee. The 30-page agreement, on page 25, contained an arbitration provision that required the parties to arbitrate their disputes in Boston, and to equally bear the costs of arbitration. The provision also gave MailCoups (D) the ability to seek redress either through arbitration or judicially to obtain provisional remedies to protect its intellectual property. After two years of unprofitable operation of her franchise, Nagrampa (P) unilaterally terminated the agreement, and MailCoups (D) initiated arbitration proceedings to recover over $80,000 in fees it claimed Nagrampa (P) owed under the agreement. Nagrampa (P), through her attorney, objected to proceeding with arbitration and questioned the validity of the arbitration clause. Ultimately, Nagrampa (P) refused to participate in the arbitration proceedings and filed suit against MailCoups (D) in California state court, and the case was removed to federal district court. MailCoups (D) moved, inter alia, to compel arbitration. Nagrampa (P) opposed principally on the ground that the arbitration clause was unconscionable. The district court sidestepped the question under California law of whether the provision was procedurally unconscionable, and rendered judgment. The court of appeals granted review. [The complete procedural posture of the case is not presented in the casebook extract.]

ISSUE: Is an arbitration clause in a franchise agreement unconscionable where, procedurally, it is adhesive and oppressive, even if minimally so, and where, substantively, it strongly exhibits a lack of mutuality?

HOLDING AND DECISION: (Wardlaw, J.) Yes. An arbitration clause in a franchise agreement is unconscionable where, procedurally, it is adhesive and oppressive, even if minimally so, and where, substantively, it strongly exhibits a lack of mutuality. Here, the law of California applies. Under that law, the doctrine of unconscionability applies to franchise agreements, and, to determine whether a provision in a franchise agreement is unconscionable, the provision must be analyzed for both procedural and substantive unconscionability. While both these types of unconscionability must be present to some degree, they do not have to be present to the same degree. Instead, a sliding scale is used, so the greater the substantive unconscionability is shown to be, the less evidence of procedural unconscionability is needed to render the provision unenforceable. Procedural unconscionability analysis focuses on "oppression" or "surprise." Oppression arises from an inequality of bargaining power that results in no real negotiation and an absence of meaningful choice, while surprise involves the extent to which the supposedly agreed-upon terms are hidden in a prolix printed form drafted by the party seeking to enforce them. The district court's sidestepping an analysis of procedural unconscionability was erroneous. If a contract is adhesive, it is facially procedurally unconscionable. A contract is adhesive where it is a standard contract, imposed on a take-it-or-leave-it basis with no opportunity given to the subscribing party to negotiate its terms. Here, the contract was non-negotiable and Nagrampa (P) had no opportunity to negotiate its terms. MailCoups (D) argues that Nagrampa (P) had meaningful choice and bargaining power because she could have stayed at her job or entered into an agreement with another direct mail franchisor. MailCoups (D) also argues that Nagrampa (P) was a sophisticated party who could have read and understood the entire agreement. These arguments are not convincing. First, the relationship between franchisor and franchisee is characterized by a prevailing, although not universal, inequality of economic resources between the contracting parties. Typically, the franchisor is a large corporation with many resources, whereas the franchisee is typically a small businessperson, and, in many instances—as here—the franchise is the individual's first business. The agreements tend to reflect this gross bargaining disparity, as they are form contracts drafted and offered by the franchisor on a take-it-or-leave-it basis. Here, this was the case: MailCoup's (D) parent company is a very large company, and Nagrampa (P) previously had never owned her own business. As

Continued on next page.

previously noted, the contract was offered to her on a take-it-or-leave-it basis. Moreover, the availability in the market place of substitute employment, goods, or services alone does not serve to defeat a claim of procedural unconscionability. Thus, the potential availability to Nagrampa (P) of other franchise opportunities alone does not defeat her claim of procedural unconscionability. Moreover, the sophistication of a party, alone, cannot defeat a procedural unconscionability claim. Nagrampa (P) asserts that there was "surprise" because she was not informed of the existence of the arbitration provision, which was embedded toward the end of the lengthy contract. Even if there was no surprise to Nagrampa (P), such surprise need not be demonstrated if the arbitration provision is oppressive. Here, because of the factors previously noted, the provision was oppressive, even if minimally so. Therefore, regardless of whether MailCoups (D) had a duty to inform Nagrampa (P) of the clause, and the minimal evidence of procedural unconscionability, it is sufficient to establish procedural unconscionability requiring analysis of the extent of substantive unconscionability to determine, whether, on a sliding scale, the arbitration provision is unconscionable. Substantive unconscionability arises where an arbitration provision is overly harsh or generates one-sided results, so that it cannot be said to be bilateral. Rejected are Nagrampa's (P) arguments that the clause's fee-splitting provision and failure to ensure an impartial arbitrator are substantively unconscionable. However, two other provisions in the arbitration clause do exhibit a lack of mutuality supporting a finding of substantive unconscionability. First, the contract gives MailCoups (D) access to a judicial forum to obtain provisional remedies to protect its intellectual property, while it provides Nagrampa (P) with only the arbitral forum to resolve her claims. This theoretically means that MailCoups (D) could go to court relating to a breach of contract claim—which most likely would be raised by Nagrampa (P)—so long as it at all involved its intellectual property. This evidences that the party with the stronger bargaining power has restricted the weaker party to the arbitral forum, but has reserved for itself a choice of fora. Thus, this provision is clearly one-sided. Second, the arbitral forum is designated as Boston, a location considerably more advantageous to MailCoups (P). To determine whether a forum selection provision is reasonable, the respective circumstances of the parties must be analyzed. Here, requiring Nagrampa (P) to travel across the country to Boston would work a severe hardship on Nagrampa (P) and would unfairly benefit MailCoups (D). For these reasons, the arbitration clause is substantively unconscionable. Thus, even though the evidence of procedural unconscionability is slight, the evidence of substantive unconscionability is strong enough to tip the scale and render the clause unconscionable. [The disposition of the case is not indicated in the casebook extract.]

ANALYSIS

There are two types of challenges to the validity of an arbitration agreement. One type challenges specifically the validity of the agreement to arbitrate, whereas the other challenges the contract as a whole, either on a ground that directly affects the entire contract (e.g., the agreement was fraudulently induced) or on the ground that the illegality of one of the contract's provisions renders the whole contract invalid. These two types of challenges are treated differently. When the crux of the complaint challenges the validity or enforceability of the agreement containing the arbitration provision, then the question of whether the agreement, as a whole, is unconscionable must be referred to the arbitrator. However, when the crux of the complaint is not the invalidity of the contract as a whole, but rather the arbitration provision itself, then the courts must decide whether the arbitration provision is invalid and unenforceable. If the challenge is just to the provision itself, and the provision is determined to be unconscionable, just that provision may be struck, and the rest of the contract will be left intact. It is not always clear, however, when the challenge is one going to the entire contract or is just focused on the arbitration provision itself. Here, for example, a dissenting opinion would have held that because the court had to consider, in the course of analyzing the validity of the arbitration provision, the circumstances surrounding the making of the entire agreement, i.e., whether it was a contract of adhesion, that the challenge was to the entire agreement.

Quicknotes

ADHESION CONTRACT A contract, usually in standardized form, that is prepared by one party and offered to another, whose terms are so disproportionately in favor of the drafting party that courts tend to question the equality of bargaining power in reaching the agreement.

ARBITRATION CLAUSE Provision contained in a contract pursuant to which both parties agree that any disputes arising thereunder will be resolved through arbitration.

SUBSTANTIVE UNCONSCIONABILITY Rule of law whereby a court may excuse performance of a contract, or of a particular contract term, if it determines that such terms are unduly oppressive or unfair to one party to the contract and violate the subordinate party's reasonable expectations.

Washington Mutual Finance Group v. Bailey

Financial institution (P) v. Loan applicant (D)

364 F.3d 260 (5th Cir. 2004).

NATURE OF CASE: Suit to enforce an arbitration agreement.

FACT SUMMARY: Illiterate recipients of loans and various forms of insurance all signed agreements to arbitrate any disputes arising from their loan and insurance transactions.

🏛 RULE OF LAW

An arbitration agreement is not unconscionable under Mississippi law either if one party to the agreement is illiterate, and thus does not understand the agreement, or if the other party knows of the illiteracy but fails to inform the illiterate party that the agreement requires arbitration.

FACTS: Bailey (D), who was illiterate, and several other illiterate persons all received loans from Washington Mutual Finance Group (WM Finance) (P); at the same time, they also received various forms of insurance from four insurance companies. All the illiterate loan recipients (D) signed agreements governed by the Federal Arbitration Act to arbitrate any disputes that might arise with WM Finance (P). When a dispute with WM Finance (P) did arise, though, the illiterate loan recipients (D) filed suit against WM Finance (P) and the four insurance companies in Mississippi state court. WM Finance (P) then filed suit against the illiterate loan recipients (D) in federal court, asking the court to stay the state proceedings and compel the illiterate loan recipients (D) to arbitrate their claims as they had agreed to do. The insurance companies intervened in federal court, and the trial judge consolidated the matters for decision. The trial judge granted the motion to dismiss filed by the illiterate loan recipients (D), reasoning that the arbitration agreement was unconscionable and thus unenforceable because of the loan recipients' (D) illiteracy, a problem compounded, in the trial judge's analysis, by WM Finance's (P) failure to specifically inform the illiterate loan recipients (D) that they were signing an arbitration agreement. WM Finance (P) appealed.

ISSUE: Is an arbitration agreement unconscionable under Mississippi law either if one party to the agreement is illiterate, and thus does not understand the agreement, or if the other party knows of the illiteracy but fails to inform the illiterate party that the agreement requires arbitration?

HOLDING AND DECISION: (Jolly, C.J.). No. An arbitration agreement is not unconscionable under Mississippi law either if one party to the agreement is illiterate, and thus does not understand the agreement, or if the other party knows of the illiteracy but fails to inform

the illiterate party that the agreement requires arbitration. Mississippi contract law recognizes two forms of unconscionability: procedural and/or substantive. Procedural unconscionability—relied upon by the trial judge in this case—requires proof that one party to the agreement lacked knowledge or voluntariness; that the written form contained inconspicuous print or complex legal terms; that the parties had a great disparity of bargaining power or sophistication; and/or that one party had no opportunity to study and interpret the contract. Under Mississippi law, the trial judge in this case incorrectly concluded that the arbitration agreement was unconscionable because, based solely on the loan recipients' (D) illiteracy, they lacked knowledge about the arbitration agreement. Mississippi courts have consistently held all persons responsible for reading and knowing the contents of the contracts they sign. Knowledge of a contract's terms is imputed to one who signs a contract even if he does not read it, and the same reasoning applies here. Moreover, the trial judge's attempt to require WM Finance (P) to inform the illiterate loan recipients (D) about the arbitration agreement does nothing to change those basic principles of Mississippi contract law. Reversed.

▶ ANALYSIS

From a judicial perspective that strives to ensure a level playing field for all parties, the result in *Washington Mutual* is not nearly as harsh as it might seem at first blush. The illiterate loan recipients (D) presumably were all fully aware of their illiteracy when they entered their arbitration agreements with WM Finance (P). They therefore had ample reason—and ample opportunity—to take corrective measures before they conducted business in such a relatively formal setting; they could have, for example, simply asked literate friends or relatives to accompany them to the offices of WM Finance (P). Similarly, although the court of appeals confined its analysis to legal questions, there are also strong policy reasons for not shifting an illiterate person's own responsibilities to those with whom he does business: Each party to an agreement is responsible for his own interests, especially when the steps available for protecting those interests are as easy to take as they were in this case.

━━━

Quicknotes

ARBITRATION An alternative resolution process where a dispute is heard and decided by a neutral third party, rather than through legal proceedings.

Continued on next page.

SUBSTANTIVE UNCONSCIONABILITY Rule of law whereby a court may excuse performance of a contract, or of a particular contract term, if it determines that such terms are unduly oppressive or unfair to one party to the contract and violate the subordinate party's reasonable expectations.

UNCONSCIONABILITY A situation in which a contract, or a particular contract term, is unenforceable if the court determines that such terms are unduly oppressive or unfair to one party to the contract.

■━■

Broemmer v. Abortion Services of Phoenix, Ltd.

Abortion patient (P) v. Clinic (D)

Ariz. Sup. Ct., 173 Ariz. 148, 840 P.2d 1013 (1992) (en banc).

NATURE OF CASE: Appeal from summary judgment denying damages for medical malpractice.

FACT SUMMARY: When Broemmer (P) filed a malpractice complaint against Abortion Services of Phoenix (D), Abortion Services (D) argued that Broemmer (P) had given up her right to a jury trial when she signed a standardized arbitration agreement prior to treatment.

RULE OF LAW
An adhesion contract will be enforced unless it is unconscionable or beyond the reasonable expectations of the parties.

FACTS: When Broemmer (P), a 21-year-old, unmarried high school graduate, arrived for her appointment at Abortion Services of Phoenix, Ltd. (Abortion Services) (D), she was told to complete three forms, one of which was an agreement to arbitrate any dispute resulting from the fees and/or services of Abortion Services (D). The arbitration agreement included a provision requiring that any arbitrator appointed be a licensed obstetrician/gynecologist. The clinic staff did not attempt to explain the agreement to Broemmer (P) nor indicate that she was free to refuse to sign. Broemmer (P) filled out and signed the forms. When a doctor at Abortion Services (D) performed the abortion the following day, he punctured her uterus, requiring her to seek medical treatment. Broemmer (P) filed a malpractice complaint. Abortion Services (D) moved to dismiss on the ground that arbitration was required, and the trial court granted summary judgment. The court of appeals held that, although the agreement to arbitrate was an adhesion contract, it was enforceable because it did not fall outside Broemmer's (P) reasonable expectations and was not unconscionable. Broemmer (P) appealed.

ISSUE: Will an adhesion contract be enforced unless it is unconscionable or beyond the reasonable expectations of the parties?

HOLDING AND DECISION: (Moeller, V.C.J.) Yes. An adhesion contract will be enforced unless it is unconscionable or beyond the reasonable expectations of the parties. An adhesion contract is a standardized form offered on a "take it or leave it" basis which the consumer must accept without bargaining if she wants to obtain the desired product or service. The arbitration agreement signed by Broemmer (P) was an adhesion contract because it was prepared by Abortion Services (D), presented to Broemmer (P) as a condition of treatment on a "take it or leave it" basis, and its terms were nonnegotiable. Whether or not it was also enforceable depends on whether it was

beyond Broemmer's (P) reasonable expectations. In this case, it was not reasonable to expect a high school graduate to agree to arbitrate her medical malpractice claim, thus waiving her right to a jury trial, as a consequence of filling out three forms given her highly emotional state and her inexperience in commercial matters. Furthermore, it would be unreasonable to enforce the critical provision requiring that the arbitrator be an obstetrician/gynecologist when it was not a negotiated term and Abortion Services (D) failed to explain it or call attention to it. Because the arbitration agreement fell outside of Broemmer's (P) reasonable expectations and is, therefore, unenforceable, it is unnecessary to determine whether the contract is also unconscionable. Reversed and remanded.

DISSENT: (Martone, J.) The majority's decision reflects a preference for litigation over arbitration which is not in accord with current public policy considerations. There is nothing in this case that warrants a finding that an agreement to arbitrate a malpractice claim was not within the reasonable expectations of the parties. On the contrary, Broemmer (P), an adult, had an opportunity to read the document, which was legible and in bold letters, containing an agreement that was not bizarre, oppressive, or contrary to prior negotiations.

ANALYSIS

Broemmer creates an exception to the traditional duty-to-read rule where the terms of the contract are unfair under the circumstances. In cases like *Broemmer*, the manifestation of assent that is ordinarily implied by a signature is insufficient because the assent is not reasoned or knowing. Consent requires an understanding of the provision in question (which Broemmer (P) admitted she did not have) as well as a reasonable opportunity to accept or decline the provision. Even if these two criteria are present, courts will still refuse to enforce a clause that is unconscionable or contrary to public policy.

Quicknotes

ACCEPTANCE Assent to the specified terms of an offer, resulting in the formation of a binding agreement.

ADHESION CONTRACT A contract, usually in standardized form, that is prepared by one party and offered to another, whose terms are so disproportionately in favor of the

Continued on next page.

drafting party that courts tend to question the equality of bargaining power in reaching the agreement.

MUTUAL ASSENT A requirement of a valid contract that the parties possess a mutuality of assent as manifested by the terms of the agreement and not by a hidden intent.

UNCONSCIONABILITY Rule of law whereby a court may excuse performance of a contract, or of a particular contract term, if it determines that such term(s) are unduly oppressive or unfair to one party to the contract.

■≡■

We Care Hair Development, Inc. v. Engen

Franchisor (P) v. Franchisees (D)

180 F.3d 838 (7th Cir. 1999).

NATURE OF CASE: Breach of contract.

FACT SUMMARY: Franchisees (D) entered into franchise agreements with We Care Hair Development, Inc. (P), each of which contained an arbitration clause for all disputes arising out of the agreement.

🏛 RULE OF LAW
A contract is unconscionable when, viewed as a whole it is oppressive or totally one-sided.

FACTS: Franchisees (D) entered into franchise agreements with Care Hair Development, Inc. (We Care Hair) (P), each of which contained an arbitration clause for all disputes arising out of the agreement. The franchisees were required to sublease their premises from an alter ego of We Care Hair (P), which did not require arbitration. Offering circulars disclosed that the leasing company could terminate the sublease and evict the franchisee for any breach of the sublease, including a breach of the franchise agreement. The district court ordered arbitration and franchisees (D) appealed.

ISSUE: A contract is unconscionable, when viewed as a whole it is oppressive or totally one-sided.

HOLDING AND DECISION: (Wood, Jr., J.) A contract is unconscionable, when viewed as a whole it is oppressive or totally one-sided. Here the arbitration clauses cannot be viewed as creating unfair surprise. Each franchisee was provided with a copy of the offering circular which clearly disclosed that the leasing company could bring eviction proceedings for any breach of the sublease, including that of the franchise agreement. The arbitration clauses are not unconscionable.

▶ ANALYSIS

In determining whether a contract provision is unconscionable, the presence of a commercially unreasonable term is relevant. This is defined as a "term that no one is his reasonable mind would have agreed to." The court must also look to the circumstances existing at the time of the contract's formation, including the parties' relative bargaining positions and whether the provision's operation would result in unfair surprise.

Quicknotes

ARBITRATION An agreement to have a dispute heard and decided by a neutral third party, rather than through legal proceedings.

ARBITRATION CLAUSE Provision contained in a contract pursuant to which both parties agree that any disputes arising thereunder will be resolved through arbitration.

FRANCHISEE A party with whom a supplier of goods or services agrees to permit to sell the good or service or to otherwise conduct business on behalf of the franchise.

SUBLEASE A transaction in which a tenant or lessee conveys an interest in the leased premises that is less than his own or retains a reversionary interest.

UNCONSCIONABILITY Rule of law whereby a court may excuse performance of a contract, or of a particular contract term, if it determines that such term(s) are unduly oppressive or unfair to one party to the contract.

The Compensation Principle

Quick Reference Rules of Law

White v. Benkowski

Neighbor (P) v. Neighbor (D)

Wis. Sup. Ct., 37 Wis. 2d 285, 155 N.W.2d 74 (1967).

NATURE OF CASE: Action in damages for breach of contract.

FACT SUMMARY: The Whites (P) contracted with the Benkowskis (D) to supply water for their house.

🏛 RULE OF LAW
Damages may be awarded for inconvenience for breach of contract, but no punitive damages may be awarded.

FACTS: The Whites (P) purchased a home which had no water supply. The Whites (P) entered into a contract with their next-door neighbors, the Benkowskis (D), to use their well for water. A contract for 10 years was entered into by the parties. After a few years, the relationship between the parties deteriorated. The Benkowskis (D) shut off the water several times allegedly to clear the pipes and to remind the Whites (P) that they were using too much water. The Whites (P), during these periods, had to bathe their children elsewhere and put up with bathroom odors. The Whites (P) filed suit for exemplary and punitive damages. The jury awarded the Whites (P) $10 in exemplary damages, no pecuniary loss being proved or pled, and $2,000 in punitive damages. The court reduced the exemplary damages to $1 since no pecuniary loss was proved and disallowed all punitive damages.

ISSUE:
(1) May a jury take into account inconvenience in awarding exemplary damages?
(2) May punitive damages be awarded for breach of contract?

HOLDING AND DECISION: (Wilkie, J.)
(1) Yes. A jury may take inconvenience into account in awarding exemplary damages.
(2) No. A nominal award may be rendered for personal inconvenience due to a breach of contract. $10 is such a nominal amount and is clearly sustainable under the evidence. Punitive damages are never authorized in breach of contract actions. It is immaterial whether the breach was either intentional and/or malicious. No moral penalties may be assessed for mere breach of contract. Reversed in part and affirmed in part.

▶ ANALYSIS
Some breach of contract actions include tortious conduct for which punitive damages may be awarded. To recover such damages, a tort must be separately pleaded and proved. Every breach of contract is actionable. Trivial breaches or breaches that cause no pecuniary loss will normally result in an award of minimal damages as herein. Damages for breach of contract are meant only to place the injured party in the same position he would have been in if the breach had not occurred.

Quicknotes

EXEMPLARY DAMAGES Damages exceeding the actual injury suffered for the purposes of punishment, deterrence and comfort to plaintiff.

PUNITIVE DAMAGES Damages exceeding the actual injury suffered for the purposes of punishment, deterrence and comfort to plaintiff.

City of Rye v. Public Service Mut. Ins. Co.

City (P) v. Insurance company (D)

N.Y. Ct. App., 34 N.Y.2d 470, 315 N.E.2d 458 (1974).

NATURE OF CASE: Appeal from order dismissing action to recover on bond.

FACT SUMMARY: The City of Rye, N.Y. (P) sought to recover a predetermined amount on a bond absent evidence of its actual loss.

🏛 RULE OF LAW
An action on a performance bond will not lie if the bond amount is not related to actual damages.

FACTS: Several developers contracted with the City of Rye, N.Y. (the "City") (P) to construct six cooperative apartments. The developers had to post a $100,000 bond to ensure liquidated damages of $200 per day for each day past the projected completion date for the buildings. Five hundred days past that date, the buildings had not been completed. The City (P) brought an action to recover on the bond, which had been issued by Public Service Mut. Ins. Co. (D). The trial court denied the City's (P) motion for summary judgment. The appellate division affirmed, and the New York Court of Appeals granted review.

ISSUE: Will an action on a performance bond lie if the bond amount is not related to actual damages?

HOLDING AND DECISION: (Breitel, C.J.) No. An action on a performance bond will not lie if the amount is not related to actual damages. When damages flowing from a breach of contract would be difficult to ascertain, the parties may provide for liquidated damages that reasonably approximate likely actual damages. However, if liquidated damages are so disproportionate as to constitute a penalty, they will not be permitted. Here, there was no evidence that the $200 per day liquidated damages provision was commensurate with actual damages; in fact, there was no convincing evidence that any damages were incurred by the City (P). For these reasons, the liquidated damages provision constituted a penalty and may not be enforced. Affirmed.

▶ ANALYSIS

The rule stated here is fairly universal. Liquidated damages are allowable, but only if they are commensurate with actual damages. To provide otherwise would constitute a penalty, which would be at odds with contract law's purpose of compensation, not punishment. In addition, it would often violate the rule of contract damages which generally limits recover to that amount which would restore the damaged party, rather than place that party in a better position than he would have been had there been no breach.

Quicknotes

ACTUAL DAMAGES Measure of damages necessary to compensate victim for actual injuries suffered.

LIQUIDATED DAMAGES An amount of money specified in a contract representing the damages owed in the event of breach.

McCallister v. Patton

Buyer (P) v. Seller (D)

Ark. Sup. Ct., 214 Ark. 293, 215 S.W.2d 701 (1948).

NATURE OF CASE: Appeal from dismissal of an action for specific performance of a contract.

FACT SUMMARY: McCallister (P) sued Patton (D), alleging the breach of a contract for the sale of a car, demanding specific performance of the contract.

RULE OF LAW
Equity does not grant specific performance of a contract for the sale of personal property if damages in an action at law afford a complete and adequate remedy.

FACTS: On September 14, 1945, McCallister (P) entered into a contract with Patton (D) for the sale of a Ford automobile. Patton (D) had no cars in stock and took orders by contract, numbering the contracts in the order they were executed. McCallister (P) put down a $25 deposit on the car. McCallister (P) was number thirty-seven, but even though Patton (D) received more than thirty-seven cars, Patton (D) never sold one to McCallister (P). McCallister (P) claimed that Ford cars were difficult to obtain and sued Patton (D) for breach of contract, demanding specific performance for the delivery of a Ford automobile. Patton (D) demurred to the complaint on the grounds that it did not state facts sufficient to entitle McCallister (P) to the relief of specific performance. The trial court sustained the demurrer, and McCallister (P) appealed.

ISSUE: Does equity grant specific performance of a contract for the sale of personal property if damages in an action at law afford a complete and adequate remedy?

HOLDING AND DECISION: (Millwee, J.) No. Equity does not grant specific performance of a contract for the sale of personal property if damages in an action at law afford a complete and adequate remedy. One exception to this general rule is for contracts relating to personal property which have a peculiar, unique, or sentimental value. Such items are not measurable in money damages. Here, damages in an action at law will afford a complete and adequate result. A number of Ford cars had been produced since 1945, and McCallister (P) did not allege facts stating that this particular automobile had a unique and irreplaceable value. While Ford cars were hard to obtain, this case involves no harm that money damages would not adequately cure. Specific performance is not warranted here. Affirmed.

ANALYSIS

This case highlights the different types of relief available within expectation remedies: damages and specific performance. Both are designed to give the non-breaching party the "benefit of the bargain." That is, the aggrieved party will be allowed to obtain his contractual expectation interests.

Quicknotes

BENEFIT OF THE BARGAIN Calculation of assessing damages in actions for breach of contract measured as the difference between the actual value and the purported value of the goods being bought.

EQUITY Fairness; justice; the determination of a matter consistent with principles of fairness and not in strict compliance with rules of law.

EXPECTANCY INTEREST The expectation or contingency of obtaining possession of a right or interest in the future.

SPECIFIC PERFORMANCE An equitable remedy whereby the court requires the parties to perform their obligations pursuant to a contract.

London Bucket Co. v. Stewart

Heating installation company (D) v. Motel owner (P)

Ky. Ct. App., 314 Ky. 832, 237 S.W.2d 509 (1951).

NATURE OF CASE: Appeal of grant of specific performance.

FACT SUMMARY: Stewart (P) sought specific performance when London Bucket Co. (D) contracted to properly provide and install a heating system for Stewart's motel.

🏛 RULE OF LAW
Specific performance will not be granted unless the ordinary common law remedy for breach of contract is an inadequate and incomplete remedy.

FACTS: Stewart (P) entered into a contract with London Bucket Co. (London) (D) for the provision and installation of a heating system in Stewart's motel. Stewart (P) alleged that London (D) installed the heating system in an unskilled and unprofessional manner, to the extent that the heating system would not properly provide heat during the cold season. Stewart (P) demanded specific performance and also asked for damages in the amount of $8,250. Required to elect his remedy, Stewart (P) opted for specific performance, dismissing without prejudice his action for damages. The trial court granted specific performance, and London (D) appealed.

ISSUE: Will specific performance be granted if the ordinary common law remedy for breach of contract is an adequate and complete remedy?

HOLDING AND DECISION: (Stanley, Comm.) No. Specific performance will not be granted unless the ordinary common law remedy for breach of contract is an inadequate and incomplete remedy. With respect to building construction contracts, the general rule is that such contracts will not be specifically enforced because ordinarily damages are an adequate remedy and because of the incapacity of the court to supervise the performance. The present case involves a building construction contract, in that it covers the proper installation of a heating system in a motel. As a result, Stewart (P) could be adequately protected with an award of monetary damages. Therefore, the granting of specific performance was an error by the lower court. Reversed.

▶ ANALYSIS

When deciding between damages or specific performance, courts look to the expectation interests of the parties and how sufficient money damages will compensate for the loss. In analyzing expectation interests, courts often look to two components: First, out-of-pocket losses sustained in reliance on the contract; and second, the forgone opportunities experienced due to the breach of the contract.

Quicknotes

DAMAGES Monetary compensation that may be awarded by the court to a party who has sustained injury or loss to his or her person, property or rights due to another party's unlawful act, omission or negligence.

EXPECTANCY INTEREST The expectation or contingency of obtaining possession of a right or interest in the future.

SPECIFIC PERFORMANCE An equitable remedy whereby the court requires the parties to perform their obligations pursuant to a contract.

Neri v. Retail Marine Corp.

Buyer (P) v. Seller (D)

N.Y. Ct. App., 30 N.Y.2d 393, 285 N.E.2d 311 (1972).

NATURE OF CASE: Action for breach of a sales contract.

FACT SUMMARY: Neri (P) contracted to purchase a boat from Retail Marine Corp. (Marine) (D). Later Neri (P) wrongfully rescinded the contract and then brought suit for recovery of his deposit. Marine (D) counterclaimed seeking damages for its lost sale.

🏛 RULE OF LAW
A seller may recover his lost profit from a sales contract when the buyer defaults on the purchase if the contract market differential measure of damages is inadequate to put the seller in as good a position as performance would have done.

FACTS: Neri (P) contracted to purchase a boat from Retail Marine Corp. (Marine) (D). Neri (P) gave a deposit of $4,250 and Marine (D) ordered the boat from the factory. A week later Neri (P) rescinded the contract stating that because he was about to undergo an operation he would be unable to make the payments on the boat. In his rescission, Neri (P) requested a refund on his deposit which Marine (D) refused, whereupon Neri (P) brought suit for restitution. Marine (D) counterclaimed alleging that they were entitled to damages of $4,250, which included their lost profit on the sale of the boat to another buffer. The trial court held that Marine (D) was only entitled to $500 of its incidental damages—the costs of holding the boat for four months, at which time Marine (D) was able to resell the boat to another purchaser for the same price. On the issue of damages, Marine (D) appealed.

ISSUE: May a seller recover his lost profit when a buyer defaults on a purchase contract if the contract market differential measure of damages is inadequate to put the seller in as good a position as performance would have done?

HOLDING AND DECISION: (Gibson, J.) Yes. A seller may recover his lost profit when a buyer defaults on a sales contract if the contract market differential measure of damages is inadequate to put the seller in as good a position as performance would have done. Uniform Commercial Code (UCC) § 2-708(1) provides that the measure of damages for non-acceptance or repudiation by the buyer is the difference between the market price, plus incidentals, at the time and place of tender and the unpaid contract price. UCC § 2-708(2) provides that if UCC § 2-708(1) is inadequate to make the seller whole (to put him in the same position as if the contract had been performed) then the measure is the lost profit on the contract. In this case Marine

(D) resold the boat within four months for the same price. Thus UCC § 2-708(1) is inadequate to make the seller whole, and UCC § 2-708(2) would apply, as Marine's (D) real damage was its lost profit on the contract. We conclude that Marine (D) is entitled to an offset of $2,579 (lost profit) plus $674 in incidental damages against Neri's (P) claim for restitution. Judgment should be modified, and, as so modified, affirmed.

▌ ANALYSIS

The principal case is an example of the UCC provisions to protect sellers of goods from defaulting purchasers. Here the code gives a specific remedy which does justice for the seller by allowing the seller to recover his lost profit. The principal case is also noteworthy as an illustration of the Code position on restitution for defaulting purchasers. UCC § 2-718 allows a defaulting purchaser to acquire restitution for money advanced by allowing the defaulting purchaser to recover that money in excess of the seller's damages. Prior to the code a defaulting purchaser was usually without remedy.

Quicknotes

COUNTERCLAIM An independent cause of action brought by a defendant to a lawsuit in order to oppose or deduct from the plaintiff's claim.

INCIDENTAL DAMAGES Those damages reasonably incurred and arising from the subject matter of a claim for actual damages; such damages generally arise from activities undertaken by the nonbreaching party as a result of the breach.

REPUDIATION The actions or statements of a party to a contract that evidence his intent not to perform, or to continue performance, of his duties or obligations thereunder.

RESCISSION The canceling of an agreement and the return of the parties to their positions prior to the formation of the contract.

RESTITUTION The return or restoration of what the defendant has gained in a transaction to prevent the unjust enrichment of the defendant.

Fertico Belgium S.A. v. Phosphate Chemicals Export Assn.

Buyer (P) v. Seller (D)

N.Y. Ct. App., 70 N.Y.2d 76, 510 N.E.2d 334 (1987).

NATURE OF CASE: Appeal from an award of damages for breach of contract.

FACT SUMMARY: Phosphate Chemicals Export Assn. (D) breached a contract for the sale of fertilizer, but Fertico Belgium S.A. (P) still obtained possession of the late delivered goods and resold them at a profit after covering for the breach.

RULE OF LAW

Gains made by an injured party on other transactions after the breach are not deducted from recoverable damages unless such gains resulted from the breach.

FACTS: Fertico Belgium S.A. (Fertico) (P), a buyer-trader of fertilizer, contracted with Phosphate Chemicals Export Assn. (Phosphate) (D) for the purchase of two shipments of fertilizer to be delivered on very specific dates. Phosphate (D) informed Fertico (P) that the deliveries would be late. Fertico (P), in order to meet contractual obligations to a third party, bought cover fertilizer for the entire transaction at an increased cost of $700,000. Fertico (P) also canceled the second Phosphate (D) shipment, but had no other choice but to accept the late first shipment, as Phosphate (D) already had possession of Fertico's (P) honored letter of credit. In possession of this extra fertilizer, Fertico (P) sold it at a profit of $454,000. Fertico (P) sued Phosphate (D) for breach of contract, and the jury awarded Fertico (P) $1.07 million in damages, including an award for Fertico's (P) cost of cover ($700,000) and did not subtract the profit made ($454,000) on the subsequent sale. The appellate court overturned the award and ordered a new trial to determine the proper damages. Fertico (P) appealed.

ISSUE: Are gains made by an injured party on other transactions after the breach deducted from the damages that are otherwise recoverable?

HOLDING AND DECISION: (Bellacosa, J.) No. Gains made by an injured party on other transactions after the breach are not deducted from the recoverable damages unless such gains resulted from the breach. Uniform Commercial Code (UCC) § 1-106 requires that the provisions of the UCC be administered liberally in order to put aggrieved parties in as good a position as if the other party had fully performed. Here, Fertico's (P) profit on the late sale should not be deducted from the cost of cover because this transaction is to be viewed as a separate transaction occurring independently and after the breach. Phosphate's (D) breach forced Fertico (P) to obtain cover

in the amount of $700,000. Upon breaching, Phosphate (D) knew the time requirements of Fertico (P) and forced Fertico (P) to obtain cover. Therefore, the late delivery of the fertilizer can be viewed as a separate transaction from the original contract which caused the breach. Fertico (P) was left with an overage of fertilizer and needed to sell it off. The fact that Fertico (P) made a profit from this fourth-party sale should not affect the damages awarded for the cost of cover. As a result, the judgment is reversed and final damages are awarded in the amount of $700,000—the cost of cover, without subtracting the fourth-party profits. Reversed.

DISSENT: (Titone, J.) Allowing Fertico (P) to obtain damages for the cost of cover and to retain the profit from the fourth-party sale would result in a double award for Fertico (P). In this case, had Phosphate (D) fully performed, Fertico (P) would not have had to cover for $700,000, but would also not have made the profit of $454,000.

ANALYSIS

This case highlights the need to look at the specific facts of each case to precisely determine what would be the proper amount in the award of general damages. Often, general damages are based on certain patterns, such as the difference between the market price and the purchase price, but each case must be examined independently. The dissent's logic is not persuasive. Since Fertico (P) could have made a fourth-party sale at a profit by obtaining the goods elsewhere, the profit was not a result of Phosphate's (D) breach.

Quicknotes

GENERAL DAMAGES Measure of damages necessary to compensate victim for actual injuries suffered and which are the direct result of the wrongful act.

Vitex Mfg. Corp. v. Caribtex Corp.

Cloth manufacturer (P) v. Cloth importer (D)

377 F.2d 795 (3d Cir. 1967).

NATURE OF CASE: Appeal of an award of damages for breach of contract.

FACT SUMMARY: Vitex Mfg. Corp. (P) claimed lost profits damages resulting from Caribtex Corp.'s (D) breach of a manufacturing contract.

> ### 🏛 RULE OF LAW
> Overhead should be treated as a part of gross profits and recoverable as damages and is not considered part of the seller's costs.

FACTS: Vitex Mfg. Corp. (Vitex) (P) ran a business in the Virgin Islands which chemically shower-proofed imported cloth so that it could enter the United States duty free. Caribtex Corp. (D) was a cloth importer. In 1963, Vitex (P) temporarily closed down its plant due to a lack of customers. Caribtex (D) then approached Vitex (P) with a deal to chemically shower-proof some of Caribtex's (D) wool. The parties entered into the contract, and Vitex (P) reopened its plant, rehired the workers, and prepared for the project. Subsequently, Caribtex (D) refused to deliver the wool claiming it doubted Vitex's ability to sufficiently prepare the wool for importation. Vitex (P) sued Caribtex (D) for breach of contract and sued to obtain its lost profits, which it estimated at $21,114, plus interest. Vitex (P) arrived at this number by subtracting costs ($10,136) from gross profits under the contract ($31,250). The district court awarded Vitex (P) its requested damages, and Caribtex (D) appealed, claiming that overhead expenses should have been deducted from the award.

ISSUE: Should overhead be treated as a part of gross profits and recoverable as damages?

HOLDING AND DECISION: (Staley, C.J.) Yes. Overhead should be treated as a part of gross profits and recoverable as damages and is not considered part of the seller's costs. Overhead costs are basically the nonfluctuating, continuous costs a business incurs, regardless of a particular contract. Because overhead expenses are not affected by the performance of the particular contract, there is no need to deduct them in computing lost profits. The only costs that need to be deducted are those that particularly apply to the individual contract. Here, Vitex's (P) overhead costs were not affected by the Caribtex (D) contract. Therefore, only the costs specifically allocated to the Caribtex (D) contract should be deducted. While this case is not governed by the Uniform Commercial Code, such a result follows the policy standards espoused by the Code that recovery of overhead expenses in such circumstances are allowed. Affirmed.

▶ ANALYSIS

Expectation interests can often be calculated using two particular criteria. One such way involves the expenses a party incurs meeting the costs of the contract in reliance on the promise of the other party. The other such way is the value of opportunities not taken in reliance on the contract.

■■■

Quicknotes

EXPECTATION DAMAGES Damages awarded in actions for non-performance of a contract, which are calculated by subtracting the injured party's actual dollar position as a result of the breach from that party's expected dollar position had the breach not occurred.

OVERHEAD The necessary costs associated with the operation of a business that are constant and are unrelated to the costs of production.

■■■

Parker v. Twentieth Century-Fox Film Corp.

Actress (P) v. Film company (D)

Cal. Sup. Ct., 3 Cal. 3d 176, 474 P.2d 689 (1970).

NATURE OF CASE: Appeal from summary judgment in a breach of contract action.

FACT SUMMARY: Parker (P) sued Twentieth Century-Fox Film Corp. (Twentieth) (D) for damages resulting from Twentieth's (D) breach of an employment contract with her.

🏛 RULE OF LAW
Projected earnings from other employment opportunities only offset damages if the employment is substantially similar to that of which the employee has been deprived.

FACTS: Parker (P) was a well-known actress who entered into a contract with Twentieth Century-Fox Film Corp. (Twentieth) (D) in August 1965 to star in a musical film called "Bloomer Girl." The contract contained many specific clauses, including payment of $53,571.42 per week for fourteen weeks to commence in May 1966, shooting in California. Twentieth (D) decided not to produce "Bloomer Girl" and, as compensation for the broken contract, offered Parker (P) the lead in the western film "Big Country," for the same fee. "Big Country" was scheduled to be shot in Australia. Parker (P) refused the lead in "Big Country" and sued Twentieth (D) for the profits she would have made on her original contract. At trial, Twentieth (D) admitted to the existence of the contract and to its anticipatory breach, but argued that Parker (P) was required to mitigate damages by accepting other work, which she did not by turning down "Big Country." Parker (P) filed a motion for summary judgment which the trial court granted. Twentieth (D) appealed.

ISSUE: Do projected earnings from other employment opportunities offset damages for breach of an employment contract?

HOLDING AND DECISION: (Burke, J.) No. Projected earnings from other employment opportunities only offset damages if the other employment was substantially similar to that of which the employee has been deprived. Generally, there is some duty to mitigate damages by the nonbreaching party. Thus, if an employee is offered a similar job after an employment contract is breached, the projected earnings would offset the damages. In the present case, the two movies offered to Parker (P) were different—one was a musical and one was a western—thereby, requiring different types of work. Also, other factors were substantially changed, such as the location of the shoot. Therefore, the offered employment was not substantially similar and the projected earnings cannot be used to offset the damages Twentieth (D) owed for breaching the original contract. Affirmed.

DISSENT: (Sullivan, C.J.) Summary judgment was not appropriate in this case because the trial court should have carefully examined the kind of work offered. Simply because the work is different does not automatically make it incomparable. New work will always be different in certain respects.

▌ ANALYSIS

This case demonstrates one type of remedy—the award of money damages. Another type of remedy based on expectations is specific performance. Specific performance is limited to situations in which damages would not adequately protect the parties' expectations.

Quicknotes

ANTICIPATORY BREACH Breach of a contract subsequent to formation but prior to the time performance is due.

EXPECTATION DAMAGES Damages awarded in actions for non-performance of a contract, which are calculated by subtracting the injured party's actual dollar position as a result of the breach from that party's expected dollar position had the breach not occurred.

SPECIFIC PERFORMANCE An equitable remedy whereby the court requires the parties to perform their obligations pursuant to a contract.

Peevyhouse v. Garland Coal & Mining Co.

Lessor (P) v. Lessee (D)

Okla. Sup. Ct., 382 P.2d 109 (1962).

NATURE OF CASE: Cross-appeals of an award of $5,000 in damages for breach of contract.

FACT SUMMARY: Garland Coal & Mining Co. (D) refused to do certain restorative work on the property it had leased from Peevyhouse (P) when it was finished with its mining operation.

🏛 RULE OF LAW
Where the economic benefit to a nonbreaching party by full performance of a contract would be grossly disproportionate to the cost of performance, the damages which the party may recover are limited to the diminution in value resulting to its property because of the nonperformance.

FACTS: Peevyhouse (P) owned land that contained numerous coal deposits. Garland Coal & Mining Co. (Garland) (D) contracted with Peevyhouse (P) to enter into a lease agreement whereby Garland (D) would perform strip-mining activities on the land and then do restorative work to the land when it was finished. The contract was fulfilled, except that Garland (D) did not perform the restorative work on the land. Peevyhouse (P) sued Garland (D) for damages for breach of contract, asking for the cost of the restorative work to be done—$25,000. Garland (D) claimed that the diminution in value to the land was minimal and the cost of the restorative work would be disproportionate. In fact, the diminution in value to the land was approximately $300. The trial court found in favor of Peevyhouse (P) and returned a verdict in the amount of $5,000. Both parties appealed.

ISSUE: Where the economic benefit to a nonbreaching party by full performance of a contract would be grossly disproportionate to the cost of performance, are the damages which the party may recover limited to the diminution in value of its property because of the non-performance?

HOLDING AND DECISION: (Jackson, J.) Yes. Where the economic benefit to a nonbreaching party by full performance of a contract would be grossly disproportionate to the cost of performance, the damages which the party may recover are limited to the diminution in value resulting to its property because of the nonperformance. The general rule is that, in a coal mining lease, when a lessee agrees to perform certain remedial work on the premises concerned at the end of the lease period, and thereafter the contract is fully performed by both parties except that the remedial work is not done, the measure of damages in an action by the lessor against the lessee for

damages for breach of contract is the reasonable cost of performance of the work. However, when a restorative provision is mostly incidental to a contract and would result in economic waste, the measure of damages is the diminution in value of the land. The main contract provision in this case was merely incidental, as the purpose of the contract was for strip-mining and the land was generally not used for other purposes. Additionally, the economic benefit to Peevyhouse (P) if the work were fully performed would be grossly disproportionate to the cost of the work. The diminution in value was only $300. Such a price drop does not warrant forcing Garland (D) to conduct $25,000 worth of restoration work. While the parties did contract for such terms, the restorative term was not the main purpose of the agreement and as such should not dictate an unreasonable result. The award to Peevyhouse (P) is affirmed, but the amount of the damages is reduced to $300, which is the amount of the diminution in value. Affirmed as modified.

DISSENT: (Irwin, J.) The breach of the contract in this case was willful and not in good faith and, therefore, Garland (D) should not be allowed to escape its obligations under the contract. The costs of the work could have been reasonably anticipated; allowing Garland (D) to rescind on its obligations would be to revoke the solemn obligation of contract law: obtaining the benefit of one's bargain.

SUPPLEMENTAL OPINION ON REHEAR-ING: (Jackson, J.) While Peevyhouse (P) asserts that the trial court excluded critical evidence as to the actual value of the property, he failed to raise these issues earlier. Peevyhouse (P) had every opportunity to bring the information before the court previously and cannot do so now. Motion for rehearing denied.

▶ ANALYSIS

This case highlights the need to measure general damages specifically, as determined by the type of contract and the facts of the case. While general damages are those which are suffered generally by general categories of people, the amount that should be awarded in each case cannot follow a clear-cut pattern. Each award depends on the circumstances of the individual case.

■━■

Continued on next page.

Quicknotes

BENEFIT OF THE BARGAIN Calculation of assessing damages in actions for breach of contract measured as the difference between the actual value and the purported value of the goods being bought.

ECONOMIC WASTE An act done by someone in lawful possession of an interest in land, causing injury to other estate holders in the same property, that diminishes the value of the mineral resources that may be produced from the property.

GENERAL DAMAGES Measure of damages necessary to compensate victim for actual injuries suffered and which are the direct result of the wrongful act.

■▬■

Locke v. United States

Typewriter supplier (P) v. Federal government (D)

Ct. Cl., 151 Ct. Cl. 262, 283 F.2d 521 (1960).

NATURE OF CASE: Appeal from judgment in an action for lost profits due to breach of requirements contract.

FACT SUMMARY: Locke (P) sued the Government (D) for breach of a requirements contract for the supply and repair of typewriters, which guaranteed that upon meeting certain requirements Locke (P) would be placed on a list of businesses that the Government (D) would be required to use.

🏛 RULE OF LAW
Where the chance for a profit is not outweighed by a countervailing risk of loss, and where it is fairly measurable, courts should be allowed to value that lost opportunity.

FACTS: Locke (P) entered into a requirements-contracts with the Government (D) for the supply and repair of typewriters. Pursuant to the contract, once Locke (P) met certain requirements, he would be put on a list of possible suppliers and repairmen that the Government (D) would be required to use. Locke (P) remained on the list and received some work for several months, but on February 2, 1956 the Government (D) terminated the contract and struck Locke (P) from the list. Other contractors on the list continued to receive work for the remainder of their contracts. Locke (P) sued the Government (D) before the General Service Administration's Board of Review for breach of contract. The Board found that the Government (D) terminated the contract without proper cause, but Locke (P) did not suffer any calculable damages because the requirements contract did not guarantee any work. Therefore, Locke (P) received no damages. Locke (P) appealed.

ISSUE: Where the chance for profit is not outweighed by a countervailing risk of loss and where it is fairly measurable by calculable odds, should courts be allowed to value that lost opportunity?

HOLDING AND DECISION: (Jones, C.J.) Yes. Where the chance for profit is not outweighed by a countervailing risk of loss and where it is fairly measurable by calculable odds, courts should be allowed to value that lost opportunity. Damages depend on certainty. If a reasonable probability of damage can be clearly established, uncertainty as to the amount will not preclude recovery. Here, Locke's (P) expectation in entering into the contract was the reasonable probability of obtaining work. That probability of obtaining work was of value to Locke (P) and should be compensated. Additionally, Locke's (P) chance for profit outweighed any risk of loss. In fact, because Locke (P) was one of the lowest bidders, there was a real likelihood that he would receive work. Therefore, the trial commissioner is directed to determine the damages Locke (P) sustained judged by his proportionate share of the work received by the members on the list.

▶ ANALYSIS

Special damages, also known as consequential damages, compensate the nonbreaching party for losses that are particular to the injured party's situation, as well as general damages. Such damages might include lost profits or good will. However, such damages are limited by requirements that they be reasonably foreseeable and proven with reasonable certainty.

■=■

Quicknotes

REQUIREMENTS CONTRACT An agreement pursuant to which one party agrees to purchase all his required goods or services from the other party exclusively for a specified time period.

SPECIAL DAMAGES Damages caused by a specific act that are not the usual consequence of that act and which must be specifically pled and proven.

■=■

Kenford Co., Inc. v. County of Erie

Stadium operator (P) v. County (D)

N.Y. Ct. App., 67 N.Y.2d 257, 493 N.E.2d 234 (1986).

NATURE OF CASE: Appeal in action for damages for breach of contract.

FACT SUMMARY: Kenford Co., Inc. (P) filed suit for loss of profits when County of Erie (D) failed to construct a domed stadium that Kenford (P) was going to operate.

🏛 RULE OF LAW
To establish loss of future profits as damages for breach of contract, a party must demonstrate with certainty that such damages have been caused by the breach, and the alleged loss must be capable of proof with reasonable certainty.

FACTS: In 1969, pursuant to a resolution adopted by its legislature, the County of Erie (D) entered into a contract with Kenford Co., Inc. (P) and Dome Stadium, Inc. (DSI) (P) for the construction and operation of a domed stadium facility near Buffalo. The contract provided that construction of the facility would begin within twelve months of the contract date, and that a mutually acceptable forty-year lease between Erie (D) and DSI (P) for the operation of the facility would be negotiated within three months of the receipt by Erie (D) of preliminary plans, drawings, and cost estimates. Although extensive negotiations followed, the terms of the lease were never agreed upon and the construction of a domed facility never occurred. In June 1971, Kenford (P) and DSI (P) commenced an action for breach of contract. The trial court awarded a multimillion dollar judgment for Kenford (P) and DSI (P), but the appellate division modified the judgment and remanded on the issue of loss of profits during the twenty-year period of the proposed management contract. The appellate court concluded that the use of expert opinion to present statistical projections of future business operations involved the use of too many variables to provide a rational basis on which lost profits could be calculated, and it was therefore insufficient as a matter of law to support an award of lost profits.

ISSUE: To establish loss of future profits as damages for breach of contract, must a party demonstrate with certainty that such damages have been caused by the breach and that the alleged loss is capable of proof with reasonable certainty?

HOLDING AND DECISION: (Per curiam) Yes. To establish loss of future profits as damages for breach of contract, a party must demonstrate with certainty that such damages have been caused by the breach, and the alleged loss must be capable of proof with reasonable certainty.

Damages may not be merely speculative, possible, remote, or caused by intervening events. The procedure for computing damages selected by DSI (P) was in accord with contemporary economic theory and was presented through the testimony of recognized experts. Nonetheless, the proof is insufficient to meet the required standard. The provisions in the contract addressing remedy for a default do not suggest or provide for such a heavy responsibility on the part of Erie (D). Furthermore, the multitude of assumptions required to establish projections over the twenty-year life of the contract do not add up to reasonable certainty no matter how sophisticated the calculations. Although the appellate court's verdict was correct, their application of a "rational basis" test was not. Affirmed.

▶ ANALYSIS

The expectation measure seeks to compensate an aggrieved party even when they have not changed their position in reliance on the breaching party. The goal of this measure is to put the party in the same position they would have been in had the contract been performed. The court's analysis follows the traditional definition of the expectation measure; however, it places a very high burden of proof on the party seeking damages.

Quicknotes

EXPECTATION DAMAGES Damages awarded in actions for non-performance of a contract, which are calculated by subtracting the injured party's actual dollar position as a result of the breach from that party's expected dollar position had the breach not occurred.

RATIONAL BASIS TEST A test employed by the court to determine the validity of a statute in equal protection actions, whereby the court determines whether the challenged statute is rationally related to the achievement of a legitimate state interest.

Hadley v. Baxendale

Mill operator (P) v. Carrier (D)

Ex. Ch., 9 Exch. 341, 156 Eng. Rep. 145 (1854).

NATURE OF CASE: Action for damages for breach of a carrier contract.

FACT SUMMARY: Hadley (P), a mill operator in Gloucester, arranged to have Baxendale's (D) company, a carrier, ship his broken mill shaft to the engineer in Greenwich for a copy to be made. Hadley (P) suffered a £300 loss when Baxendale (D) unreasonably delayed shipping the mill shaft, causing the mill to be shut down longer than anticipated.

> ## 🏛 RULE OF LAW
> The injured party may recover those damages as may reasonably be considered arising naturally from the breach itself and, second, may recover those damages as may reasonably be supposed to have been in contemplation of the parties, at the time they made the contract, as the probable result of a breach of it.

FACTS: Hadley (P), a mill operator in Gloucester, arranged to have Baxendale's (D) shipping company return his broken mill shaft to the engineer in Greenwich who was to make a duplicate. Hadley (P) delivered the broken shaft to Baxendale (D), who, in consideration for his fee, promised to deliver the shaft to Greenwich in a reasonable time. Baxendale (D) did not know that the mill was shut down while awaiting the new shaft. Baxendale (D) was negligent in delivering the shaft within a reasonable time. Reopening of the mill was delayed five days, costing Hadley (P) lost profits and paid-out wages of £300. Hadley (P) had paid Baxendale (D) £24 to ship the mill shaft. Baxendale (D) paid into court £25 in satisfaction of Hadley's (P) claim. The jury awarded an additional £25 for a total £50 award.

ISSUE: May the injured party recover those damages as may reasonably be considered arising naturally from the breach itself, and may damages as may reasonably be supposed to have been in contemplation of the parties, at the time they made the contract, as the probable result of a breach of it, be recovered?

HOLDING AND DECISION: (Alderson, B.) Yes. The jury requires a rule for its guidance in awarding damages justly. When a party breaches his contract, the damages he pays ought to be those arising naturally from the breach itself and, in addition, those as may reasonably be supposed to have been in contemplation of the parties, at the time they made the contract, as the probable result of the breach of it. Therefore, if the special circumstances under which the contract was made were known to both parties, the resulting damages upon breach would be those reasonably contemplated as arising under those communi-cated and known circumstances. But if the special circumstances were unknown, then damages can only be those expected to arise generally from the breach. Hadley's (P) telling Baxendale (D) that he ran a mill and his mill shaft which he wanted shipped was broken did not notify Baxendale (D) that the mill was shut down. Baxendale (D) could have believed reasonably that Hadley (P) had a spare shaft or that the shaft to be shipped was not the only defective machinery at the mill. Here, it does not follow that a loss of profits could fairly or reasonably have been contemplated by both parties in case of breach. Such a loss would not have flowed naturally from the breach without the special circumstances having been communicated to Baxendale (D). New trial ordered.

▶ ANALYSIS

This case lays down two rules guiding damages. First, only those damages as may fairly and reasonably be considered arising from the breach itself may be awarded. Second, those damages which may reasonably be supposed to have been in contemplation of the parties at the time they made the contract as the probable result of a breach of it may be awarded. The second is distinguished from the first because, with the latter, both parties are aware of the special circumstances under which the contract is made. Usually those special circumstances are communicated by the plaintiff to the defendant before the making of the contract. But that is not an absolute condition. If the consequences of the breach are foreseeable, the party which breaches will be liable for the lost profits or expectation damages. Foreseeability and assumption of the risk are ways of describing the bargain. If there is an assumption of the risk, the seller or carrier must necessarily be aware of the consequences. A later English case held that there would be a lesser foreseeability for a common carrier than a seller as a seller would tend to know the purpose and use of the item sold, while the common carrier probably would not know the use of all items it carried. If all loss went on to the seller, this would obviously be an incentive not to enter into contracts. Courts balance what has become a "seller-beware" attitude by placing limitations on full recovery. The loss must be foreseeable when the contract is entered into. It cannot be overly speculative. The seller's breach must be judged by willingness, negligence, bad faith, and availability of replacement items. Restatement, First, § 331(2) would allow recovery in the situation in this case under an alternative theory. If the breach were one preventing the use and operation of property from

Continued on next page.

which profits would have been made, damages can be measured by the rental value of the property or by interest on the value of the property. Uniform Commercial Code § 2-715(2) allows the buyer consequential damages for any loss which results from general or particular needs of which the seller had reason to know.

Quicknotes

EXPECTATION DAMAGES Damages awarded in actions for non-performance of a contract, which are calculated by subtracting the injured party's actual dollar position as a result of the breach from that party's expected dollar position had the breach not occurred.

FORESEEABILITY A reasonable expectation that an act or omission would result in injury.

Security Stove & Mfg. Co. v. American Ry. Express Co.

Shipper (P) v. Carrier (D)

Mo. Ct. App., 227 Mo. App. 175, 51 S.W.2d 572 (1932).

NATURE OF CASE: Action for damages.

FACT SUMMARY: American Railway Express Co. (D) was late in delivering an exhibit shipped by Security Stove & Mfg. Co. (Security) (P). Security (P) was awarded its expenses as damages.

🏛 RULE OF LAW
Where a carrier has notice that a delay will cause a shipper an unusual loss, and where the notice was such that the carrier will be presumed to have contracted with reference thereto, he is responsible for the actual damages occasioned by his delay.

FACTS: Security Stove & Mfg. Co. (Security) (P) contracted with American Railway Express Co. (American) (D) to have the latter ship an exhibit to Atlantic City for a convention. Security (P) emphasized that the exhibit had to be there by October 8. American (D) assured Security (P) that it could deliver it by that date; however, a package containing part of the shipment did not arrive until after the convention had closed. The trial court allowed as damages: the express charges, transportation expenses, and hotel costs incurred by the employees who Security (P) had sent to the convention, as well as the cost of the booth rental at the convention.

ISSUE: Can a carrier be held liable for actual damages sustained as a result of its delay in delivery of a shipment?

HOLDING AND DECISION: (Bland, J.) Yes. Ordinarily, the measure of damages for a carrier's failure to deliver a shipment within a reasonable time is the difference between the market value of the goods at the time of delivery and their value at the time they should have been delivered. However, where the carrier has notice that a delay will cause the shipper an unusual loss, and where the notice was such that the carrier can be presumed to have contracted with reference thereto, he is responsible for the actual damages occasioned by the delay in delivery. Here, the suit was not to recover loss of profits or goods. Hence, unless Security (P) is allowed to recover its actual expenses it will be deprived of any substantial compensation for its loss. In cases like the one at bar, the method of estimating damages should be the one which is the most definite and best serves the purpose of compensation. Thus, although Security (P) would have incurred its expenses whether or not the contract had been breached, it should be allowed to recover them. Affirmed.

▶ ANALYSIS

The principle that damages, to be recoverable, must have been in the contemplation of the parties at the time the contract was entered into does not require that the defaulting party could have foreseen the specific details of the injury or damages which did occur. For example, it has been held sufficient that the defaulting party could have foreseen that its failure to make delivery would cause the other party's factory to shut down, since details of the losses that resulted may be determined at trial. This same principle is applied in other types of cases provided, of course, that the losses are proved with reasonable certainty.

Quicknotes

ACTUAL DAMAGES Measure of damages necessary to compensate victim for actual injuries suffered.

Goodman v. Dicker

Franchisor (D) v. Franchisee (P)

169 F.2d 684 (D.C. Cir. 1948).

NATURE OF CASE: Action for damages for breach of a contract for granting of a franchise.

FACT SUMMARY: Dicker (P) made certain expenditures after applying for an Emerson radio and phonograph franchise in the District of Columbia upon the inducement of an Emerson representative, Goodman (D). While Goodman (D) had represented that the franchise would be granted and radios would be delivered, no franchise was approved.

🏛 RULE OF LAW
One who by his language or conduct leads another to do what he would not otherwise have done shall not subject such person to loss or injury by disappointing the expectation upon which he acted.

FACTS: Dicker (P) was encouraged by Goodman (D), a local representative for Emerson Radio and Phonograph Co., to apply for an Emerson dealer franchise for the District of Columbia. Dicker (P) was induced by Goodman's (D) representations to make certain expenditures including hiring salesmen and soliciting orders. Dicker (P) was told by Goodman (D) that the franchise application had been accepted and would be granted plus an initial delivery of radios was on the way. None were delivered and the franchise was not granted.

ISSUE: Was Goodman (D) estopped from denying the existence of a contract by reason of his statements and conduct upon which Dicker (P) relied to his detriment?

HOLDING AND DECISION: (Proctor, J.) Yes. Dicker (P) justifiably relied upon Goodman's (D) statement and conduct. Even though under a formal franchise agreement, a franchise would have been terminable at will and would have imposed no duty on the manufacturer, this is a defense inconsistent with the assurance that a franchise would be granted. Justice and fair dealing require that one who acts to his detriment on the faith of conduct such as seen here should be protected by estopping the party whose conduct is responsible from alleging anything opposite to the natural consequences of his course of conduct. Expenses of $1,150 expended in preparation for doing business are recoverable. However, the $350 loss of profits on the undelivered radios is not recoverable as it was not a loss incurred in reliance upon the assurance of a dealer franchise. Affirmed.

▶ ANALYSIS

Goodman's (D) promise is enforced because there was justifiable reliance by Dicker (P). The one who desires the franchise assumes more of a risk because had the radios been delivered, the franchise would have been granted and then become terminable at will. Good faith by the party offering the franchise is required by the court so that negotiations may be conducted with a sense of fair play. The appeals court apparently did not want to award $350 loss of profits to a business that really had not started—it may be a simple desire on the court's part to avoid speculation. The loss of profits was probably considered to have been covered by the award of reliance damages so that any award of loss of profits damages would have put Dicker (P) in a better position than had a franchise been granted. If it had been proven that Goodman (D) did not deal in good faith, expectation profits could then be awarded.

■=■

Quicknotes

DETRIMENTAL RELIANCE Action by one party, resulting in loss that is based on the conduct or promises of another.

ESTOPPEL An equitable doctrine precluding a party from asserting a right to the detriment of another, who justifiably relied on the conduct.

■=■

Walters v. Marathon Oil Co.

Perspective franchisee (P) v. Franchisor (D)

642 F.2d 1098 (7th Cir. 1981).

NATURE OF CASE: Appeal of district court award of damages for breach of contract.

FACT SUMMARY: Walters (P) purchased a service station and made improvements to it based upon promises made by Marathon Oil Co. (D) during negotiations.

RULE OF LAW

Lost profits, if ascertained with reasonable certainty, may be properly included with reliance damages where the sole theory for damages is promissory estoppel.

FACTS: Walters (P) purchased a vacant gasoline service station after entering into three-way talks with Marathon Oil Co. (Marathon) (D) and Time Oil Company. Marathon (D) made repeated assurances to Walters (P) that the service station arrangement would proceed normally. He invested a substantial sum in preparing the site for business. After his proposal had been submitted to Marathon (D), but before it was approved, Marathon (D) placed a moratorium on new applications for dealerships. Accordingly, Marathon (D) refused to sign the three-party agreement. Walters (P) filed suit in district court on a theory of promissory estoppel and received damages, including $22,200 as a calculation of first-year profits based upon the number of gallons he would have been entitled to receive. Marathon (D) appealed the calculation of the damages.

ISSUE: May lost profits, if ascertained with reasonable certainty, properly be included with reliance damages where the sole theory for damages is promissory estoppel?

HOLDING AND DECISION: (Spears, J.) Yes. Lost profits, if ascertained with reasonable certainty, may be properly included with reliance damages where the sole theory for damages is promissory estoppel. A court of equity possesses the discretionary power to ensure justice through the award of damages. In this case, Marathon (D) argued that damages should be reliance measure only. It contended that Walters (P) could be placed back in his original position in this fashion. But this overlooks the fact that Walters (P) entered into his efforts with the full expectation of receiving profits for his efforts. The profits, based upon the experience of numerous dealers, were calculated with fair certainty. If Marathon (D) is going to induce an individual to act in expectation of future profit, then equity requires that Marathon (D) pay a portion of that frustrated profit when it backs out of its bargain. Affirmed.

▶ ANALYSIS

The decision in this case is not clearly consistent with other cases proceeding on a promissory estoppel theory. Some courts have held that the appropriate damage figure in such cases is only the losses sustained in reliance. However, it does seem equitable to include any lost profits where they can be calculated with fair certainty.

Quicknotes

LOST PROFITS The potential value of income earned or goods which are the subject of the contract; may be used in calculating damages where the contract has been breached.

PROMISSORY ESTOPPEL A promise that is enforceable if the promisor should reasonably expect that it will induce action or forbearance on the part of the promisee, and does in fact cause such action or forbearance, and it is the only means of avoiding injustice.

RELIANCE DAMAGES The injury suffered by a party to a breached contract as the result of that party's dependence on the agreement.

Sullivan v. O'Connor

Patient (P) v. Doctor (D)

Mass. Sup. Jud. Ct., 363 Mass. 579, 296 N.E.2d 183 (1973).

NATURE OF CASE: Action for breach of contract.

FACT SUMMARY: O'Connor (D), a plastic surgeon, promised to enhance Sullivan's (P) beauty by performing an operation on her nose.

🏛 RULE OF LAW
Where an offer promises to enhance physical beauty, breach of the contract would permit recovery for pain and suffering, mental distress, and a worsening of the condition.

FACTS: O'Connor (D), a plastic surgeon, promised to enhance Sullivan's (P) beauty by performing an operation on her nose. Three operations were required, and the nose ended up looking worse than before the operations. Sullivan (P) sued for breach of contract and negligence. The jury found for Sullivan (P) on the breach of contract count but for O'Connor (D) on the negligence issue. Damages were awarded for Sullivan's (P) out-of-pocket expenses, the worsening of her condition, and for pain, suffering, and mental distress from the third operation. O'Connor (D) appealed, alleging that pain, suffering, and mental distress were not proper elements of damages in breach of contract actions.

ISSUE: Where it is reasonably foreseeable that nonperformance of a contract will cause pain, suffering, and mental distress are these proper measures of damage?

HOLDING AND DECISION: (Kaplan, J.) Yes. A party may recover those elements of damages which flow naturally and foreseeably from a breach. In most situations there is no recovery allowed for pain, suffering, or mental distress. The offeror could not normally be expected to foresee such damages, and monetary relief for actual damages will normally be adequate to compensate the injured party. Where, as herein, pain, suffering, and mental distress are not only foreseeable but are highly likely to occur upon a breach, there is no reason why recovery for such damages should not be allowed. In the normal case, no contract will be found between a physician and his patient. Rarely is a cure actually promised. Normally, words of encouragement cannot be read as a promise, and the law will not find a contract absent a very clear showing that a definite contractual relationship was intended. This was the case herein, and recovery for out-of-pocket expenses alone would be inadequate to compensate Sullivan (P) for the breach. Sullivan (P) was properly awarded damages for her expenditures, the worsening of her condition, and pain, suffering, and mental distress caused by the third operation. Affirmed.

▶ ANALYSIS

Generally, actions for breach of contract where the physician has allegedly promised to cure the patient will be decided in favor of the physician on public policy grounds. Most physicians do not absolutely promise a cure, only that they will use their best efforts to cure the patient. *Gault v. Sideman*, 42 Ill. App. 2d 96 (1963). To establish the existence of a contract, the law will generally require clear, unequivocal proof that the parties intended to and did enter into a contract (43 A.L.R.3d 1225).

Quicknotes

ACTUAL DAMAGES Measure of damages necessary to compensate victim for actual injuries suffered.

FORESEEABILITY A reasonable expectation that an act or omission would result in injury.

NEGLIGENCE Conduct falling below the standard of care that a reasonable person would demonstrate under similar conditions.

Oliver v. Campbell

Attorney (P) v. Client (D)

Cal. Sup. Ct., 43 Cal. 2d 298, 273 P.2d 15 (1954).

NATURE OF CASE: Review of trial court decision denying recovery for services rendered pursuant to an express contract.

FACT SUMMARY: After Oliver (P) had represented Campbell (D) in a legal matter, Campbell (D) fired Oliver (P) before the final resolution of the case and refused to pay Oliver (P) the fee stipulated in their express contract.

🏛 RULE OF LAW

One who has been injured by a breach of contract may elect to pursue any of three remedies: (1) proceed in quantum meruit so far as performance has been completed, (2) keep the contract alive for both parties, or (3) treat the breach as a repudiation and sue for the profits that would have been realized through performance.

FACTS: Oliver (P) was hired as an attorney by Mr. Campbell to represent him in an action for separate maintenance brought by Mrs. Campbell (D). Mr. Campbell cross-complained for a divorce. Oliver (P) agreed to represent Mr. Campbell for a flat sum of $750 plus court costs of $100. The fees were to be paid after trial. Oliver (P) represented Mr. Campbell at the trial, which lasted 29 days. After the trial ended, but before the court had entered a final judgment, Mr. Campbell substituted himself for Oliver (P), thereby terminating Oliver's (P) representation. Oliver (P) signed the substitution document. Oliver (P) received $450 from Mr. Campbell plus the $100 in costs. The reasonable value of Oliver's (P) services was $5,000. Mr. Campbell subsequently died. Oliver (P) sued the estate of Mr. Campbell, and the administrator of the estate, Mrs. Campbell (D), for $10,000. The trial court found in favor of Mrs. Campbell (D), awarding nothing. Oliver (P) appealed.

ISSUE: Where there is a contract of employment for a definite term, is the employee limited to an action on the contract for the fixed compensation or damages for the breach of the contract?

HOLDING AND DECISION: (Carter, J.) No. One who has been injured by a breach of contract may elect to pursue any of three remedies: (1) proceed in quantum meruit so far as performance has been completed, (2) keep the contract alive for both parties, or (3) treat the breach as a repudiation and sue for the profits that would have been realized through performance. If a party to a contract has performed partially, and is then prevented from completing performance, recovery for the fair value of the services rendered may be recovered. But if all, or virtually all, of the performance has been completed, and the party would be entitled to payment under the contract, then payment of the contracted fee is warranted, rather than the value of the completed performance. In this way, a contracting party cannot receive compensation greater than that contemplated in the contract for services performed pursuant to the contract. Here, Oliver (P) agreed to work at a flat rate of $750 for the case. He completed the trial proceedings, and was merely awaiting the entry of final determinations by the court. His performance was so substantially completed, that he is entitled to the full $750 under the contract. Therefore, although his services were worth more based upon his time, he contracted at a lower rate and is bound by that decision. He was free to charge an hourly fee to more properly reflect the amount of work performed, but he did not. Judgment reversed; an award in the sum of $300 is entered for Oliver (P).

▶ ANALYSIS

Had there been no contract, Oliver (P) might well have recovered the $5,000 in quantum meruit. However, once an agreement had been negotiated, the parties were bound by their folly. Although a deal might be a poor one from a business standard, a major policy goal of contract law is to ensure that individuals negotiate agreements carefully and with the understanding that they are bound to their agreement.

▬▭■

Quicknotes

QUANTUM MERUIT Equitable doctrine allowing recovery for labor and materials provided by one party, even though no contract was entered into, in order to avoid unjust enrichment by the benefited party.

REPUDIATION The actions or statements of a party to a contract that evidence his intent not to perform, or to continue performance, of his duties or obligations thereunder.

RESTITUTION The return or restoration of what the defendant has gained in a transaction to prevent the unjust enrichment of the defendant.

▬▭■

United States v. Algernon Blair, Inc.

Federal government (P) v. General contractor (D)

479 F.2d 638 (4th Cir. 1973).

NATURE OF CASE: Action to recover in quantum meruit the value of labor and equipment furnished.

FACT SUMMARY: Coastal Steel Erectors, a subcontractor, brought suit in the name of the United States (P) against Algernon Blair, Inc. (D), the prime contractor on a government project, to recover in quantum meruit the value of the labor and materials it had furnished up to the point at which it justifiably ceased work.

🏛 RULE OF LAW
A promisee is allowed to recover in quantum meruit the value of services he gave to a defendant who breached their contract irrespective of whether he would have lost money had the contract been fully performed and would thus be precluded from recovering in a suit on the contract.

FACTS: Algernon Blair, Inc. (Algernon) (D) was the prime contractor on a government project. Coastal Steel Erectors, a subcontractor on the project, furnished materials and labor up to the point that Algernon (D) breached its contract with Coastal. At that point, Coastal ceased work and brought an action under the Miller Act, in the name of the United States (P), to recover in quantum meruit the value of the equipment and labor it had theretofore supplied. The district court found Algernon (D) had breached the contract, but held that Coastal would have lost money on the contract had it been fully performed. For this reason, it denied recovery, and Coastal appealed.

ISSUE: Even if a promisee would have lost money had he completed the contract, can he nonetheless recover in quantum meruit the value of services he gave to a defendant who breached the contract?

HOLDING AND DECISION: (Craven, J.) Yes. Regardless of whether or not the promisee would have lost money had he completed the contract, he can recover in quantum meruit the value of the services he gave to a defendant who breached the contract. It is an accepted principle of contract law, often applied in the case of construction contracts, that the promisee upon breach has the option to forgo any suit on the contract and claim only the reasonable value of his performance. Thus, Coastal can recover for the equipment and labor it supplied despite the fact that it would have lost money on the contract and would thus have been unable to recover in a suit on the contract. Recovery in quantum meruit is measured by the reasonable value of the performance and is undiminished by any loss which would have been incurred by complete performance. Reversed and remanded for findings as to the reasonable value of the equipment and labor supplied by Coastal.

▶ ANALYSIS

The applicable standard in determining the "reasonable value" of services rendered is the amount for which such services could have been purchased from one in the plaintiff's position at the time and place the services were rendered. Some courts have held that the contract price is not only evidence of the reasonable value but is a ceiling on recovery, but others disagree. The rationale is that one should not recover more for part performance than he would have upon full performance.

■■■■■

Quicknotes

QUANTUM MERUIT Equitable doctrine allowing recovery for labor and materials provided by one party, even though no contract was entered into, in order to avoid unjust enrichment by the benefited party.

■■■■■

The Autonomy and Security Principles Again

Quick Reference Rules of Law

Gianni v. R. Russel & Co., Inc.

Store operator (P) v. Property owner (D)

Pa. Sup. Ct., 281 Pa. 320, 126 A. 791 (1924).

NATURE OF CASE: Appeal of a damage award for breach of an oral contract.

FACT SUMMARY: Gianni (P) entered into a written lease agreement to operate a store, but Gianni (P) claimed that certain oral representations not included in the lease persuaded him to enter into the agreement.

🏛 RULE OF LAW
An oral agreement falls outside the field embraced by the written one where parties, situated as the ones in the contract, would naturally and normally refrain from including the oral agreement within the written one.

FACTS: Gianni (P) was a tenant in an office building where he operated a small store, selling tobacco, fruit, candy, and similar goods. Russel (D) acquired the entire property, and an agent for Russel (D) began negotiating for a further lease of the premises. Gianni (P) agreed to a three-year lease which allowed him to continue his business, subject to the condition that he no longer sells tobacco. Gianni (P) claimed that in the course of negotiations, he was promised the exclusive right to sell soft drinks in the building; however, no such stipulation was present in the lease, which had been read over by two other people for Gianni (P). Shortly after the lease was signed, a drug company occupied an adjoining room and commenced selling soft drinks. Gianni (P) brought an action for breach of oral contract, and recovered damages. Russel (D) appealed.

ISSUE: Are all oral representations made prior to the formation of a written agreement embraced by the written agreement even if not specifically mentioned in the writing?

HOLDING AND DECISION: (Schaffer, J.) No. An oral agreement falls outside the field embraced by the written one where parties, situated as the ones in the contract, would naturally and normally refrain from including the oral agreement within the written one. Once parties have reduced an agreement to writing, the law regards that writing generally as the best and only evidence of that agreement. However, circumstances may exist where parties might make an oral agreement that is not appropriately included in their writing. To determine when such a circumstance exists, the specific situation must be analyzed from the view of similarly situated persons. In this case, the lease contained terms that Gianni (P) argues have no part in the agreement. The lease specified what Gianni (P) could and could not sell in his store. Certainly, parties in similar circumstances would include any agreement to confer exclusive sales rights on the goods mentioned in the lease. Thus, it must be presumed that the writing contains the sum total of the final agreement between Gianni (P) and Russel (D). Any evidence of an alleged oral contract is inadmissible under the parol evidence rule. Reversed.

▶ *ANALYSIS*

The parol evidence rule stands between competing concerns. There are certainly cases where the rule will operate to prevent enforcement of an oral agreement that was actually made. On the other hand, since a writing is by far the most reliable evidence of an agreement, the parol evidence rule serves to promote a complete integration of terms into the final contract.

■▬■

Quicknotes

PAROL EVIDENCE RULE Doctrine precluding parties to an agreement from introducing evidence of prior or contemporaneous agreements in order to repudiate or alter the terms of a written contract.

■▬■

Masterson v. Sine

Transferor (P) v. Transferee (D)

Cal. Sup. Ct., 68 Cal. 2d 222, 436 P.2d 561 (1968).

NATURE OF CASE: Appeal of declaratory relief action authorizing a trustee in bankruptcy to enforce an option to purchase real property.

FACT SUMMARY: Masterson (P) conveyed a property to Sine (D), reserving an option to purchase for ten years; Masterson (P) was later adjudged bankrupt, and his trustee brought an action to enforce the option to purchase.

RULE OF LAW
Even where a writing appears complete on its face, evidence to prove the existence of a collateral agreement may be offered if the collateral agreement is such that it might naturally be made as a separate agreement by parties similarly situated.

FACTS: Masterson (P) conveyed a ranch to Sine (D) by a grant deed which reserved for Masterson (P) an option to purchase the property within ten years. Masterson (P) was adjudged bankrupt after the conveyance. Masterson's (P) wife and trustee in bankruptcy brought a declaratory relief action to enforce the option. At trial, Sine (D) was precluded from introducing extrinsic evidence showing that the intention of the parties was to keep the property in the Masterson family, since Mrs. Sine (D) was Mr. Masterson's (P) sister. Judgment was entered for the Masterson (P) trustee. Sine (D) appealed.

ISSUE: If a writing appears complete on its face, does the parol evidence rule prohibit the introduction of evidence to prove the existence of collateral oral agreements?

HOLDING AND DECISION: (Traynor, C.J.) No. Even where a writing appears complete on its face, evidence to prove the existence of a collateral agreement may be offered if the collateral agreement is such that it might naturally be made as a separate agreement by parties similarly situated. When only part of an agreement is integrated, the parol evidence rule operates to prevent extrinsic evidence from modifying the integrated terms, but parol evidence may be offered to prove elements not reduced to writing. While the writing must be given a presumption of complete integration, the circumstances of each case must be examined to see if parties in such a situation might naturally have left terms out of the writing. In this case, the parties had an agreement in the form of a deed. Although the formal structure of a deed makes modifications somewhat difficult, it is common for family members to enter into agreements that lack complete formality. The transfer met legal formality, but a brother and sister might naturally intend to keep an option on property personal to each other without even thinking to include the term in the deed. Reversed.

DISSENT: (Burke, J.) The majority has done an exceptional job of undermining the parol evidence rule as it has stood since at least 1872. Now all instruments of conveyance, absolute on their face, are suspect. A door has been opened to a new method for defrauding creditors.

ANALYSIS

While this decision might have been equitable on the specific facts, it causes problems in the larger scheme. Jurisprudence is aided whenever contracting parties include the entire agreement in a writing. By making a special inquiry as to whether collateral agreements might naturally be excluded from the integrated writing, triers of fact have substantially more work to do.

Quicknotes

COLLATERAL AGREEMENT An agreement made prior to or contemporaneous with a written agreement, which is admissible in evidence as long as it is consistent with the written document.

DECLARATORY RELIEF A judgment of the court establishing the rights of the parties.

EXTRINSIC EVIDENCE Evidence that is not contained within the text of a document or contract but which is derived from the parties' statements or the circumstances under which the agreement was made.

PAROL EVIDENCE RULE Doctrine precluding parties to an agreement from introducing evidence of prior or contemporaneous agreements in order to repudiate or alter the terms of a written contract.

Interform Co. v. Mitchell

Construction supply company (P) v. Construction company (D)

575 F.2d 1270 (9th Cir. 1978).

NATURE OF CASE: Suit for unjust enrichment; counterclaim for breach of contract.

FACT SUMMARY: Mitchell (D) used Interform Co.'s (P) concrete-molding forms twice but failed to pay for the second use.

RULE OF LAW

Extrinsic evidence is admissible under Idaho law to determine the intent of the parties to a contract.

FACTS: Interform Company (P), a construction supply company, and Mitchell Construction Company (Mitchell) (D) entered into a contract under which Mitchell (D) would lease Interform's (P) forms for molding concrete on one of Mitchell's (D) jobs. Mitchell (D) used the forms once and paid Interform (P) the amount required by the contract. Mitchell (D) then claimed ownership of the forms, kept them, and used them on a second job without making further payment to Interform (P). Mitchell (D) knew, all the while, that Interform (P) still claimed ownership of the forms and demanded payment for additional uses of them. Mitchell (D) based his claim to ownership on a portrayal of the contract as a sale contract instead of a lease contract; Mitchell (D) claimed that the parties had orally agreed to a purchase of the forms, and that Mitchell's (D) subsequent so-called "purchase order" for the items established a contract for sale. Interform's (P) representative, however, claimed not to have had the authority to enter an oral agreement during the conversation portrayed by Mitchell (D) as the basis for an oral contract. After Mitchell (D) sent its purchase order to Interform (P), Interform (P) sent six documents to Mitchell, all of which referred to the transaction as being for a rental, not a purchase, of the concrete-molding forms. Mitchell (D) did not object to these documents' portrayal of the transaction as a lease. Nonetheless, Mitchell (D) used the forms a second time without making an additional payment to Interform (P). Interform (P) sued, seeking return of the forms, as well as recovery for the value of Mitchell's (D) second use. Mitchell (D) counterclaimed, seeking a declaration of its ownership of the forms. After a bench trial, the trial judge entered judgment for Interform (P), finding that the parties entered a lease agreement for one use of the forms. In addition to evidence of the circumstances and the parties' conduct at the contract's formation, evidence that it was common for construction companies to request rentals of equipment by using purchase orders was also instrumental in the trial judge's decision. Mitchell (D) appealed, arguing that the trial judge should have deter-mined the parties' intent from the purchase orders without hearing extrinsic evidence of intent.

ISSUE: Is extrinsic evidence admissible under Idaho law to determine the intent of the parties to a contract?

HOLDING AND DECISION: (Sneed, C.J.) Yes. Extrinsic evidence is admissible under Idaho law to determine the intent of the parties to a contract. Courts use two competing approaches to determining the parties' intent in forming a contract. The first, championed by Williston, treats an integrated written contract as having a unique claim upon determinations of intent. The second view, championed by Corbin, accords no special force to a writing as an expression of intent; this view is much more receptive to extrinsic evidence of what the parties in fact did intend. Idaho follows this more flexible latter view. Accordingly, the trial judge here did not err by hearing evidence beyond Mitchell's (D) purchase orders. The trial judge did err, however, in declining Interform's (P) request for attorney's fees. Affirmed in part, reversed in part, and remanded for further proceeding on attorney's fees.

ANALYSIS

If Interform's (P) claim for attorney's fees was not based on contract, such that the claim must stand or fall based solely on Mitchell's (D) own conduct, how strong was the evidence in *Interform* that the contract was for a lease and not for a sale? Strong enough that the appellate court reversed the trial judge's denial of Interform's (P) request for attorney's fees. In assessing the strength of Interform's (P) case, the appellate court noted that "[p]reliminary negotiations . . . without question centered entirely upon the rental of forms." The appellate court also could have relied on Mitchell's (D) total failure to object to Interform's (P) six portrayals of the transactions as being for a lease of the equipment, as well as on Mitchell's (D) presumed knowledge of the customary practice of requesting rentals of equipment on documents that are only nominally "purchase orders." As excerpted in the casebook, then, the opinion in *Interform* gives the distinct impression that Mitchell's (D) assertion of ownership of the forms contained an element of bad faith that overcame the strong presumption against awarding attorney's fees.

Continued on next page.

Quicknotes

COUNTERCLAIM An independent cause of action brought by a defendant to a lawsuit in order to oppose or deduct from the plaintiff's claim.

EXTRINSIC EVIDENCE Evidence that is not contained within the text of a document or contract, but which is derived from the parties' statements or the circumstances under which the agreement was made.

Lee v. Joseph E. Seagram & Sons, Inc.

Seller (P) v. Buyer (D)

552 F.2d 447 (2d Cir. 1977).

NATURE OF CASE: Action for damages on an oral contract.

FACT SUMMARY: Joseph E. Seagram & Sons, Inc. (Seagram) (D) orally promised to set Lee's (P) sons up in a distributorship as part of the consideration for the sale of Lee's (P) business to Seagram (D) under a written contract.

> ## 🏛 RULE OF LAW
> A collateral oral agreement not covering or contradicting the terms of the contemporary written agreement may be proved by parol unless the written agreement is deemed completely integrated.

FACTS: Lee (P) agreed to sell his distributorship to Joseph E. Seagram & Sons, Inc. (Seagram) (D). Lee (P) had a long, close association with Seagram (D) and had been one of its officers. Lee (P) had begun the distributorship, partially at Seagram's (D) request and also to give his sons some experience in the business. As part of the sale, Seagram (D) orally promised to set the sons up in a distributorship as soon as one opened. The written sales contract did not refer to the oral agreement and did not cover this point in any manner. Seagram (D) refused to perform the contemporary oral contract, and Lee (P) brought suit. The contract was not deemed to be completely integrated, i.e., no contemporary or prior oral promises or warranties have been made, and parol evidence was permitted since the oral contract did not contradict or alter the written contract. Seagram (D) did not refute the evidence as to the oral agreement. Seagram's (D) only contention on appeal was that parol evidence should not have been admitted to prove its existence.

ISSUE: Where a written contract is not integrated, may parol evidence be admitted to establish the existence of a contemporary oral agreement which neither alters nor contradicts the terms of the written contract?

HOLDING AND DECISION: (Gurfein, J.) Yes. The Parol Evidence Rule was adopted to prevent the fraudulent assertion of oral promises not contained in the written contract. If the writing contains an integration clause or the asserted oral promises vary or contradict the reasonable, unambiguous construction of written clauses, parol evidence is barred. The rule does not bar parol evidence as to contemporary oral contracts which neither vary nor contradict the written contract if it has no integration clause. Normally, the subject of the oral agreement must be something which the parties would not necessarily have included in the written contract. Here, there was a long

and close association between the parties; the distributorship could reasonably be considered the subject of a second contract since the parties were different, i.e., the sons. The lack of an integration clause where one is customary is also evidence that the oral agreement was valid. Judgment for the sons is affirmed.

▶ ANALYSIS

Integration is more easily inferred in simple contracts, e.g., the sale of land. *Mitchill v. Lath*, 247 N.Y. 377 (1928). In more complex cases, in which customary business practices may be more varied, an oral agreement can be treated as separate and independent of the written contract, even though a strong integration clause is present. *Gem Corrugated Box Corp. v. National Kraft Container Corp.*, 427 F.2d 499 (2d Cir. 1970). Agreements not covered under the written contract are far more likely in such situations.

■■■

Quicknotes

COLLATERAL AGREEMENT An agreement made prior to or contemporaneous with a written agreement, which is admissible in evidence as long as it is consistent with the written document.

INTEGRATION An agreement between two parties to a contract that the document represents the total and final expression of their agreement.

PAROL EVIDENCE RULE Doctrine precluding parties to an agreement from introducing evidence of prior or contemporaneous agreements in order to repudiate or alter the terms of a written contract.

■■■

Nelson v. Elway

Car dealerships (P) v. Buyer of dealerships (D)

Colo. Sup. Ct., 908 P.2d 102 (1995).

NATURE OF CASE: Appeal from summary judgment dismissing claims for civil conspiracy, breach of contract, and promissory estoppel.

FACT SUMMARY: Prospective buyers of a car dealership discussed, but did not execute a written contract memorializing, a reduced sale price in exchange for a $50 fee on each car sold by the dealership over a seven-year period.

> ### 🏛 RULE OF LAW
> A plain and unambiguous merger clause bars extrinsic evidence where sophisticated parties, with the assistance of counsel, have extensively negotiated a detailed written contract.

FACTS: Nelson (P) owned two car dealerships, Metro Auto and Metro Toyota, for both of which General Motors Acceptance Corporation (GMAC) provided all financing. A representative of Metro Toyota negotiated a sale of Metro Toyota to Elway (D) after both dealerships began having financial difficulties. Elway (D) eventually signed a "buy-sell agreement" and a separate real-estate contract to purchase Metro Toyota. After the buy-sell agreement for Metro Toyota was executed, the parties began discussing Elway's (D) purchase of both dealerships. Elway (D), however, was either unable or unwilling to pay Nelson's (P) asking price for the two dealerships. During those expanded negotiations, though, the parties also discussed an arrangement by which Nelson (P) would reduce his price for Metro Toyota in exchange for Elway's (D) payment of a $50 fee for each car sold from both dealerships over a seven-year period. The parties reduced these specific terms to a writing, which the parties called the "service agreement," but neither party signed that document. Shortly thereafter, the parties signed a buy-sell agreement for the sale of Metro Auto. Both of the buy-sell agreements contained a merger clause that plainly and unambiguously precluded any consideration of any other agreements the parties might have reached except for the buy-sell agreements themselves. Before the closing on the real-estate purchase of Metro Toyota, GMAC informed Elway (D) that its financing of Elway's (D) purchase of the dealerships required that Nelson (P) not receive any proceeds from the sale. Elway (D) did not execute the service agreement before the closing, despite Nelson's (P) demand that he do so. Nelson (P) sued, alleging breach of contract and several other theories of recovery. The trial judge granted Elway's (D) motion for summary judgment on the claims for breach of contract, civil conspiracy, and promissory estoppel. The intermediate appellate court affirmed, and

Nelson (P) petitioned the Colorado Supreme Court for further review.

ISSUE: Does a plain and unambiguous merger clause bar extrinsic evidence where sophisticated parties, with the assistance of counsel, have extensively negotiated a detailed written contract?

HOLDING AND DECISION: (Vollack, C.J.) Yes. A plain and unambiguous merger clause bars extrinsic evidence where sophisticated parties, with the assistance of counsel, have extensively negotiated a detailed written contract. The merger clauses in the buy-sell agreements in this case preclude any consideration of whether the parties intended for the service agreement to be part of their transaction. Extrinsic evidence generally is not admissible to prove intent in the face of a merger clause; even when it is admissible, it may not contradict or supplement the intent as expressed by the written contract itself. The merger clauses here—plain, unambiguous provisions of detailed written agreements—were negotiated by sophisticated parties with the assistance of counsel. Extrinsic evidence on other alleged agreements therefore may not be admitted. Affirmed.

DISSENT: (Lohr, J.) Extrinsic evidence should be admitted because the parties' intent with respect to the service agreement is the very essence of this case. Nelson (P) supported his position with sufficient evidence to create a triable issue for a finder of fact. Merger clauses are presumptively valid, but the presumption may be rebutted when giving effect to them would frustrate the parties' actual intentions. Here, despite the strict letter of the two merger clauses, the parties' entire transaction indisputably encompassed two buy-sell agreements and two real-estate purchase agreements. Evidence of the service agreement, therefore, also should have been admitted to prove the parties' actual intent.

▶ ANALYSIS

A practical danger in Judge Lohr's dissenting position is that the exception he notes can all too easily swallow the rule. Under that exception, a complaining party apparently need only allege an actual intent that differs from the plain language of a written agreement to justify admission of the very contradictory or supplementary evidence that the majority's reasoning seeks to exclude.

▪▬▪

Continued on next page.

Quicknotes

EXTRINSIC EVIDENCE Evidence that is not contained within the text of a document or contract but which is derived from the parties' statements or the circumstances under which the agreement was made.

PROMISSORY ESTOPPEL A promise that is enforceable if the promisor should reasonably expect that it will induce action or forbearance on the part of the promisee, and does in fact cause such action or forbearance, and it is the only means of avoiding injustice.

SUMMARY JUDGMENT Judgment rendered by a court in response to a motion by one of the parties, claiming that the lack of a question of material fact in respect to an issue warrants disposition of the issue without consideration by the jury.

■▬■

Pacific Gas & Electric Co. v. G.W. Thomas Drayage & Rigging Co.

Electric company (P) v. Contractor (D)

Cal. Sup. Ct., 69 Cal. 2d 33, 442 P.2d 641 (1968).

NATURE OF CASE: Action for damages for breach of a contract.

FACT SUMMARY: G.W. Thomas Drayage & Rigging Co. (Thomas) (D) contracted to repair Pacific Gas & Electric Co.'s (Pacific) (P) steam turbine and to perform work at its own risk and expense and to indemnify Pacific (P) against all loss and damage. Thomas (D) also agreed not to procure less than $50,000 insurance to cover liability for injury to property. But when the turbine rotor was damaged, Pacific (P) claimed it was covered under that policy, while Thomas (D) said it was only to cover injury to third persons.

🏛 RULE OF LAW
The test of admissibility of extrinsic evidence to explain the meaning of a written instrument is not whether it appears to the court to be plain and unambiguous on its face but whether the offered evidence is relevant to prove a meaning to which the language of the instrument is reasonably susceptible.

FACTS: Thomas (D) contracted to replace the upper metal cover on Pacific's (P) steam turbine and agreed to perform all work "at [its] own risk and expense" and to "indemnify" Pacific (P) against all loss, damage, expense, and liability resulting from injury to property arising out of or in any way connected with performance of the contract. Thomas (D) agreed to obtain not less than $50,000 insurance to cover liability for injury to property. Pacific (P) was to be an additional named insured, but the policy was to contain a cross-liability clause extending the coverage of Pacific's (P) property. During the work, the cover fell, damaging the exposed rotor in the amount of $25,144.51. Thomas (D) during trial offered to prove that its conduct and, under similar contracts entered into by Pacific (P), the indemnity clause were meant to cover injury to third person's property only, not to Pacific's (P).

ISSUE: Was Thomas' (D) offered evidence relevant to proving a meaning to which the language of the instrument was susceptible?

HOLDING AND DECISION: (Traynor, C.J.) Yes. While the trial court admitted that the contract was "the classic language for a third party indemnity provision," it held that the plain language of the contract would give a meaning covering Pacific's (P) damage. However, this admission by the court clearly shows the ambiguous nature of the agreement and the need for extrinsic evidence in order to clarify the intentions of the parties. Extrinsic evidence for the purpose of showing the intent of the parties could be excluded only when it is feasible to determine the meaning of the words from the instrument alone. Rational interpretation requires at least an initial consideration of all credible evidence to prove the intention of the parties. Reversed.

▶ ANALYSIS

This case strongly disapproves of the "plain meaning rule," which states that if a writing appears clear and unambiguous on its face, the meaning must be determined from "the four corners" of the writing without considering any extrinsic evidence at all. The trial court applied this rule. However, the rule, while generally accepted but widely condemned, would exclude evidence of trade usage, prior dealings of the parties, and even circumstances surrounding the creation of the agreement. Uniform Commercial Code § 2-202 expressly throws out the plain meaning rule. Instead, it allows use of evidence of a course of performance or dealing to explain the writing "unless carefully negated." Here, Chief Justice Traynor greatly expanded the admission of extrinsic evidence to show intent. When he says it should not be admitted only when it is feasible "to determine the meaning the parties gave to the words from the instrument alone," he is saying in all practicality that extrinsic evidence to show intent should be admissible in just about any case, and that rarely will the instrument be so exact as to clearly show intent.

━━

Quicknotes

EXTRINSIC EVIDENCE Evidence that is not contained within the text of a document or contract but which is derived from the parties' statements or the circumstances under which the agreement was made.

INDEMNIFICATION Reimbursement for losses sustained or security against anticipated loss or damages.

━━

W.W.W. Associates, Inc. v Giancontieri

Developers (P) v. Sellers (D)

N.Y. Ct. App., 77 N.Y.2d 157, 566 N.E.2d 639 (1990).

NATURE OF CASE: Suit for specific performance of a contract to sell real property.

FACT SUMMARY: Developers (P) sought to compel specific performance of a contract to sell certain property.

RULE OF LAW

When parties set down a writing in a clear, complete document, their writing should be enforced according to their terms, and extrinsic evidence is generally inadmissible to add to or vary the writing.

FACTS: Owners (D) of two acres of property contracted to sell the property to developers (P). The parties signed a contact of sale containing a reciprocal cancellation provision and merger clause, In particular, paragraph 31 of the contract provided that if pending litigation were not concluded by 6-1-87, then either party had the right to cancel the contract, and the down payment was to be returned. The owners (D) moved for summary judgment and the court dismissed holding that the agreement unambiguously conferred the right to cancel on both parties. The appellate division reversed, awarding specific performance of the contract to developers (P).

ISSUE: When parties set down a writing in a clear, complete document, should their writing be enforced according to their terms and is extrinsic evidence generally inadmissible to add to or vary the writing?

HOLDING AND DECISION: (Kaye, J.) Yes. When parties set down a writing in a clear, complete document, their writing should be enforced according to their terms and extrinsic evidence is generally inadmissible to add to or vary the writing. Here the contract plainly manifests the intent that all prior understandings be merged into the contract, which expresses the parties' full agreement. Furthermore there is no ambiguity as to the cancellation clause, which confers a reciprocal right of cancellation on either party. Reversed.

▌ *ANALYSIS*

The court declines to accept extrinsic evidence here as well to create an ambiguity in the document. The general rule is that if a document is clear on its face, extrinsic evidence is inadmissible to create an ambiguity where apparently there is none.

Quicknotes

EXTRINSIC EVIDENCE Evidence that is not contained within the text of a document or contract but which is derived from the parties' statements or the circumstances under which the agreement was made.

MERGER CLAUSE A clause in a contract prohibiting modification of its terms by prior or oral agreements since all such agreements are assumed to have been merged into the document.

Brinderson-Newberg Joint Venture v. Pacific Erectors, Inc.

General contractor (P) v. Subcontractor (D)

971 F.2d 272 (9th Cir. 1992), *cert. denied*, 507 U.S. 914 (1993).

NATURE OF CASE: Appeal of district court denial of motions for a directed verdict and judgment n.o.v.

FACT SUMMARY: A contractor and a subcontractor disagreed upon the meaning of certain construction phrases in the building contract.

🏛 RULE OF LAW
Where a dispute exists as to the meaning of a term or phrase in a contract, parol evidence may be offered to explain the term; however, the written contract must be reasonably susceptible to the meaning given by the parol evidence on an objective standard.

FACTS: The Navy awarded Brinderson-Newberg Joint Venture (Brinderson) (P) a contract to construct a coal-fired power plant. Brinderson (P) entered into negotiations with Pacific Erectors, Inc. (Pacific) (D), a subcontractor submitting a low bid for certain erection work. The negotiations focused on erection of a Flue Gas System (FGS). As part of a $1.54 million bid, Pacific (D) offered to erect the support steel for the FGS for $257,000. But Brinderson (P) wanted Pacific (D) to erect the large steel FGS components along with the support steel. A draft contract required Pacific (D) to "erect complete" the FGS equipment. During negotiations on a final draft, Pacific (D) asked to have its work on the FGS limited to "picks and sets." There was a disagreement as to whether Brinderson (P) agreed to this change. No change was made, the contract was signed, and an integration clause in the contract specified that it was the whole agreement. Pacific (D) performed until a dispute arose concerning the FGS erection. Brinderson (P) filed suit under the contract. A jury found for Pacific (D), based in part on parol evidence Pacific (D) offered to explain the term "erect complete" in the contract to mean that Pacific (D) was to complete only a portion of the FGS. According to Pacific (D), Brinderson (P) orally agreed to that interpretation. Brinderson (P) requested a directed verdict and a judgment n.o.v., but was denied. Brinderson (P) appealed.

ISSUE: If a dispute exists between parties on the meaning of a phrase or term in a contract, may parol evidence be offered to explain the disputed term?

HOLDING AND DECISION: (Wiggins, J.) Yes. Where a dispute exists as to the meaning of a term or phrase in a contract, parol evidence may be offered to explain the term; however, the written contract must be reasonably susceptible to the meaning given by the parol

evidence on an objective standard. While a contract may be a complete agreement on its face, the terms therein may be so complex or contentious as to require extrinsic evidence to divine the most reasonably intended meaning. In this case, the normal industry meaning of the phrase "erect complete" includes field assembly, picking and setting, and bolting and welding the relevant components into permanent position. Even if Pacific's (D) argument is accepted, and there was in fact an oral agreement to alter the normal industry meaning of the terms in the contract, Pacific (D) lost the opportunity to make such an argument when it accepted the integration clause in the contract. If strained interpretations of terms are accepted as reasonable, the parol evidence rule will be eviscerated. The contract must be reasonably susceptible to the proffered meaning before parol evidence may be introduced. Reversed.

▶ ANALYSIS

Since one goal of contact law is to promote writings that can serve as good evidence of an agreement, the use of parol evidence for interpretation of disputed terms must be restricted. As the court observes, if the terms of a contract were subject to strained interpretations, even written contracts would be almost unenforceable as written. Thus the threshold test of reasonable susceptibility must be overcome before parol evidence is considered.

Quicknotes

DIRECTED VERDICT A verdict ordered by the court in a jury trial.

JUDGMENT N.O.V. A judgment entered by the trial judge reversing a jury verdict if the jury's determination has no basis in law or fact.

PAROL EVIDENCE RULE Doctrine precluding parties to an agreement from introducing evidence of prior or contemporaneous agreements in order to repudiate or alter the terms of a written contract.

Frigaliment Importing Co. v. B.N.S. International Sales Corp.

Buyer (P) v. Seller (D)

190 F. Supp. 116 (S.D.N.Y. 1960).

NATURE OF CASE: Action for breach of warranty of a contract for the sale of goods.

FACT SUMMARY: Frigaliment Importing Co. (Frigaliment) (P) ordered a large quantity of "chicken" from B.N.S. International Sales Corp. (BNS) (D), intending to buy young chicken suitable for broiling and frying, but BNS (D) believed, in considering the weights ordered at the prices fixed by the parties, that the order could be filled with older chicken, suitable for stewing only, and termed "fowl" by Frigaliment (P).

> ### 🏛 RULE OF LAW
> The party who seeks to interpret the terms of the contract in a sense narrower than their everyday use bears the burden of persuasion to so show, and if that party fails to support its burden, it faces dismissal of its complaint.

FACTS: Frigaliment Importing Co. (Frigaliment) (P), a Swiss corporation, and B.N.S. International Sales Corp. (BNS) (D), a New York corporation, made two almost identical contracts for the sale of chicken by the latter to the former as follows: U.S. fresh frozen chicken, Grade A, government inspected, eviscerated, all wrapped and boxed suitably for export, 75,000 lbs. 2.5-3 lbs. at $33.00 per 100 lbs. and 25,000 lbs. 1.5-2 lbs. at $36.50 per 100 lbs. The second contract was the same except for 25,000 lbs. less of the heavier chicken and a price of $37.00 per 100 lbs. for the lighter birds. BNS (D), which was new to the poultry business, believed any kind of chicken could be used to fill the order including stewing chickens. Most of the order for heavier birds was filled with stewers, as that was the only way BNS (D) could make a profit on the contract.

ISSUE: Did Frigaliment support its burden of persuasion that the word "chicken" should be used in its narrower sense so as to exclude stewing chicken?

HOLDING AND DECISION: (Friendly, J.) No. Frigaliment (P) failed to support its burden. While cables leading up to negotiations were predominantly in German, the use of the English word "chicken" as meaning "young chicken" rather than the German word "huhn" meaning "broilers and stewers" lost its force when BNS (D) asked if any kind of chickens were wanted to which an affirmative answer meaning "huhn" was given. BNS (D), being new to the chicken trade, the other party must show the other's acceptance of the trade use of a term. Frigaliment (P) failed to offer such proof. There was conflicting evidence anyway as to the trade use of the word "chicken." BNS's (D) price of $33.00 per 100 lbs. for the larger birds was $2.00 to $4.00

less than for broilers. Frigaliment (P) could not say that the price appeared reasonable because it was closer to the $35.00 broiler price than the $30.00 stewer price. BNS (D) could be expected not to sell at a loss. While the evidence is generally conflicting, overall it appeared that BNS (D) believed it could comply by supplying stewing chicken. This did conform with one dictionary meaning, with the definition in the department of animal regulations to which at least there was a contractual reference, and with some trade usage. This evidence must be relied upon as the contract language itself could not settle the question here.

▶ ANALYSIS

In determining the intent of the parties the court will turn first to the language of the contract to see whether the meaning of the ambiguous term can be raised. If this is unsuccessful, the court must look to other evidence. Under Restatement, First, § 235, certain guidelines aid in determining meaning. First, the ordinary meaning of language throughout the country is given to words unless circumstances show that a different meaning is applicable. Also, all circumstances surrounding the transaction may be taken into consideration. Also, if after consideration of all factors, it is still uncertain what meaning should be given, a reasonable, lawful, and effective meaning to all manifestations of intention is preferred to an interpretation which leaves a part of such unreasonable, unlawful, or ineffective. Restatement, First, § 236(a). Even so, the principal apparent purpose of the parties should be given greater weight in determining the meaning to be given.

━━■

Quicknotes

AMBIGUITY Language that is capable of more than one interpretation.

WARRANTY An assurance by one party that another may rely on a certain representation of fact.

━━■

Nanakuli Paving and Rock Co. v. Shell Oil Co., Inc.

Buyer (P) v. Seller (D)

664 F.2d 772 (9th Cir. 1981).

NATURE OF CASE: Appeal of judgment n.o.v. setting aside a jury verdict and damage award for breach of contract.

FACT SUMMARY: Nanakuli Paving and Rock Co. (P) entered into long-term supply contracts with Shell Oil Co., Inc. (Shell) (D) to buy asphalt and objected when Shell (D) raised the price from $44 to $76.

RULE OF LAW
Under the Uniform Commercial Code, an agreement goes beyond the written words to mean the bargain of the parties in fact, as found in their language or by implication from other circumstances, including course of dealing, usage of trade, and course of performance.

FACTS: Nanakuli Paving and Rock Co. (Nanakuli) (P) was a large asphaltic paving contractor in Hawaii. It had been purchasing all its asphalt requirements from Shell Oil Co., Inc. (Shell) (D) under two long-term contracts. Nanakuli (P) incorporated the price of asphalt into bids. However, on 7,200 tons of committed asphalt, Shell (D) suddenly raised the price from $44 to $76, costing Nanakuli (P) $220,800 on the committed asphalt. Nanakuli (P) argued, with substantial support, that price protection was the convention of the asphalt paving trade in Hawaii. Price protection required that the price of committed asphalt be held constant so that contracts would remain at the same profit level as initially negotiated. During the time in question, the management structure of Shell (D) was completely altered. Prior to this time, Shell (D) had always price protected Nanakuli (P). Nanakuli (P) filed a breach of contract action and was awarded $220,800. But the court set aside the verdict, and Nanakuli (P) appealed the judgment n.o.v.

ISSUE: Can evidence of trade usage or course of dealing be offered under the Uniform Commercial Code to modify the apparent meaning of express terms in a written contract?

HOLDING AND DECISION: (Hoffman, J.) Yes. Under the Uniform Commercial Code, an agreement goes beyond the written words to mean the bargain of the parties in fact, as found in their language or by implication from other circumstances, including course of dealing, usage of trade, and course of performance. Several factors must be analyzed to determine if a trade usage is implied in a contract. First, the breadth of the trade must be examined to determine if the practice in question was sufficiently widespread to place a party to a contract on notice. Second,

the course of dealing or trade usage must be reasonably consistent with the express terms of the contract before a party will be bound beyond the writing. In this case, the appropriate trade in question is the asphaltic paving trade on the island of Oahu. Since Government agencies in Hawaii refused to accept escalation clauses, the entire asphalt industry practiced price protection. Shell (D) should have been on notice that everyone in the trade assumed this practice was normal. The express term at issue is the term that allowed Shell (D) to charge its posted price at the time of delivery. However, the trade practice modified the term, through a regular course of dealing, to include price protection for committed asphalt. This implied term, while modifying the writing, could reasonably have been found to be incorporated into the contract. The judgment is reversed and the jury verdict is reinstated with interest.

ANALYSIS

The Uniform Commercial Code acknowledges that an agreement is the bargain in fact, and it may extend beyond the written words. Such a consideration is due, in part, to the fact that certain industries use language in a way peculiar to the trade. Unfortunately, members of a trade may not even be aware that their turns of phrase are incomprehensible to others, and they may not draft a contract accordingly.

Quicknotes

COURSE OF DEALING Previous conduct between two parties to a contact which may be relied upon to interpret their actions.

J.N.O.V. Judgment notwithstanding the verdict—a judgment entered by the trial judge reversing a jury verdict if the jury's determination has no basis in law or fact.

REQUIREMENTS CONTRACT An agreement pursuant to which one party agrees to purchase all his required goods or services from the other party exclusively for a specified time period.

TRADE USAGE A course of dealing or practice commonly used in a particular trade.

Corenswet, Inc. v. Amana Refrigeration, Inc.

Distributor (P) v. Manufacturer (D)

594 F.2d 129 (5th Cir. 1979).

NATURE OF CASE: Consolidated appeals from injunction forbidding termination of a distribution in diversity litigation.

FACT SUMMARY: Corenswet, Inc. (P) was the exclusive distributor of Amana Refrigeration, Inc. (Amana) (D) merchandise in southern Louisiana, and their agreement included a right to terminate the relationship at any time, which Amana (D) exercised over Corenswet's (P) objections.

🏛 RULE OF LAW
Where a contract expressly provides that either party may terminate the agreement for any reason, no obligation exists requiring there be a good faith reason for the termination.

FACTS: Corenswet, Inc. (P) was an independent wholesale distributor of appliances. It was also the exclusive Amana Refrigeration, Inc. (Amana) (D) distributor in southern Louisiana and had been since 1969. The distribution agreement was of infinite duration, but was terminable by either party at any time "with or without cause" on ten days' notice. The term was modified in 1975 to allow for termination by either party "at any time for any reason" on ten days' notice. Corenswet (P) made substantial investments in an organization designed to distribute Amana (D) products. Annual sales of Amana (D) products rose from $200,000 in 1969 to $2.5 million in 1976. However, Amana (D) was concerned that Corenswet (P) was underfinanced. Corenswet (P) complied with each of Amana's (D) requests regarding its financial structure and credit arrangements, but Amana (D) persisted in changing its requirements as quickly as Corenswet (P) could respond. Finally, Amana (D) gave notice of termination. Corenswet (P) filed suit for damages and injunctive relief in state court. A preliminary injunction was issued by the federal district court after removal to that venue. Amana (D) appealed.

ISSUE: Does a good faith obligation extend to express terms of a contract which permit termination of the agreement for any reason by either party?

HOLDING AND DECISION: (Wisdom, J.) No. Where a contract expressly provides that either party may terminate the agreement for any reason, no obligation exists requiring there be a good faith reason for the termination. The concept of good faith has generally been used as a rationale when implying contract terms. It has not, however, been regularly used to strike down express terms in a contract. In this case, the distribution contract contained very clear language that termination was available to either party for any reason. The clear meaning of this language is that a simple desire to end the relationship is a good enough reason. There is no room in such a clear express term to imply some other agreement between the parties. The hope that one party would never use termination to the other's detriment is insufficient to imply new terms to the contract. As a last note, Corenswet (P) argued that the termination term was unconscionable, but it never pressed the issue; the district court could make no finding in that regard based upon the record. Reversed.

▶ ANALYSIS

If the appliance distribution trade operated under the assumption that termination clauses required good cause, then Corenswet (P) might have argued its position more effectively. Corenswet (P) might also have found more fertile ground arguing that an unrestricted termination clause is unconscionable, as suggested by the court. But Corenswet (P) also had the power to terminate under the agreement, making complaints somewhat hollow.

━━

Quicknotes

DIVERSITY The authority of a federal court to hear and determine cases involving $10,000 or more and in which the parties are citizens of different states, or in which one party is an alien.

GOOD FAITH An honest intention to abstain from any unconscientious advantage of another.

INJUNCTION A court order requiring a person to do, or prohibiting that person from doing, a specific act.

━━

Spaulding v. Morse

Trustee (P) v. Settlor (D)

Mass. Sup. Jud. Ct., 322 Mass. 149, 76 N.E.2d 137 (1947).

NATURE OF CASE: Appeal of judgment in suit in equity ordering enforcement of trust provisions.

FACT SUMMARY: Morse (D) hired Spaulding (P), a trustee, to handle funds paid by Morse (D) and held in trust for the college education of Morse's (D) son, but Morse (D) ceased making payments while his son was in the Army.

🏛 RULE OF LAW

If a contract as a whole produces a conviction that a particular result was fixedly desired although not expressed by formal words, the defect may be supplied by implication and the underlying intention effectuated if sufficiently declared.

FACTS: Morse (D) and his wife divorced; they had a child, Richard. After divorcing, a trust was established to provide for the future education of Richard in college. The trust agreement required that Morse (D) pay $1,200 a year to the trust until Richard entered college. Thereafter, Morse (D) was to pay $2,200 a year for a maximum of four years to cover the cost of college. Trouble arose when Richard graduated from high school and was inducted into the Army. Morse (D) sought to suspend his payments to the trust until Richard entered college. Spaulding (P), the trustee, filed suit to compel Morse (D) to continue his payments to the trust. Spaulding (P) prevailed, and Morse (D) appealed.

ISSUE: If a contract as a whole produces a conviction that a particular result was fixedly desired although not expressed by formal words, may the defect be supplied by implication and the underlying intention effectuated if sufficiently declared?

HOLDING AND DECISION: (Dolan, J.) Yes. If a contract as a whole produces a conviction that a particular result was fixedly desired although not expressed by formal words, the defect may be supplied by implication and the underlying intention effectuated if sufficiently declared. Every instrument is to be construed so as to give effect to the intent of the parties. An omission cannot be supplied by conjecture. But if the intent is sufficiently clear in the entire agreement, then it may be implied. Here, the purpose of the trust was to provide for Richard's education. The assumption was that Richard would enter college after high school. But induction into the Army during World War II thwarted that plan. Clearly, the intent was to apply $1,200 toward Richard's college savings for the years in school until graduation from high school. There was no suggestion that the payments continue indefinitely should Richard be unable to attend college. Morse (D) will have to pay the $2,200 a year for four years when and if Richard attends college, but for now he may properly suspend payment to the trust, given that its educational purpose cannot now be met. Reversed.

▶ ANALYSIS

The problem in this case is that the parties did not plan for the contingency that occurred. The court, in essence, used the existing agreement to supply an omitted term consistent with the remainder of the agreement. There isn't a good doctrinal explanation for this case; the court did its best to find an equitable solution to an unexpected situation.

■=■

Quicknotes

CONTINGENCY Based on the uncertain happening of another event.

EQUITY Fairness; justice; the determination of a matter consistent with principles of fairness and not in strict compliance with rules of law.

SETTLOR The grantor or donor of property that is to be held in trust for the benefit of another.

■=■

Bloor v. Falstaff Brewing Corp.

Brewery trustee (P) v. Marketing agent (D)

601 F.2d 609 (2d Cir. 1979).

NATURE OF CASE: Action for damages for breach of contract.

FACT SUMMARY: Bloor (P), Reorganization Trustee of the once-successful Ballantine Brewery, brought suit alleging that Falstaff Brewing Corp. (Falstaff) (D) had breached its contractual obligation to use its "bests efforts to promote and maintain a high volume of sales" of the Ballantine brands.

🏛 RULE OF LAW
A contractual provision obligating one to use its "best efforts" to promote and maintain a high volume of sales of a certain product is breached by a policy which emphasizes profit without fair consideration of the effect on sales volume.

FACTS: Falstaff Brewing Corp. (Falstaff) (D) contracted to purchase Ballantine's brewing labels, trademarks, etc., for $4,000,000 plus a $0.50 royalty on each barrel of Ballantine brands sold between 1972 and 1978. The contract provided Falstaff (D) would use its best efforts to promote and maintain a high volume of sales of Ballantine products and contained a liquidated damages clause operative if Falstaff (D) ever substantially discontinued distribution of beer under the brand name "Ballantine." With policies based on profit to Falstaff (D), there was a continual decline in sales volume, and Bloor (P), the Reorganization Trustee of the company which had been Ballantine & Sons, sued to recover damages for breach of contract. The trial court found Falstaff (D) had breached the best efforts clause, for which damages were to be awarded, but that such did not trigger the liquidated damages clause.

ISSUE: Does one breach a contract obligating him to use best efforts to maintain a high volume of sales of an item if he makes policy based primarily on considerations of profit?

HOLDING AND DECISION: (Friendly, J.) Yes. Where, as in this case, a party contractually obligates itself to use its best efforts to promote and maintain a high volume of sales of a particular item, its action in making policies and decisions based primarily on considerations of profit and without fair consideration of the effect on sales volume constitutes a breach of that contractual provision, and damages may be sought. Even taking into account Falstaff's (D) right to give reasonable consideration to its own interest, including the profit interest, it breached its duty to use best efforts to maintain and promote a high sales volume with regard to Ballantine brands. It must,

therefore, pay damages based on a reasonable estimate of the royalties which would have been paid had such breach not occurred. That was the standard used by the lower court. Affirmed.

▶ *ANALYSIS*

Uniform Commercial Code § 2-306(2) provides for the imposition of an obligation on the part of both parties to an agreement for exclusive dealing in goods to use their "best efforts." It is a codification of the judicially made rule that was formed over the years, i.e., that certain contracts carried an implied obligation to use "best efforts" because they would otherwise lack mutuality of obligation.

◼◼◼

Quicknotes

ILLUSORY AGREEMENT An agreement that is not legally enforceable because performance of the obligation by the promisor is completely within his discretion.

LIQUIDATED DAMAGES An amount of money specified in a contract representing the damages owed in the event of breach.

MUTUALITY OF OBLIGATION Requires that both parties to a contract are bound or else neither is bound.

◼◼◼

Greer Properties, Inc. v. LaSalle National Bank

Buyer (P) v. Seller (D)

874 F.2d 457 (7th Cir. 1989).

NATURE OF CASE: Appeal of district court's grant of a summary judgment enforcing a contract termination.

FACT SUMMARY: Greer Properties, Inc. (P) entered into a contract to purchase a property specifying that the owners (D) would clean up environmental contamination at their own expense but could terminate the contract if the cleanup became "economically impracticable."

RULE OF LAW
A party vested with contractual discretion must exercise that discretion reasonably.

FACTS: Old Orchard (D), a partnership, purchased a property for $700,721.70, with legal title held by LaSalle National Bank (LaSalle) (D). They intended to develop the land, but later chose to sell the property. Two buyers expressed interest: G.D. Searle Co., and Greer Properties, Inc. (Greer) (P), the real estate subsidiary of Marriott Corporation. Searle agreed to pay $1,100,000, subject to the right to terminate if the soil was contaminated by environmental waste. The soil was contaminated, and Searle received an estimate that cleanup would cost $500,000. Searle terminated. Greer (P) then offered to buy the property for $1,250,000. As part of the agreement, Old Orchard (D) and LaSalle (D) were to remove the soil waste at their own expense, but could terminate if the cleanup became "economically impracticable." Old Orchard (D) and LaSalle (D) retained a consultant who estimated cleanup costs at between $100,000 and $200,000. Without formally terminating, Old Orchard (D) began to negotiate again with Searle. Searle offered $1,455,000. Old Orchard (D) then terminated the agreement with Greer (P). Actual cleanup cost around $250,000. Greer (P) filed suit, seeking specific performance, but the district court issued a summary judgment against Greer (P). Greer (P) appealed.

ISSUE: May a contracting party vested with broad discretion to terminate the contract do so simply to recapture the opportunity to receive a better price?

HOLDING AND DECISION: (Wood, Jr., J.) No. A party vested with contractual discretion must exercise that discretion reasonably. Otherwise a breach of contract has occurred, and the court must grant relief to the aggrieved party. Every contract implies good faith and fair dealing. This implication sets limits on the extent of discretionary power. In the present case, Old Orchard's (D) decision to terminate must be analyzed to determine if it acted in good faith. Evidence suggests that the sellers terminated to get a better price. Such an act constitutes bad faith. Once a specific price has been agreed upon, the opportunity to search for a better price has passed. The district court issued a summary judgment in favor of Old Orchard (D). This was in error. Material issues of fact exist as to whether Old Orchard (D) did terminate to sell at a higher price. The issue of bad faith cannot be settled without addressing this underlying factual matter. Summary judgment is reversed.

ANALYSIS

Other cases have held that an absolute right to terminate need not comply with any standard of good faith if the absolute right is expressly stated in the contract. Here, however, termination was authorized only in the case of economic impracticability. But with the help of a little math, it is clear that Greer's (P) offer was well above Old Orchard's (D) basis in the property plus the $250,000 cleanup cost and therefore not economically impracticable.

Quicknotes

FAIR DEALING An implied warranty that the parties will deal honestly in the satisfaction of their obligations and without an intent to defraud.

GOOD FAITH An honest intention to abstain from any unconscientious advantage of another.

IMPRACTICABILITY A doctrine relieving the parties to a contract from liability for nonperformance of their duties thereunder, if the subject matter of the contract ceases to exist.

SPECIFIC PERFORMANCE An equitable remedy whereby the court requires the parties to perform their obligations pursuant to a contract.

Market Street Associates Limited Partnership v. Frey

Lessee assignee (P) v. [Party not identified] (D)

941 F.2d 588 (7th Cir. 1991).

NATURE OF CASE: Appeal from summary judgment dismissing action seeking specific performance of a lease provision.

FACT SUMMARY: A principal of Market Street Associates Limited Partnership (Market Street) (P) allegedly deliberately failed to notify General Electric Pension Trust (General Electric) (D), the lessor, of a clause in a lease that could result in General Electric (D) having to sell the leased property at less than market value. Market Street (P) contended that its failure to point out the clause did not constitute bad faith, and that it was, therefore, entitled to specific performance.

> 🏛 **RULE OF LAW**
> A determination of good faith that depends on a contracting party's state of mind cannot be made on summary judgment.

FACTS: J.C. Penney (Penney) entered into a sale-lease-back arrangement with General Electric Pension Trust (General Electric) (D) on a property. A clause in the lease (paragraph 34) provided that if General Electric (D) failed to negotiate with the lessee regarding future financing, the property could be purchased at less than market value. Years later, Market Street Associates Limited Partnership (Market Street) (P), J.C. Penney's assignee, attempted to negotiate financing with General Electric (D). In its correspondence with General Electric (D), Market Street (P) failed to mention paragraph 34. General Electric (D), no longer being aware of the clause, refused to negotiate. Market Street (P) then sought to exercise its option and sued for specific performance. At his deposition, the principal of Market Street (P) primarily responsible for the property testified that he suspected that his counterpart at General Electric (D) might not be aware of the clause and that he had realized this during negotiations. However, he also testified that he believed this was unlikely because someone at General Electric (D) would have read the lease and realized its ramifications. Based on this testimony, the district court inferred that Market Street (P) was not really interested in financing from General Electric (D), but really just wanted the opportunity to buy the property at a bargain price. From this, the district court determined that Market Street (P) should have advised General Electric (D) that it was requesting financing pursuant to paragraph 34, and concluded that because Market Street (P) failed to do so, it had prevented the negotiations over financing that were a condition precedent to the lessee's exercise of the purchase option from taking place, and it had acted in bad faith. Accordingly, the district court entered summary

judgment dismissing the action. Market Street (P) appealed, and the court of appeals granted review.

ISSUE: Can a determination of good faith that depends on a contracting party's state of mind be made on summary judgment?

HOLDING AND DECISION: (Posner, J.) No. A determination of good faith that depends on a contracting party's state of mind cannot be made on summary judgment. That parties to a contract must act in good faith does not mean, as some courts seem to believe, that the parties must act in an altruistic or fiduciary manner toward each other; they need not do so. Furthermore, it is quite legitimate for a party to use his superior knowledge to drive an advantageous bargain. However, it is one thing to have superior knowledge, but it is quite another to know that the other party is unaware of a crucial fact and take advantage of this ignorance. This constitutes sharp practice, which departs from good faith. Thus, a party to a contract may not intentionally exploit the other party's oversight of an important fact. Implying good faith in the contracting process promotes the overriding purpose of contract law, which is to give the parties what they would have stipulated for expressly if at the time of making the contract they had had complete knowledge of the future and the costs of negotiating and adding provisions to the contract had been zero. Here, the dispositive question is whether Market Street (P) tried to trick General Electric (D) and succeeded in doing so. If that was the case, Market Street (P) violated the duty of good faith. Here, the district court held that Market Street's (P) principal had engaged in such conduct. While there are arguments to be made for that conclusion, it could also be argued that construing the facts as favorably to Market Street (P) as the record permits—as must be done at this stage of the litigation—an entirely different picture emerges, one where Market Street (P) acted honestly, reasonably, without ulterior motive, in the face of circumstances as they actually and reasonably appeared to it. However, because choosing between these alternatives is a matter for a trier of fact, the district court jumped the gun in making that choice, without the benefit of a trial, at the summary judgment stage. The case must be remanded to decide what Market Street's (P) principal's state of mind was and what he believed. Reversed and remanded.

> ▎ **ANALYSIS**
>
> A mutual mistake is grounds for nullifying a contract or a term thereof. Unilateral mistake may or may not be. As the

Continued on next page.

court stated here, unilateral mistake combined with an opponent's overreaching may be grounds for rescission.

∎══∎

Quicknotes

GOOD FAITH An honest intention to abstain from any unconscientious advantage of another.

MUTUAL MISTAKE A mistake by both parties to a contract, who are in agreement as to what the contract terms should be, but the agreement as written fails to reflect that common intent; such contracts are voidable or subject to reformation.

SPECIFIC PERFORMANCE An equitable remedy whereby the court requires the parties to perform their obligations pursuant to a contract.

SUMMARY JUDGMENT Judgment rendered by a court in response to a motion by one of the parties, claiming that the lack of a question of material fact in respect to an issue warrants disposition of the issue without consideration by the jury.

UNILATERAL MISTAKE A mistake or misunderstanding as to the terms of a contract made by one party which is generally not a basis for relief by rescission or reformation.

∎══∎

Eastern Air Lines, Inc. v. Gulf Oil Corp.

Airlines (P) v. Oil company (D)

415 F. Supp. 429 (S.D. Fla. 1975).

NATURE OF CASE: Suit in district court for breach of contract seeking specific performance.

FACT SUMMARY: Eastern Air Lines, Inc. (P) bought jet fuel from Gulf Oil Co. (D), but price changes after an oil embargo brought the parties into contention on the source of the reference price and other contract elements.

> 🏛 **RULE OF LAW**
> If the established course of dealing, the established usages of the trade, and the basic contract have existed without dispute for a substantial length of time, a party may not defend its breach by complaining about practices in the trade unless the other party has in fact acted in bad faith.

FACTS: Eastern Air Lines, Inc. (Eastern) (P) entered into an agreement with Gulf Oil Co. (Gulf) (D) whereby Gulf (D) would supply jet fuel at certain specific cities in the Eastern (P) system. A similar contract had existed between the parties for years. The latest contract contained a reference to reflect changes in the price of raw materials to make jet fuel, specifically crude oil. The parties selected, as their indicator of the market value of oil, the average price of West Texas Sour, a crude oil bought in large quantity. The U.S. government subsequently imposed a two-tiered price control on crude oil. Then the 1973 oil embargo disturbed what had been a fairly stable system. The end result was that the West Texas Sour was held to a lower price than the typical price of crude oil. Eastern (P), like all airlines, could to some degree select between different fuel prices by controlling how much fuel a plane would "lift" in a particular city; in other words, a plane could carry more fuel than necessary to reduce the amount required at the next stop, a practice known as "fuel freighting." However, the reality was that this practice did not dramatically affect prices, as Gulf (D) would claim at trial, and it was standard practice for the industry. Gulf (D) demanded that Eastern (P) accept a price increase or be cut off in fifteen days. Eastern (P) filed suit, claiming breach of contract. Gulf (D) countered that Eastern (P) had breached first by manipulating its fuel requirements by fuel freighting.

ISSUE: If the established course of dealing, the established usages of the trade, and the basic contract have existed without dispute for a substantial length of time, may one of the parties defend its breach by complaining of these long-established practices?

HOLDING AND DECISION: (King, J.) No. If the established course of dealing, the established usages of the trade, and the basic contract have existed without dispute for a substantial length of time, a party may not defend its breach by complaining about practices in the trade unless the other party has in fact acted in bad faith. Good faith, according to the Uniform Commercial Code (UCC), requires honesty in fact in the conduct or transaction concerned. However, good faith between merchants is more precisely defined. In the case of merchants, good faith requires honesty in fact and the observance of reasonable commercial standards of fair dealing in the trade. Here, Gulf (D) complains that Eastern (P) engaged in bad faith when it utilized its ability to control fuel "lifts" at different cities. But fuel requirements change dramatically from day to day. Gulf (D) has known of this fuel freighting practice in the airline industry for years, including thirty years of dealings with Eastern (P). The UCC protects the seller if a buyer's requirements become unreasonable. However, these parties have a thirty-year history of dealing with the variable nature of airline fuel requirements. Nothing in Eastern's (P) behavior as a buyer has changed, and Gulf (D) only now complains of the situation it helped to design. Eastern (P) has not breached the contract.

⏵ ANALYSIS

At first viewing, it seems that Gulf (D) was treated unfairly. However, the price rise from the oil embargo was not as surprising to the industry as it was to the general public. Gulf (D) actually profited greatly in its overseas divisions because of the price hikes. And Gulf (D) had been at the forefront of lobbying the U.S. Congress to lift price controls on domestic oil, the very action that caused the pricing problem under which Gulf (D) was required to operate.

■━■

Quicknotes

COMMERCIAL IMPRACTICABILITY A doctrine relieving the parties to a contract from liability for nonperformance of their duties thereunder, if the subject matter of the contract ceases to exist.

■━■

Orange and Rockland Utilities, Inc. v. Amerada Hess Corp.

Utility companies (P) v. Oil company (D)

N.Y. App. Div., 59 A.D.2d 110, 397 N.Y.S.2d 814 (1977).

NATURE OF CASE: Appeal of trial court dismissal of a complaint alleging breach of requirements contract.

FACT SUMMARY: Orange and Rockland Utilities, Inc. (Orange and Rockland) (P) entered into a requirements contract with Amerada Hess Corp. (D), specifying estimates of Orange and Rockland's (P) oil requirements and setting a fixed price, but when the market price nearly doubled, Orange and Rockland (P) dramatically increased its demand for oil.

🏛 RULE OF LAW
A buyer in a rising market has acted in bad faith if the fixed price in a requirements contract is used for speculation, or if conditions at the time of contracting are unilaterally changed by the buyer to take advantage of the market at the seller's expense.

FACTS: Amerada Hess Corp. (Hess) (D) agreed to supply the fuel oil requirements of Orange and Rockland Utilities, Inc. (Orange and Rockland) (P). A fixed price of $2.14 per barrel was agreed upon. Estimates for the yearly requirements were included in the contract; the year of highest demand was estimated at 1.75 million barrels, and the lowest year was estimated at 1.38 million barrels. Orange and Rockland (P) reserved the right to use as much natural gas as might become available, thereby reducing its requirements of fuel oil. However, the price of fuel oil began to rise dramatically, climbing to $4.30 in just one year. As the price rose, Orange and Rockland (P) repeatedly revised upward its requirements with Hess (D). For 1970, Orange and Rockland (P) projected requirements at more than one million barrels over the contract estimate of 1.75 million, a 63 percent increase. Orange and Rockland (P) was making more money selling natural gas than burning it for power, shifting upward the need for fuel oil. Hess (D) protested, offering to supply the contract estimates plus an additional 10 percent. Hess (D) did supply the contract amounts plus an additional 10 percent for the rest of 1970, and Orange and Rockland (P) purchased other oil from elsewhere. Orange and Rockland (P) subsequently sued Hess (D), seeking the difference between what it had paid on the open market for oil and the cost it would have incurred had Hess (D) delivered the entire amount at $2.14 per barrel as contracted. The court found for Hess (D), citing bad faith on the part of Orange and Rockland (P). Orange and Rockland (P) appealed.

ISSUE: May a buyer in a requirements contract use the presence of a fixed price term to take advantage of unex-

pected market conditions by substantially increasing his requirement demands at the fixed price?

HOLDING AND DECISION: (Margett, J.) No. A buyer in a rising market has acted in bad faith if the fixed price in a requirements contract is used for speculation, or if conditions at the time of contracting are unilaterally changed by the buyer to take advantage of the market at the seller's expense. When a requirements contract is negotiated, the underlying assumption is that the agreement is exclusively between the buyer and the seller. But if the buyer uses an advantageous price to effectively become another seller, then other parties have, in effect, become entangled in the contract. In this case, Orange and Rockland (P) used the unexpected price rise in fuel oil to change the circumstances that were presumed in the original contract. Natural gas that would have been burned for power production became more profitable when sold by Orange and Rockland (P) to other utilities. Thus, far more fuel oil was required than originally anticipated since natural gas was not being used. Hess (D) had entered into the contract with a good faith expectation that it would be supplying the needs of one utility, not a region's entire demand for power production. Orange and Rockland (P) effectively made others silent partners in the contract and unilaterally changed conditions to take advantage of the market. These actions constitute bad faith. Affirmed.

▶ ANALYSIS

A buyer in a requirements contract setting does not have to keep requirements consistent and level to have still acted in good faith. Demands can change dramatically, but only where change is the nature of the industry, or an expectation reasonably foreseen at the time of contracting, will it be deemed legitimate. If the buyer changes his position unilaterally so as to profit from the requirements contract at the seller's expense, effectuating an arbitrage on the contract price, he has acted in bad faith.

Quicknotes

ARBITRAGE Contemporaneous purchase and sale of securities in two different markets for the purpose of profiting from their price differences.

BAD FAITH Conduct that is intentionally misleading or deceptive.

Continued on next page.

REQUIREMENTS CONTRACT An agreement pursuant to which one party agrees to purchase all his required goods or services from the other party exclusively for a specified time period.

■━■

Citizens for Preservation of Waterman Lake v. Davis

Non-profit organization (P) v. Contractor (D)

R.I. Sup. Ct., 420 A.2d 53 (1980).

NATURE OF CASE: Appeal of judgment denying injunctive and declarative relief for alleged breach of contract.

FACT SUMMARY: Davis (D) contracted with a town (P) to operate certain property as a commercial dump; however, he operated the dump in a manner contrary to representations he had made to the Department of Natural Resources and others.

RULE OF LAW
While existing law is an implied term of every contract, it acts only to clarify ambiguous contracts and cannot give rise to a cause of action where the law itself grants none.

FACTS: Davis (D) and the Town of Glocester (P) entered into a contract whereby Davis (D) would use certain property as a commercial dump. Davis (D), contrary to representations he made to the Department of Health and the Department of Natural Resources, deposited waste in wetlands on his property. A non-profit group, Citizens for Preservation of Waterman Lake (Citizens) (P), filed suit. Citizens (P) and the Town (P), as an intervenor, alleged that the operation of the dump violated local refuse ordinances and the Fresh Water Wetlands Act by dumping trash in a wetlands without a permit. Enforcement of the Fresh Water Wetlands Act was vested in the Department of Natural Resources director. Citizens (P) sought injunctive relief and money damages, but the trial court rejected their arguments, finding that neither Citizens (P) nor the Town (P) had standing to enforce the Wetlands Act. Citizens (P) then appealed.

ISSUE: May existing law be enforced as an element of a contract where the law itself does not give rise to a cause of action for the party in question?

HOLDING AND DECISION: (Bevilacqua, C.J.) No. While existing law is an implied term of every contract, it acts only to clarify ambiguous contracts and cannot give rise to a cause of action where the law itself grants none. Existing law is an implied term of every contract. But existing law is a term only for the purpose of divining unclear intent in the contracting parties, or as an express term if it creates a specific obligation between the parties. Here, Citizens (P) is attempting to enforce the Wetlands Act as a term of the contract where they have no cause of action under the Act itself. If injunctive relief is not available to them under the Act, the contract does not create the remedy. Likewise, a contract does not allow for equitable enforcement of local ordinances. The refuse ordinances

that Davis (D) may have violated contain penal sanctions. The implication of existing law into a contract does not provide a civil cause of action where common law or a statute, do not so provide. Affirmed.

ANALYSIS

The terms of a contract must comply with the law. However, if a party violates the law in the course of performance, the violation of the law does not automatically place that party in breach. The contract can remain intact even when penal sanctions result from the unlawful performance.

Quicknotes

DECLARATORY RELIEF A judgment of the court establishing the rights of the parties.

INJUNCTIVE RELIEF A court order issued as a remedy, requiring a person to do, or prohibiting that person from doing, a specific act.

INTERVENOR A party, not an initial party to the action, who is admitted to the action in order to assert an interest in the subject matter of a lawsuit.

STANDING Whether a party possesses the right to commence suit against another party by having a personal stake in the resolution of the controversy.

Jungmann & Co., Inc. v. Atterbury Brothers, Inc.

[Parties not identified.]

N.Y. Ct. App., 249 N.Y. 119, 163 N.E. 123 (1928).

NATURE OF CASE: Suit for breach of contract.

FACT SUMMARY: Two companies entered an agreement for the shipment of thirty tons of casein, and the shipper failed to notify the recipient about the shipments in conformity with the shipping agreement.

🏛 RULE OF LAW
A party to a contract may not recover damages if the party has not performed all its conditions precedent under the contract.

FACTS: Under a written contract, Plaintiff agreed to sell and ship thirty tons of casein to Defendant. During contract negotiations, Defendant insisted on a clause requiring Plaintiff to notify Defendant "of shipment . . . by cable immediately goods are dispatched" [*sic*]. Plaintiff shipped fifteen tons of casein on June 9th but failed to notify Defendant at all, and Defendant refused tender of the shipment on June 20th. Defendant eventually offered to accept that first shipment "and call the contract filled," but Plaintiff declined. Plaintiff sent Defendant a letter on June 23rd informing Defendant that the second fifteen tons would ship June 26th; Plaintiff, however, did not notify Defendant of the second shipment "by cable" immediately after the casein shipped. By letter on June 28th, Plaintiff informed Defendant that all thirty tons of the order would be delivered to Defendant when the final shipment arrived. Plaintiff did tender all thirty tons of the order, but Defendant refused the tender. Plaintiff sued for breach of contract. [Procedural history is not reported in the casebook excerpt.]

ISSUE: May a party to a contract recover damages if the party has not performed all its conditions precedent under the contract?

HOLDING AND DECISION: (Lehman, J.) No. A party to a contract may not recover damages if the party has not performed all its conditions precedent under the contract. Defendant demanded that the "advice by cable" provision be included in the contract, and Plaintiff was therefore obligated to perform that condition in order to recover under the contract. Plaintiff did not advise Defendant by cable, and it is of no consequence Plaintiff provided Defendant some form of notice when the form did not comply with the contract's requirements. Plaintiff barred from recovery.

▌ *ANALYSIS*

The court's enforcement of the strict letter of the contract in *Jungmann* amply illustrates judicial deference to the right of bargaining parties to create their own obligations by contract. *Jungmann,* strict though it is, is still good law. Most recently in 1995, the New York Court of Appeals discussed *Jungmann* with approval in a larger discussion of conditions precedent in contract law. See *Oppenheimer & Co., Inc. v. Oppenheim*[sic], *Appel, Dixon & Co., Inc.,* 660 N.E.2d 415, 419 (N.Y. Ct. App. 1995) ("substantial performance is ordinarily not applicable to excuse the non-occurrence of an express condition precedent").

━■

Quicknotes

DAMAGES Monetary compensation that may be awarded by the court to a party who has sustained injury or loss to his or her person, property or rights due to another party's unlawful act, omission or negligence.

━■

Peacock Construction Co., Inc. v. Modern Air Conditioning, Inc.

General contractor (P) v. Subcontractor (D)

Fla. Sup. Ct., 353 So. 2d 840 (1977).

NATURE OF CASE: Consolidation on appeal of action for breaches of identical contractual provisions.

FACT SUMMARY: Modern Air Conditioning, Inc. (P) had subcontracted to do work for Peacock Construction Co., Inc. (D) under a contract calling for final payment of subcontractors "within 30 days after the completion of the work . . . and full payment therefor by the Owner."

🏛 RULE OF LAW
Ambiguous provisions in subcontracts which do not expressly shift the risk of payment failure by the owner to the subcontractor will be interpreted as constituting absolute promises to pay and not as setting payment by the owner as a condition precedent to payment.

FACTS: As builder of a condominium project, Peacock Construction Co., Inc. (Peacock) (D) subcontracted the heating and air conditioning work to Modern Air Conditioning, Inc. (Modern Air) (P) and the "rooftop swimming pool" work to Overty (P). Both subcontractors signed agreements providing that they would receive final payment "within 30 days after the completion of the work included in this subcontract, written acceptance by the Architect and full payment therefor by the Owner." When the work was completed, both subcontractors requested final payment, which Peacock (D) withheld because it had not received full payment from the owner. Although Peacock (D) urged payment by the owner was a condition precedent to its duty to pay the subcontractors, the trial court disagreed and granted summary judgments to the subcontractors when they sued for damages for breach of contract. The decisions were affirmed on appeal.

ISSUE: Will a subcontract be interpreted as making the owner's payment a condition precedent to payment of the subcontractors only if such is unambiguously provided for in the contract?

HOLDING AND DECISION: (Boyd, C.J.) Yes. This case will be decided under the rule adopted in the majority of jurisdictions, that a subcontract will not be interpreted as making the owner's payment a condition precedent to payment of the subcontractors unless such is unambiguously provided for in the contract. In the typical subcontracting situation, it is not intended that the subcontractor will assume the risk of the owner's failure to pay the general contractor. That is the reason for this majority rule. Of course, the parties can, by express and unambiguous contractual language, shift the risk of payment failure by the owner to the subcontractor. In this case, there was no such express provision. Thus, payment by the owner is not a condition precedent to paying the subcontractors. Affirmed, overruling *Edward J. Gerrits, Inc. v. Astor Electric Service, Inc.*, 328 So. 2d 522 (1976).

▶ ANALYSIS

Restatement, Second, § 224 defines a "condition" as "an event, not certain to occur, which must occur, unless its nonoccurrence is excused, before performance under a contract becomes due." Conditions can be express, implied in fact (inferred from the contract's express provisions), or "constructive" (created by operation of law).

Quicknotes

CONDITION PRECEDENT The happening of an uncertain occurrence, which is necessary before a particular right or interest may be obtained or an action performed.

CONSTRUCTIVE CONDITION A condition that is not expressly stated in or implied by the terms of an agreement, but is imposed by law.

EXPRESS CONDITION A condition that is expressly stated in the terms of a written instrument.

IMPLIED CONDITION A condition that is not expressly stated in the terms of an agreement, but which is inferred from the parties' conduct or the type of dealings involved.

Burger King Corp. v. Family Dining, Inc.

Licensor (P) v. Licensee (D)

426 F. Supp. 485 (E.D. Pa.), *aff'd mem.* 566 F.2d 1168 (3d Cir. 1977).

NATURE OF CASE: Motion to dismiss action seeking declaratory judgment voiding a contract.

FACT SUMMARY: Burger King Corp. (P), after years of not requiring strict compliance with a contractual term, sought to void the contract for violation thereof.

🏛 RULE OF LAW
A party to a contract may, by its actions, excuse the other from compliance with a contractual condition.

FACTS: Burger King Corp. (P) granted Family Dining, Inc. (D) an exclusive territorial license to operate Burger King Restaurants. The contract called for Family Dining (D) to open one additional restaurant every year for 10 years and then to operate at least 10 for the remainder of the duration of the contract. Family Dining (D) did not always strictly comply with this term, although Burger King Corp. (P) did not make an issue of this. Toward the tenth year of the contract, Family Dining (D) was operating only eight restaurants, although it was getting ready to open two others. Burger King Corp. (P) brought an action seeking to terminate the contract for failure to comply with the term mandating the number of restaurants. After trial, Family Dining (D) moved to dismiss.

ISSUE: May a party to a contract, by its actions, excuse the other from compliance with a contractual condition?

HOLDING AND DECISION: (Hannum, J.) Yes. A party to a contract may, by its actions, excuse the other from compliance with a contractual condition. As a general rule, a condition may be excused without other reason if its requirement will involve extreme forfeiture or penalty, and its existence or occurrence forms no essential part of the exchange for the promisor's performance. When a party indicates, by its actions, that it does not consider strict compliance with a condition important, it demonstrates that the condition does not form an essential part of the contract. Here, Burger King (P) for several years did not demand strict compliance, indicating that strict compliance was not essential. Since Family Dining (D) has invested substantial time and capital into the contract, to void the contract would constitute extreme penalty. This being so, the elements for excusing compliance with the term at issue are present. Motion granted.

▌ *ANALYSIS*

This was an action for declaratory relief. Strictly speaking, declaratory relief actions are not equitable in nature. Nevertheless, the court, in deciding upon whether to grant relief, can seek reference to equitable principles. This is essentially what the court did here.

■≡■

Quicknotes

CONDITION Requirement; potential future occurrence upon which the existence of a legal obligation is dependent.

DECLARATORY JUDGMENT An adjudication by the courts which grants not relief but is binding over the legal status of the parties involved in the dispute.

■≡■

Fry v. George Elkins Co.

Offeror (P) v. Real estate broker (D)

Cal. Dist. Ct. App., 162 Cal. App. 2d 256, 327 P.2d 905 (1958).

NATURE OF CASE: Appeal of damage award in suit to recover a deposit in a real estate contract.

FACT SUMMARY: Fry (P) made an offer to purchase a home, with certain loan conditions on his purchase, but he made little effort to effectuate the conditions of the sale.

RULE OF LAW
The failure to make a good faith effort to carry out an obligation essential to the consummation of a deal constitutes breach of contract.

FACTS: Fry (P) made an offer, through George Elkins Co. (D), to purchase the Miller home for $42,500. Fry (P) placed $4,540 down as a deposit. His offer contained certain conditions. One condition was that Fry (P) would purchase only if he could obtain a $20,000 loan at 5 percent for twenty years. The owners accepted the offer and agreed to pay the broker a 5 percent commission, or one-half of the deposit if Fry (P) forfeited. Western Mortgage Co. handled a loan on the owner's property, which it was willing to refinance. Fry (P) made no effort to discuss refinancing the loan on the house to meet with his requirements. Several efforts were made to contact Fry (P) about securing a loan. A George Elkins Co. (D) representative called Fry (P) to tell him that Western Mortgage Co. was prepared to lend to him on the terms he specified in his offer. Fry (P) failed to submit a loan application to Western Mortgage. Fry (P) had, however, applied for the loan at two banks, but was denied. Fry (P) then wrote the Millers, attempting to rescind his offer because the conditions had not been met. The Millers incurred costs of $937.50 and $250 selling the home to another buyer. The Millers also paid George Elkins Co. (D) the $2,125 commission fee for the failed sale. Fry (P) sued for return of his deposit, but the court awarded him only $937.50, having deducted $3,312.50 in expenses and broker fees from his deposit. Fry (P) appealed the award.

ISSUE: Does the failure to make a good faith effort to carry out an obligation essential to the consummation of a deal constitute a breach of contract?

HOLDING AND DECISION: (Fox, J.) Yes. The failure to make a good faith effort to carry out an obligation essential to the consummation of a deal constitutes breach of contract. Implicit in every term of a contract is the obligation to act in good faith. Nowhere is this more important than where a party to the contract can influence the occurrence of a condition precedent to performance. If this were not so, then a contractual duty could be avoided simply by preventing a condition from occurring. In this case, Fry (P) conditioned his own performance on the success of his efforts to secure a particularized loan. While he did apply to two banks, he ignored repeated contacts from George Elkins Co. (D) and the mortgage company about borrowing through Western Mortgage Co. At one point he was told that the loan was ready and waiting if he would only fill out the paperwork. Fry's (P) own recalcitrance prevented the condition from coming to pass; his failure to act in good faith was a breach of contract. Therefore, the expenses and broker's fees were properly deducted from the deposit. Affirmed.

ANALYSIS

If a party is in control of a condition to performance, the general approach is to analyze behavior with an objective standard of review. Here, it was objectively unreasonable for Fry (P) to refuse an offered loan when he had conditioned the agreement on securing such a loan. Furthermore, there was evidence that he had changed his plans and was no longer interested in buying the property, thereby calling his motives for failing to refinance into question, pursuant to a subjective standard of inquiry.

Quicknotes

CONDITION PRECEDENT The happening of an uncertain occurrence, which is necessary before a particular right or interest may be obtained or an action performed.

GOOD FAITH An honest intention to abstain from any unconscientious advantage of another.

Pannone v. Grandmaison

Buyer (P) v. Seller (D)

Conn. Super. Ct., 1990 WL 265273 (1990).

NATURE OF CASE: Suit seeking the return of a deposit on a real estate sales contract.

FACT SUMMARY: Pannone (P), highly fearful of radiation, conditioned the purchase of a home on the results of a radon gas inspection, the results of which, though easily within safe limits, caused Pannone (P) to cancel the contract.

> ## RULE OF LAW
> If an agreed-upon contractual condition leaves one party the discretion to approve whether the condition has been met that party must act in accordance with a standard of subjective good faith.

FACTS: Pannone (P) placed an $18,000 deposit down on the purchase of the home. Pannone (P) conditioned his offer on his approval of the result of a radon gas inspection. He hired an inspector. The inspector found some radon gas, but at levels well below the level that would concern the Environmental Protection Agency. Lower readings were not likely to be found in the entire state. However, Pannone (P) was highly worried about exposure to radiation. He had served in the Air Force, monitoring radiation levels resulting from Soviet atomic testing. Pannone's (P) concern was long-standing and well documented, but he had no health problems from any radiation exposure. After much argumentation, Pannone (P) sent a notice of cancellation. He then filed suit to recover his deposit.

ISSUE: Where a contract condition depends upon the approval of a party, must the discretion exercised in refusing to approve the condition meet an objective good faith standard?

HOLDING AND DECISION: (McWeeny, J.) No. If an agreed-upon contractual condition leaves one party the discretion to approve whether the condition has been me, that party must act in accordance with a standard of subjective good faith. Every contract imposes on each party a duty of good faith and fair dealing in its performance and its enforcement. Where a condition to performance lies in the hands of one party to the contract that party must seek to meet the condition in good faith. Normally, the sufficiency of effort is judged by an objective standard, but where personal satisfaction is a condition, the standard becomes more subjective. In the instant case, Pannone (P) could not justify his irrational fear of minute levels of radon gas by any objective standard. But the parties to the agreement had stipulated that inspections were subject to Pannone's (P) approval. In this instance, Pannone (P) had only to exercise his approval in good faith, given his

unusual proclivities. There was a long history of Pannone (P) fearing anything radioactive. His exacting standards were not unique to this transaction. His refusal to approve the inspection, given his negotiated right to approve on his terms, cannot be said to lack good faith. The court finds for Pannone (P), and he is awarded the return of his deposit.

► ANALYSIS

When a subjective taste controls the condition to performance, the court will look beyond the surface of the actions to consider the motivation. It is the intent of the party controlling the condition that is at issue. Thus, an action unreasonable on its face, which prevents a condition, can still be made in good faith if there is a valid subjective motivation.

Quicknotes

GOOD FAITH An honest intention to abstain from any unconscientious advantage of another.

OBJECTIVE STANDARD A standard that is not personal to an individual but is dependent on some external source.

SUBJECTIVE STANDARD A standard that is based on the personal belief of an individual.

Godburn v. Meserve

Life tenant (P) v. Executor (D)

Conn. Sup. Ct., 130 Conn. 723, 37 A.2d 235 (1944).

NATURE OF CASE: Appeal of plaintiff's verdict in suit to recover awarded damages for breach of contract.

FACT SUMMARY: The Godburns (P) agreed to live as tenants in the home of Wells for the remainder of her life, providing food and basic care in exchange for a promise by Wells to leave the Godburns (P) the home in her will.

🏛️ **RULE OF LAW**
In order to constitute prevention of performance, the conduct on the part of the party who is alleged to have prevented performance must be wrongful, and, accordingly, in excess of his legal rights.

FACTS: The Godburns (P) agreed to live as tenants in the home of Carrie Wells, seventy-six years of age. They further agreed to provide food and basic care for Wells for the remainder of her life. In exchange for the care and maintenance, Wells promised to leave the Godburns (P) her property by will at her death. Wells adjusted her will to reflect the agreement. The agreement also stipulated that the Godburn family was limited to the Godburns (P) and their daughter. For two years the parties lived together agreeably. But thereafter increasing friction developed. Wells objected to the Godburns' (P) grandchildren staying as guests. There was also evidence that Wells complained incessantly about the food she was served. The Godburns (P) finally moved out. One year later, Wells died after revoking her will. The Godburns (P) sued the executors (D) of the Wells estate to recover damages for breach of contract and value for services rendered. At trial, the jury awarded damages to the Godburns (P). The judge denied a motion to set aside the verdict, and the executors (D) appealed.

ISSUE: Will merely disagreeable conduct by one party to an ongoing bilateral contract be sufficient to excuse the other party's performance?

HOLDING AND DECISION: (Brown, J.) No. In order to amount to prevention of performance, the conduct on the part of the party who is alleged to have prevented performance must be wrongful, and, accordingly, in excess of his legal rights. Where a party stipulates that another shall do a certain thing, he thereby impliedly promises that he will himself do nothing that will hinder or obstruct that other in doing that thing. But if one party acts in a manner that makes performance by the other merely unpleasant, then there is no discharge of the obligation. Here, Wells was evidently very difficult to get along with, becoming more caustic over time. But the Godburns

(P) agreed to the arrangement and knew her for some time before agreeing to it. They knew she was quite old, and they faced the risks attendant with caring for someone so aged. The only question is whether Wells behaved in a manner that was wrongful with respect to her obligation under the contract. Since she made no promise to be agreeable and did not force the Godburns (P) to leave, it must be concluded that she did not violate her obligations under the contract. The judgment is set aside and a new trial is ordered.

▶ **ANALYSIS**

Performance under a contract does not have to be pleasant. Performance must be rendered unreasonable or impossible by the other party before the obligation is discharged. The question that has not been answered is whether there exists behavior that is technically within legal rights, but so outrageous as to make performance unbearable for any reasonable person.

■═■

Quicknotes

LIFE TENANT An individual whose estate in real property is measured either by his own life or by that of another.

■═■

The Security Principle

Quick Reference Rules of Law

Kingston v. Preston

Buyer (P) v. Seller (D)

K.B., 99 Eng. Rep. 606 (1773).

NATURE OF CASE: Action to recover damages for breach of contract.

FACT SUMMARY: Preston (D) agreed to sell his business to Kingston (P), and Kingston (P) agreed to, but did not, give security for the payments.

🏛 RULE OF LAW
Breach of a covenant by one party to a contract relieves the other party's obligation to perform another covenant which is dependent thereon, the performance of the first covenant being an implied condition precedent to the duty to perform the second covenant.

FACTS: Preston (D) agreed (among other things) to sell his business to Kingston (P). Kingston (P) agreed (among other things) to give sufficient security for his payments. Kingston's (P) personal worth was negligible. Kingston (P) failed to provide sufficient security, and thereafter Preston (D) refused to sell.

ISSUE: When one party agrees to sell and a second party agrees to give sufficient security for his payments, are those covenants mutual and independent so that it is no excuse for nonperformance by the first party for him to allege breach of covenant by the second party?

HOLDING AND DECISION: (Lord Mansfield, J.) No. When one party covenants to sell and a second party covenants in return to give sufficient security for his payments, those covenants are dependent. Therefore, Kingston (P) must show that he has provided or is ready and willing to provide sufficient security as a condition precedent to Preston's (D) duty to sell. The dependence or independence of covenants is to be determined from the intention of the parties which in turn will normally be determined by the "order of time in which the intent of the transaction requires their performance." Here, the security was to be given "at and before the sealing and delivery of the deeds" conveying the business. Thus, according to the "temporal sequence" test, Preston's (D) duty to convey his business was dependent on Kingston's (P) giving of sufficient security. Furthermore, "it would be the greatest injustice if the plaintiff [Kingston (P)] should prevail." The giving of sufficient security was the essence of this agreement and "therefore, must necessarily be a condition precedent."

▶ ANALYSIS

Although Lord Mansfield in this famous decision focused on the time sequence of the contract provisions (e.g., a provision to be performed after another provision is

dependent on that other provision), he was very likely reacting primarily to the personal poverty of Kingston (P) and the "injustice" that would be done by making Preston (D) go through with his performance and then sue poor Kingston (P) for damages. (Kingston (P), presumably, might run the business into the ground very quickly, leaving Preston's (D) court victory a purely theoretical one.) Note that Lord Mansfield, in determining the time sequence (which he felt was so important) apparently looked not only to the contract itself but also to what he thought must have been the reasonable intentions of the parties.

Quicknotes

CONDITION PRECEDENT The happening of an uncertain occurrence, which is necessary before a particular right or interest may be obtained or an action performed.

COVENANT A written promise to do, or to refrain from doing, a particular activity.

IMPLIED CONDITION A condition that is not expressly stated in the terms of an agreement, but which is inferred from the parties' conduct or the type of dealings involved.

Hochster v. De La Tour

Employee (P) v. Employer (D)

Q.B., 2 E. & B. 678, 118 Eng. Rep. 922 (1853).

NATURE OF CASE: Action to recover damages for breach of contract.

FACT SUMMARY: Before Hochster (P) was due to perform his contract of employment for De La Tour (D), De La Tour (D) announced his intention to repudiate the contract, whereupon Hochster (P) immediately commenced an action for breach of contract.

RULE OF LAW

A party to a contract who renounces his intention to perform may not complain if the other party, instead of waiting until performance is due, elects to sue immediately for breach of contract.

FACTS: In April, Hochster (P) contracted to serve as De La Tour's (D) employee beginning on June 1. On May 11, De La Tour (D) wrote to Hochster (P) that he had changed his mind and declined Hochster's (P) services. On May 22, Hochster (P) brought this action for breach of contract.

ISSUE: When the time for performance has not arrived, but one party nevertheless indicates his intention not to perform, must the other party wait until the performance should have occurred before bringing action for breach of contract?

HOLDING AND DECISION: (Lord Campbell, C.J.) No. "The man who wrongfully renounces a contract into which he has deliberately entered cannot justly complain if he is immediately sued for compensation in damages by the man whom he has injured; and it seems reasonable to allow an option to the injured party, either to sue immediately, or to wait till the time when the act was to be done." If Hochster (P) had to wait until June 1 to sue, he would not be able to enter any employment which would interfere with his promise to begin work at that time. But it is surely more rational that after renunciation by De La Tour (D), Hochster (P) should be at liberty to consider himself absolved from any future performance. Thus, he would be free to seek other employment in mitigation of damages. De La Tour's (D) renunciation may be treated as a breach of contract. Judgment for the plaintiff.

ANALYSIS

This is the leading case on the so-called doctrine of anticipatory breach. The court's reasoning is erroneous insofar as it felt that Hochster (P) would otherwise be caught in a dilemma: to remain idle and hope for a favorable future judgment or to obtain other employment and thereby for-

feit his rights against De La Tour (D). The court overlooked the rule that where a party manifests prospective unwillingness to perform, the other party may suspend his performance and change his position without surrendering his right to sue after the breach occurs. In other words, the court could have considered the repudiation as (1) a defense to an action brought by De La Tour (D) and (2) an excuse of the constructive condition that Hochster (P) is ready, willing, and able to perform on June 1.

Quicknotes

ANTICIPATORY REPUDIATION Breach of a contract subsequent to formation but prior to the time performance is due.

CONSTRUCTIVE CONDITION A condition that is not expressly stated in or implied by the terms of an agreement, but is imposed by law.

United States v. Seacoast Gas Co.

Federal government (P) v. Supplier (D)

204 F.2d 709 (5th Cir. 1953).

NATURE OF CASE: Action for damages for anticipatory breach of a contract for the sale of goods.

FACT SUMMARY: The Govenment (P) sued when Seacoast Gas Co. (Seacoast) (D), a supplier of natural gas to a government housing project, wrote the Government (P), alleging it guilty of breach. The Government (P) did not recognize any right of Seacoast (D) to breach and notified it that if the Government (P) did not receive assurance of continued performance, it would find a new supplier and charge to Seacoast (D) the difference.

🏛 RULE OF LAW
A repudiation may be retracted up until the other party has commenced an action thereon or otherwise changed his position.

FACTS: Seacoast Gas Co. (Seacoast) (D) supplied gas to a Government (P) housing project under a contract running from April 15, 1947, to June 15, 1948. On October 7, 1947, during performance, Seacoast (D) anticipatorily breached by writing the Government (P) that it felt the Government (P) had breached so that Seacoast (D) would, as a result, terminate performance November 15, 1947. The Government (P) immediately notified Seacoast (D) that it did not recognize any right to cease performance and would advertise for bids for a new supplier to insure a continued gas supply. On November 6, 1947, having advertised for bids, the Government (P) notified Seacoast (D) that it would accept Trion's low bid within three days of the letter date unless Seacoast (D) retracted its repudiation. Not having received a retraction, the Government (P) accepted Trion's bid and began preparations to complete a contract agreement at a higher cost. Seacoast (D) claimed that its retraction, though after November 10, 1947, was received by the Government (P) before it signed its new contract with Trion so that, in fact, the Government (P) had not suffered any damage and that the breach had been cured.

ISSUE: Had the Government (P) altered its position before Seacoast (D) retracted its repudiation?

HOLDING AND DECISION: (Hutcheson, C.J.) Yes. Even though the Trion contract was signed on November 17, 1947 and Seacoast's (D) retraction was received before that date, it was still after November 10, 1947, the day the United States (P) accepted the Trion bid. As late as November 13, 1947, Seacoast (D) had reasserted its position that no retraction would be made. The Government (P) notified Seacoast (D) that it had three days to retract the *locus poenitentiae*, place for repentance, vended in three

days, not when the contract was signed. The only reason the Trion contract was not signed earlier was that Trion had not yet furnished a bond. Considering that Mr. Zell was president and practically sole owner of Seacoast (D) and of Trion, the latter which was formed for the sole purpose of bidding on the contract in question, Seacoast's (D) grounds are not very firm. Reversed and remanded.

▸ ANALYSIS

Under Uniform Commercial Code § 2-611 (1), the view of this case will be found stated, "Until the repudiating party's next performance is due he can retract his repudiation unless the aggrieved party has, since the repudiation, canceled or materially changed his position or otherwise indicated that he considers the repudiation final." The Government's (P) three-day notice was the indication of when repudiation would be deemed final. No other act is necessary than a statement by the aggrieved party that it is relying on the repudiation. This case was obviously affected on appeal by the curious fact that the same man was president and virtually sole owner of Seacoast (D) and Trion. Mr. Zell was apparently attempting to find an out on the Seacoast (D) contract and get a higher price on the Trion contract. It would appear under Restatement, First, § 319, that without bringing an action or otherwise materially altering its position, the repudiation would be able to be retracted. Note that under § 320, urging performance in spite of repudiation does not affect the aggrieved party's rights.

◼▬◼

Quicknotes

ANTICIPATORY REPUDIATION Breach of a contract subsequent to formation but prior to the time performance is due.

LOCUS POENITENTIAE The time period within which a party may withdraw from an agreement or transaction before he is bound thereby.

◼▬◼

Pittsburgh-Des Moines Steel Co. v. Brookhaven Manor Water Co.

Manufacturer (P) v. Buyer (D)

532 F.2d 572 (7th Cir. 1976).

NATURE OF CASE: Action alleging repudiation of contract.

FACT SUMMARY: Pittsburgh-Des Moines Steel Co. (PDM) (P) asserted that it was entitled to demand that the purchase price of the tank it was manufacturing for Brookhaven Manor Water Co. (Brookhaven) (D) be placed in escrow or that the president of Brookhaven (D) personally guarantee the purchase price, and suspend manufacture until such was forthcoming.

🏛 RULE OF LAW
If either party under a sales contract has reasonable grounds for insecurity with respect to the performance of the other, Uniform Commercial Code (UCC) § 2-609(1) gives him the right to demand in writing adequate assurance of due performance and, if commercially reasonable, to suspend any performance for which he has not already received the agreed return until such assurance is received.

FACTS: Pittsburgh-Des Moines Steel Co. (PDM) (P) contracted to build a one-million-gallon water tank for Brookhaven Manor Water Co. (Brookhaven) (D), with the purchase price due and payable within 30 days after the tank had been tested and accepted. Just one month later, PDM (P) wrote a letter requesting assurances that the $175,000 contract price would be held in escrow until completion of the tank and stating that the order would be held in abeyance until receipt of such assurance. No action was taken on the request. Thereafter, PDM (P) learned that Brookhaven (D) was still in the process of negotiating its purchase money loan. It thus sent a letter to the president of Brookhaven (D) demanding that he mail his personal guarantee of payment of the contract price. Such was not forthcoming. PDM (P) stopped work on the tank. Within a couple of weeks, a meeting was held. There, PDM (P) said it could complete and deliver the tank in a few weeks, to which the president of Brookhaven (D) replied that he had no need for the tank until the following year. PDM (P) sued, alleging repudiation of the contract. Brookhaven (D) recovered on its counterclaim for breach of contract, the court finding that PDM (P) had requested assurances to which it was not entitled.

ISSUE: Must a party have reasonable grounds for insecurity before he can request assurance of performance under UCC § 2-609(1)?

HOLDING AND DECISION: (Pell, J.) Yes. According to UCC § 2-609(1), if either party to a sales contract has reasonable grounds for insecurity with respect to the performance of the other, he can demand in writing adequate assurance of due performance and, if commercially reasonable, suspend any performance for which he has not already received the agreed return until such assurance is received. Here, the performance to which PDM (P) was entitled was the full payment of the purchase price within a specified time after the completion of the tank. However, the letters which PDM (P) sent conveying what it wanted done before it would pursue its obligations under the contract demanded more than that to which PDM (P) was entitled. Furthermore, the demand was not founded upon what was an actuating basis for the applicability of UCC § 2-609(1). PDM's (P) actions in demanding either the escrowing of the purchase price or a personal guarantee lacked the necessary predicate of reasonable grounds for insecurity having arisen. The contract negates the existence of any basis for insecurity at the time of contracting, when PDM (P) was willing to wait 30 days beyond completion for payment. The fact that Brookhaven (D) had not completed its loan negotiations does not constitute reasonable grounds for insecurity when the money in question was not to be needed for some months. Thus, PDM's (P) action in stopping performance and in making its demands constituted a repudiation of the contract. That means that Brookhaven's (D) request to put off the contract for one year came after the contract had already been repudiated and was indicative of nothing more than that Brookhaven (D) was willing to undertake a new arrangement with PDM (P) a year hence. Therefore, Brookhaven (D) was entitled to suspend its own performance, by virtue of PDM's (P) anticipatory repudiation, and bring suit to recover damages. Affirmed.

CONCURRENCE: (Cummings, J.) Reasonable men could certainly conclude that PDM (P) had legitimate grounds to question Brookhaven's (D) ability to pay for the water tank. When the loan the parties had understood was to pay for the tank failed to materialize, a prudent businessman would have "reasonable grounds for insecurity." UCC § 2-609(1) was, I believe, designed to cover instances where an underlying condition of the contract, even if not expressly incorporated into the written document, fails to occur. Whether, in a specific case, the breach of the condition gives rise to "reasonable grounds for insecurity" is a question of fact for the jury. It is to be recognized, however, that UCC § 2-609(1) does not give the alarmed party a right to redraft the contract. Here, the district court could properly conclude that PDM (P) had demanded assurances that would work significant changes

Continued on next page.

in the contract so that its requests demanded more than a commercially "adequate assurance of due performance."

▶ *ANALYSIS*

If a party is entitled to the assurance requested, UCC § 2-609(4) provides a time frame for receipt of the requested assurance. It provides that "failure to provide within a reasonable time not exceeding 30 days such assurance of due performance as is adequate under the circumstances of the particular case is a repudiation of the contract."

Quicknotes

ANTICIPATORY REPUDIATION Breach of a contract subsequent to formation but prior to the time performance is due.

ESCROW A written contract held by a third party until the conditions therein are satisfied, at which time it is delivered to the obligee.

PURCHASE MONEY MORTGAGE A mortgage or other security in property taken in order to ensure the performance of a duty undertaken pursuant to the purchase of such property.

Cosden Oil & Chemical Co. v. Karl O. Helm Aktiengesellschaft

Manufacturer (P) v. Buyer (D)

736 F.2d 1064 (5th Cir. 1984).

NATURE OF CASE: Appeal of verdict awarding damages to a buyer in breach of contract action.

FACT SUMMARY: A contract for the sale of polystyrene was entered into by Cosden Oil & Chemical Co. (Cosden) (P) and Karl O. Helm Aktiengesellschaft (D) during a time when oil prices were driving the price of polystyrene steadily higher, but a series of other unexpected problems left Cosden (P) unable to meet the requirements of the contract.

🏛 RULE OF LAW
If a buyer learns of a seller's anticipatory repudiation before the time of performance and elects not to cover, damages may be fixed at the difference between the contract price and the market price at any commercially reasonable time after the buyer learns of the repudiation.

FACTS: Karl O. Helm Aktiengesellschaft (Helm) (D), anticipating a tight market for polystyrene due to threatened oil supply, decided to buy a large amount of polystyrene. Helm (D) began negotiating with Cosden Oil & Chemical Co. (Cosden) (P), a polystyrene manufacturer. It was agreed that 1,250 metric tons of high-impact and 250 metric tons of general polystyrene would be purchased. Options for 1000 metric tons of high-impact and 500 metric tons of general polystyrene were included in the agreement. The order called for delivery in January and February, and the optional amounts, if declared by January 31, were to be delivered in February and March. The agreement divided the polystyrene into four separate orders. On January 22, Helm (D) called for the first shipment. On January 23, Helm (D) exercised its option for extra quantity. Cosden (P) had several unrelated problems interfering with production ability at roughly the same time. On February 6, Cosden (P) canceled three of the four orders. Cosden (P) attempted to deliver as much of the first order as possible, but could not meet the entire order. What was delivered was worth $355,950. Cosden (P) canceled the balance of the first order around the end of March. Cosden (P) then filed suit, seeking damages for Helm's (D) failure to pay for delivered polystyrene. Helm (D) counterclaimed for Cosden's (P) failure to deliver as promised. In calculating damages, the jury fixed the price per pound at three different times: when Helm (D) learned of the breach, at a commercially reasonable time thereafter, and at the time for delivery. The district court selected the commercially reasonable time figure and awarded Helm (D) $628,676, against which Cosden (P) could offset the $355,950 owed. Both parties objected and the ruling was appealed.

ISSUE: If a buyer learns of a seller's anticipatory repudiation before the time of performance and does not elect to cover, are damages set at the difference between the contract price and the market price as soon as the buyer has notice of the repudiation?

HOLDING AND DECISION: (Reavley, J.) No. If a buyer learns of a seller's anticipatory repudiation before the time of performance and elects not to cover, damages may be fixed at the difference between the contract price and the market price at any commercially reasonable time after the buyer learns of the repudiation. Generally, a buyer learns of a seller's breach at or after the time for performance. In that case, market price at the time the buyer learns of the breach is the appropriate measure for damages. But in the rare case where the seller anticipatorily repudiates and the buyer does not cover, the time to set market price is not so clear. When the seller anticipatorily repudiates, the buyer may wait a commercially reasonable amount of time before acting or fixing damages. This gives the seller an opportunity to retract his repudiation. But the buyer should not be allowed to wait too long in the hope of using a rise in the market price to increase damages. Using a commercially reasonable time as the window of opportunity, the buyer can explore cover options, the seller can attempt to perform, and neither party will bear the entire burden of changing market prices. In this case, Helm (D) learned of Cosden's (P) repudiation well before the last possible date of performance. Helm (D) could have tried to cover; however, Helm (D) had the right to seek damages rather than cover. But in the face of a rising market, the longer Helm (D) waited to act, the greater the damage figure became. Allowing Helm (D) to maximize its damage remedy does not serve any equitable purpose. Determing the market price at a commercially reasonable time after Helm (D) learned of the repudiation was the appropriate decision. The district court is affirmed as to that ruling.

▸ ANALYSIS

The primary purpose of this rule is to prevent economic incentives from influencing buyers and sellers. If damages are fixed at time of repudiation, the seller sets the damages and may be induced to repudiate rather than perform. If damages are fixed at time of performance, the buyer may be induced to wait and see if the market price rises, rather than covering.

Continued on next page.

Quicknotes

ANTICIPATORY REPUDIATION Breach of a contract subsequent to formation but prior to the time performance is due.

COVER The purchase of an alternate supply of goods by a buyer, after a seller has breached a contract for sale, for which the buyer may recover the difference between the cost of the substituted goods and the price of the original goods pursuant to the contract, so long as the buyer purchases the alternate goods in good faith and without unreasonable delay.

Britton v. Turner

Recipient of services (D) v. Laborer (P)

N.H. Super. Ct. of Judicature, 6 N.H. 481 (1834).

NATURE OF CASE: Appeal of damage award on a theory of quantum meruit.

FACT SUMMARY: Turner (P) entered into a year-long labor contract, but he completed only about nine months of the contract before voluntarily abandoning it.

🏛 RULE OF LAW
Equity requires that where part of the labor of a service contract has been rendered and the party has then voluntarily abandoned the contract, recovery for the fair value of the labor completed may be had in quantum meruit, so long as it is less than the contracted compensation.

FACTS: Turner (P) entered into a year-long contract to perform labor for Britton (D) for a total of $120. Turner (P) performed for a period of nine and one-half months, and then he abandoned his efforts voluntarily. Britton (D) refused to offer any compensation for the work completed, the whole of the contract not being completed. Turner (P) sued to recover the fair value of the labor completed. A jury awarded Turner (P) $95 and Britton (D) appealed.

ISSUE: If someone contracts to perform labor for a given period at a set price and then voluntarily fails to complete the labor started, can compensation for the labor completed be recovered on a theory of quantum meruit?

HOLDING AND DECISION: (Parker, J.) Yes. While the old rule was that partial labor on a service contract was insufficient to allow any recovery for work completed, equity requires that where part of the labor has been rendered and the party has voluntarily abandoned, recovery for the fair value of the labor completed may be had in quantum meruit, so long as it is less than the contracted compensation. The rules surrounding service contracts have operated in an unequal and unjust fashion. A party that contracts to perform labor but breaches in the first instance with no attempt to perform will only have to pay damages sustained as a result of nonperformance, which are often trivial. But a party who completes nearly all of the contract and then abandons receives nothing under the contract for work completed. The reasoning has been that performance of the whole labor was a condition precedent to payment. But such a result cannot be tolerated since it promotes breach at the first instance over an attempt to perform. In this case, equity requires that Turner (P) receive compensation for the value of labor performed on a theory of quantum meruit, so long as it

is not valued greater than what he would have received had he fully performed. The jury appears to have prorated his labor over the year. Affirmed.

▶ ANALYSIS

This case raises the fundamental issue of whether a party to a contract should be entitled to recover anything when that party has willfully breached. The most common answer to this dilemma is that economic incentives should not exist which would promote breaching without any effort to perform, as this court casually observed more than 150 years ago.

Quicknotes

ABANDONMENT The surrender of rights in a trademark with the intent to abandon the mark and to permanently relinquish its use; course of conduct of a trademark owner that causes the mark to become generic in association with goods or services or to diminish in its significance.

CONDITION PRECEDENT The happening of an uncertain occurrence, which is necessary before a particular right or interest may be obtained or an action performed.

EQUITY Fairness; justice; the determination of a matter consistent with principles of fairness and not in strict compliance with rules of law.

QUANTUM MERUIT Equitable doctrine allowing recovery for labor and materials provided by one party, even though no contract was entered into, in order to avoid unjust enrichment by the benefited party.

Jacob & Youngs v. Kent

Contractor (P) v. Homeowner (D)

N.Y. Ct. App., 230 N.Y. 239, 129 N.E. 889 (1921).

NATURE OF CASE: Action for damages for breach of a construction contract.

FACT SUMMARY: Jacob (P) was hired to build a $77,000 country home for Kent (D). When the dwelling was completed, it was discovered that through an oversight, pipe not of Reading manufacture (though of comparable quality and price), which had been specified in the contract, was used. Kent (D) refused to make final payment of $3,483.46 upon learning of this.

🏛 **RULE OF LAW**
An omission, both trivial and innocent, will sometimes be atoned for by allowance of the resulting damage and will not always be the breach of a condition to be followed by forfeiture. For damages in construction contracts, the owner is entitled merely to the difference between the value of the structure if built to specifications and the value it has as constructed.

FACTS: Jacob (P) built a country home for $77,000 for Kent (D) and sued for $3,483.46, which remained unpaid. Almost a year after completion, Kent (D) discovered that not all pipe in the home was of Reading manufacture, as specified in the contract. Kent (D) ordered the plumbing replaced, but as it was encased in the walls, except in those spots where it must necessarily remain exposed, Jacob (P) refused to replace the pipe, stating that the pipe used was of comparable price and quality. It appeared that the omission was neither fraudulent nor willful and was due to oversight. Kent (D) refused to pay the balance of the construction cost still due.

ISSUE: Was the omission by Jacob (P) so trivial and innocent so as not to be a breach of the condition?

HOLDING AND DECISION: (Cardozo, J.) Yes. Where the significance of the default or omission is grievously out of proportion to the oppression of the forfeiture, the breach is considered to be trivial and innocent. A change will not be tolerated if it is so dominant and pervasive so as to frustrate the purpose of the contract. The contractor cannot install anything he believes to be just as good. It is a matter of degree judged by the purpose to be served, the desire to be gratified, the excuse for deviation from the letter, and the cruelty of enforced adherence. Under the circumstances, the measure of damages should not be the cost of replacing the pipe, which would be great. Instead, the difference in value between the dwelling as specified and the dwelling as constructed should be the measure, even though it may be nominal or nothing.

Usually, the owner is entitled to the cost of completion but not where it is grossly unfair and out of proportion to the good to be obtained. This simply is a rule to promote justice when there is substantial performance with trivial deviation. Affirmed.

DISSENT: (McLaughlin, J.) Jacob (P) failed to perform as specified. It makes no difference why Kent (D) wanted a particular kind of pipe. Failure to use the kind of pipe specified was either intentional or due to gross neglect, which amounted to the same thing.

▶ **ANALYSIS**

Substantial performance cannot occur where the breach is intentional as it is the antithesis of material breach. The part unperformed must not destroy the purpose or value of the contract. Because here there is a dissatisfied-landowner who stands to retain the defective structure built on his land, there arises the problem of unjust enrichment. Usually, it would appear that the owner would pocket the damages he collected rather than remedying the defect by tearing out the wrong pipe and replacing it with the specified pipe. The owner would have a home substantially in compliance and a sum of money greatly in excess of the harm suffered by him. Note that under the doctrine of *de minimis not curat lex*, that is, that the law is not concerned with trifles, trivial defects, even if willful, will be ignored. The party which claims substantial performance has still breached the contract and is liable for damages but in a lesser amount than for a willful breach.

■=■

Quicknotes

FORFEITURE The loss of a right or interest as a penalty for failing to fulfill an obligation.

SUBSTANTIAL PERFORMANCE Performance of all the essential obligations pursuant to an agreement.

■=■

Plante v. Jacobs

Contractor (P) v. Homeowner (D)

Wis. Sup. Ct., 10 Wis. 2d 567, 103 N.W.2d 296 (1960).

NATURE OF CASE: Action to establish a lien upon property for breach of a construction.

FACT SUMMARY: When the Jacobses (D) believed that Plante (P), whom they contracted to build a home upon their lot for $26,765, used faulty workmanship and incomplete construction, they stopped further payments to him after having paid $20,000. Plante (P) then refused to complete and sued to establish a lien on the property.

RULE OF LAW

There can be no recovery on a contract as distinguished from quantum meruit unless there is substantial performance which is defined as where the performance meets the essential purpose of the contract.

FACTS: Plante (P) contracted with Frank and Carol Jacobs (D) to furnish materials and construct a house upon their lot in accordance with plans and specifications for $26,765. Plante (P) received $20,000 during the course of construction when a dispute arose between the parties as to faulty workmanship and incomplete construction. The Jacobses (D) refused to continue payments, and Plante (P) refused to complete construction. Plante (P) then sued to establish a lien on the property so as to recover the unpaid balance plus extras. The Jacobses (D) alleged that faulty workmanship on at least 20 items plus decreasing the width of the living room by one foot did not amount to substantial performance.

ISSUE: Can there be recovery on a contract without there having been substantial performance?

HOLDING AND DECISION: (Hallows, J.) No. There can be no recovery at common law on a contract as distinguished from quantum meruit unless there is substantial performance which is determined by whether the performance meets the essential purpose of the contract. When applied to house construction, this does not mean that every detail must be in strict compliance with specifications and plans. Here, the specifications were standard printed forms, and the plan was a "stock floor plan." While the Jacobses (D) received a house with which they were dissatisfied, the contract was substantially performed. The misplacing of a wall by one foot so as to narrow the living room did not affect the value of the home. Gutters and rainspouts, kitchen cabinets, and clothes closet poles were omitted. As the measure of damages for substantial, but incomplete, performance, Plante (P) should receive the contract price less the damages caused the Jacobses (D)

by incomplete performance. For faulty construction, the "diminished value" rule pertains which is the difference between the value of the house as it would stand complete and as it stands faulty but substantially complete. The trial court applied the "cost of repair" rule which allows the cost to repair a number of small defects and omissions. If the separation of defects would lead to confusion, the diminished value rule can be applied to all defects. There was no confusion here in separating the defects. Whether a defect comes under the diminished value or cost of repair rule depends upon the magnitude of defect. However, the trial court was not in error in applying the cost of repair rule (usually applied to small items) to repairing a patio floor, plaster cracks in ceiling, and repair of a nonstructural patio wall. The misplaced wall in the living room was of a magnitude sufficient as to place it under the diminished value rule, but as misplacing the wall was of no effect to the value of the house and as it would have been economical waste to move it, no legal damage was suffered. Affirmed.

ANALYSIS

The doctrine of substantial performance is applied when the unperformed portion does not destroy the purpose or value of the contract. Of course, this is like saying that the breach must not be material. Here, when the Jacobses (D) occupied the house, they showed that it served its purpose and thereby assumed the burden to show performance was not substantial to the terms of the contract. The primary application of the doctrine of substantial performance is with building contracts where fairly large defaults have been treated as immaterial, while a small default is often sufficient to breach a sales contract due to practical considerations. The unhappy buyer can return the goods or refuse delivery. The unhappy landowner keeps the incomplete structure; hence, greater are the possibilities for unjust enrichment.

Quicknotes

LIEN A claim against the property of another in order to secure the payment of a debt.

QUANTUM MERUIT Equitable doctrine allowing recovery for labor and materials provided by one party, even though no contract was entered into, in order to avoid unjust enrichment by the benefited party.

SUBSTANTIAL PERFORMANCE Performance of all the essential obligations pursuant to an agreement.

Walker & Co. v. Harrison

Repair company (P) v. Renter (D)

Mich. Sup. Ct., 347 Mich. 630, 81 N.W.2d 352 (1957).

NATURE OF CASE: Action to recover damages for breach of contract.

FACT SUMMARY: Harrison (D) rented a neon sign and sought to repudiate the rental agreement when Walker & Co. (P) delayed in repairing the sign.

🏛 RULE OF LAW
A party attempting to repudiate a contract must convince the court that the other party has materially breached the contract.

FACTS: Walker & Co. (P) contracted to rent a neon sign to Harrison (D). The rental agreement included repair service "as deemed necessary by Walker (P) to keep sign in first class advertising condition." Shortly after the sign was installed, someone hit it with a tomato. Rust was allegedly visible on the chrome, and cobwebs had collected in the corners. Harrison (D) made several calls to Walker (P) complaining of the sign's condition, but maintenance was not forthcoming. Harrison (D) repudiated the contract, and Walker (P) sued for the rent. [Walker (P) subsequently repaired the sign.]

ISSUE: May one party to a contract repudiate that contract under circumstances which do not amount to a "material breach" by the other party?

HOLDING AND DECISION: (Smith, J.) No. It is essential to one party's repudiation of a contract that he demonstrates a "material breach" by the other party. As to the criterion for "materiality," there is no single touchstone. Here, although Walker's (P) delay in rendering service was certainly irritating, it cannot be said as a matter of law that the delay was a material breach. The trial court, on this phase of the case, held as follows: "The tomato . . . was up on the clock; that would be outside [Harrison's (D)] reach, without a stepladder or something. The cobwebs are within easy reach of Mr. Harrison, and so would the rust be. I think that [the] argument that these were not materially a breach would clearly be true as to the cobwebs, and I really can't believe in the face of all the testimony that there was a great deal of rust seven days after the installation of this sign. And that really brings it down to the tomato . . . I really can't find that that was such a material breach of the contract as to justify rescission. I really don't think so." (It is not clear whether the court defers to these findings of the trial court or whether the court draws its own independent conclusion in agreement with the trial court's judgment.) Affirmed.

▶ ANALYSIS

The primary advantage in alleging "material breach" is that the alleging party, if successful, may rescind the whole contract. If a breach is not material, the aggrieved party may recover damages flowing therefrom but may not cancel the contract. In the present case, for example, it would not be surprising to find that Harrison (D) wanted out of his contract for reasons other than the breach and alleged "materiality" as a means to that end. As the court indicates, there is no simple test for materiality (which is unfortunate since so much can hinge on the characterization). Among the factors often considered are: (1) to what extent has the contract been performed prior to the breach; (2) was the breach willful; (3) was the breach "quantitatively" serious; and (4) what will be the consequences of the determination (e.g., will it work extreme hardship on one of the parties). Some of the above factors should undoubtedly be given more weight than others, and arguably some of them overlap. Perhaps the most important factor is the last one, which openly acknowledges "materiality" as a conclusory label to be applied insofar as a sense of "justice" requires it.

Quicknotes

MATERIAL BREACH Breach of a contract's terms by one party that is so substantial as to relieve the other party from its obligations pursuant thereto.

REPUDIATION The actions or statements of a party to a contract that evidence his intent not to perform, or to continue performance, of his duties or obligations thereunder.

Plotnick v. Pennsylvania Smelting & Refining Co.

Seller (P) v. Buyer (D)

194 F.2d 859 (3d Cir. 1952).

NATURE OF CASE: Appeal of judgment awarding damages for claim and cross-claim on a breached installment contract.

FACT SUMMARY: Plotnick (P), a seller of battery lead, entered into a contract to sell installments of lead to a buyer; the seller was very late in completing the shipments and the buyer delayed payments, leading finally to an impasse.

🏛 RULE OF LAW
Where an installment contract exists and the buyer refuses to pay on one installment, it depends in each case on the terms of the contract, and the surrounding circumstances, whether the breach of contract is so material as to justify the injured party in refusing to proceed further or whether the breach is severable, giving rise to a claim for compensation, but not a right to treat the contract as broken.

FACTS: Plotnik (P) and Pennsylvania Smelting & Refining Co. (Pennsylvania Smelting) (D) had entered into a series of agreements whereby Plotnik (P) would sell battery lead to Pennsylvania Smelting (D). In the course of dealing, payments to Plotnik (P) were regularly late, but deliveries were often late as well. In the last agreement, the parties agreed that 200 tons of lead would be sold at 8.1 cents per pound, or more if quality warranted. Furthermore, 63 percent of the price would be paid shortly after each installment was shipped, and the balance within four weeks. A carload of 43,000 pounds was delivered. No part of the price was paid on that carload. Two weeks later, Pennsylvania Smelting (D) threatened to buy on the open market if the balance of the lead was not delivered. Plotnik (P) then refused to ship unless the last carload was paid for. After more discussions, Pennsylvania Smelting (D) declared the contract canceled. Plotnik (P) then sued for the price of the carload delivered but not paid for, and Pennsylvania Smelting (D) counterclaimed for damages caused by failure to deliver the remaining installments. The district court awarded recovery on both claims. Plotnik (P) appealed.

ISSUE: If a buyer refuses to pay on one shipment of an installment contract, is the seller always excused from performance on further installments?

HOLDING AND DECISION: (Hastie, J.) No. Where an installment contract exists and the buyer refuses to pay on one installment, it depends in each case on the terms of the contract, and the surrounding circumstances, whether the breach of contract is so material as to justify

the injured party in refusing to proceed further or whether the breach is severable, giving rise to a claim for compensation, but not a right to treat the contract as broken. There are two guiding considerations when evaluating whether nonpayment on an installment is a material breach warranting the withholding of future installments. First, nonpayment for a delivered shipment can make it impossible from a financial point of view to supply further installments. Second, the buyer's breach of his promise to pay for one installment may create such apprehension in the seller that the seller should not have to risk further deliveries. Applying these two factors to this case, it appears that Plotnik (P) was not justified in withholding further installments. First, Plotnik (P) had sufficient lead on hand to easily supply the entire order. There would have been no great financial burden in full performance. Second, Plotnik (P) cannot show a reasonable apprehension that payment would not be forthcoming. Over a long course of dealing, Plotnik (P) had always been paid in full. Payments at times were late, but so were deliveries. Pennsylvania Smelting (D) was concerned with getting the entire amount of lead, and withheld payment only to indicate the strong desire to see the full delivery made. Plotnik (P) was not justified in rescinding the contract. Affirmed.

▶ ANALYSIS

One factor not strongly emphasized by the court, but that most likely influenced the decision, was evidence that Plotnik (P) was selling at a much higher price to other buyers. The court suggested that Plotnik (P) wanted only to get out of a low-priced contract any way it could. Without such a prejudicial aspect to the case, Plotnik (P) might well have argued more effectively that apprehension supported rescission.

■■■

Quicknotes

INSTALLMENT CONTRACT A contract pursuant to which the parties are to render performance or payment in periodic intervals.

MATERIAL BREACH Breach of a contract's terms by one party that is so substantial as to relieve the other party from its obligations pursuant thereto.

RESCISSION The canceling of an agreement and the return of the parties to their positions prior to the formation of the contract.

■■■

McCloskey & Co. v. Minweld Steel Co.

General contractor (P) v. Subcontractor (D)

220 F.2d 101 (3d Cir. 1955).

NATURE OF CASE: Action for damages for breach of a construction contract.

FACT SUMMARY: Minweld Steel Co. (Minweld) (D), a subcontractor, had contracted to supply and erect certain steel portions for McCloskey & Co. (P), the general contractor on a state hospital project for Pennsylvania. When, because of the outbreak of the Korean War, Minweld (D) had difficulty procuring steel and requested, by letter, McCloskey's (P) aid, McCloskey (P) treated Minweld's (D) letter as an admission of breach and terminated the agreement.

> ## 🏛 RULE OF LAW
> In order to give rise to a renunciation amounting to a breach of contract, there must be an absolute and unequivocal refusal to perform or a distinct and positive statement of an inability to do so.

FACTS: McCloskey & Co. (P), a contractor on a Pennsylvania state hospital project, made three contracts with Minweld Steel Co. (Minweld) (D) for the latter to furnish and erect all structure steel for two of the hospital buildings. If Minweld (D) failed or refused to supply sufficient materials of proper quality, McCloskey (P) would have the right to terminate on two days' notice. When Minweld (D) had difficulty procuring steel due to the outbreak of the Korean War, it wrote McCloskey (P) requesting its help or the state's help in finding steel. McCloskey (P) treated this letter as notice of Minweld's (D) alleged positive intention not to perform the contracts, hence, a breach. At trial, Minweld's (D) motion for judgement on the ground McCloskey (P) had failed to state a cause of action was granted.

ISSUE: Was Minweld's (D) request for help from McCloskey (P) to find steel a failure to supply sufficient materials and, hence, a breach of contract?

HOLDING AND DECISION: (McLaughlin, J.) No. The letter conveyed no idea of contract repudiation by Minweld (D). While it was in a desperate situation, Minweld (D) realistically faced its problem and did not indicate definite abandonment or loss of all hope of finishing the project. Minweld (D) did not absolutely or unequivocally refuse to perform. Moreover, failure to take preparatory action before the time when any performance is promised is not anticipatory breach, even though such failure made it impossible for performance to take place, though the promisor at the time of failure does not intend to perform his promise. Minweld (D) was no more than

unable to give assurances as to preparatory arrangements. Affirmed.

▶ ANALYSIS

A statement such as, "I will not perform," is an anticipatory breach if it is made before performance is due. Under the doctrine of prospective unwillingness to perform, the other party may suspend his performance and change his position. As the repudiation was an anticipatory breach, the other party may sue immediately. But if the statement is basically, "I doubt that I will be able to perform," as occurred in this case, there is not repudiation. Accordingly, suit cannot be brought immediately under the doctrine of anticipatory repudiation. However, under the doctrine of prospective unwillingness to perform, the other party could suspend his performance and demand assurances and take any other steps allowable under the doctrine. This is the same for the circumstance where a party says, "I will not perform unless X occurs." It is very possible that the unforeseen circumstance, the tightening up of the steel industry resulting from the outbreak of the Korean War and subsequent presidential directive, moved the court to excuse Minweld's (D) words, which basically did have the effect of a repudiation.

Quicknotes

ANTICIPATORY REPUDIATION Breach of a contract subsequent to formation but prior to the time performance is due.

K & G Construction Co. v. Harris

General contractor (P) v. Subcontractor (D)

Md. Ct. App., 223 Md. 305, 164 A.2d 451 (1960).

NATURE OF CASE: Appeal of damage award in a breach of contract action and counterclaim for damages.

FACT SUMMARY: Harris (D), a subcontractor, damaged contractor K & G Construction Co.'s (K & G) (P) house while working, and K & G refused to pay further installments until damage to the house had been compensated.

RULE OF LAW
The failure of a party to a contract to perform in a substantial and negligence-free manner will justify the withholding of an installment payment, and so long as withholding was justified, the party will have wrongfully repudiated if work is abandoned.

FACTS: K & G Construction Co. (K & G) (P), a general contractor, hired Harris (D), a subcontractor, to do landscape grading in a housing subdivision. The contract between them required Harris (D) to carry liability insurance, which Harris (D) did. During the construction, a bulldozer operated by Harris (D) damaged K & G's (P) house. The damage was figured at $3,400. Harris (D) reported the damage to its insurance carrier. The insurance carrier and the subcontractor refused to pay for the damage, claiming there was no liability. K & G (P) withheld a monthly installment payment since the damage had not been repaired or compensated. Harris (D) worked for one month more, and then discontinued efforts on the project. Harris (D) was owed $1,484 for work done, and would have made a profit of $1,340 on the uncompleted portion of the contract had work not stopped. It cost K & G (P) $450 above the contract price to hire another excavator. K & G (P) filed suit, seeking damages for the house and the $450 extra cost incurred to finish the job. Harris (D) counterclaimed, seeking lost profits and money owed. K & G (P) was awarded $3,400 for the damage to the house, and Harris (D) was awarded $2,824 for lost profit and money owed. K & G (P) appealed.

ISSUE: If a party to a contract suffers damages through the negligent performance of the other party, may an installment payment be withheld, in partial satisfaction of the damages?

HOLDING AND DECISION: (Prescott, J.) Yes. The failure of a party to a contract to perform in a substantial and negligence-free manner will justify the withholding of an installment payment, and so long as withholding was justified, the party will have wrongfully repudiated if work is abandoned. The general rule has been that where a total price for work is fixed by contract, the work is not rendered divisible by progress payments. The entire job must be completed regardless of whether payment is by lump sum or by installment. In this case, Harris (D) promised to perform in a negligence-free manner. The return promise was for payment. When Harris (D) negligently damaged property, K & G (P) justifiably withheld an installment payment in lieu of repair or compensation for the damage. Harris (D) was not excused from performance by the withheld installment since withholding was justified. Thus, when Harris (D) refused to finish, the abandonment was a wrongful repudiation. Harris (D) cost K & G (P) $450 to finish the job. The judgment against K & G (P) is reversed. Damages are awarded to K & G (P) in the amount of $450.

ANALYSIS

This holding poses a problem for parties to contracts. It requires the parties to discern when the performance of one party has been sufficiently negligent to constitute a material breach, warranting the withholding of an installment payment. But if parties cannot agree on the terms of their own contracts, they certainly will not be able to decide when a tort has occurred.

Quicknotes

ABANDONMENT The voluntary relinquishment of a right without the intent of reclaiming it.

NEGLIGENCE Conduct falling below the standard of care that a reasonable person would demonstrate under similar conditions.

REPUDIATION The actions or statements of a party to a contract that evidence his intent not to perform, or to continue performance, of his duties or obligations thereunder.

Gill v. Johnstown Lumber Co.

Log driver (P) v. Lumber company (D)

Penn. Sup. Ct., 151 Pa. 534, 25 A. 120 (1892).

NATURE OF CASE: Appeal of directed verdict for defendant on an action in assumpsit.

FACT SUMMARY: Gill (P) agreed to drive logs down a river to Johnstown Lumber Co.'s (D) boom, but a flood carried away a considerable portion of the logs.

> 🏛 **RULE OF LAW**
> If a contract consists of several and distinct items and the price to be paid is apportioned to each item, the contract can be severed into its component parts.

FACTS: Gill (P) agreed to drive logs down a river for Johnstown Lumber Co. (Johnstown) (D). Several types of logs were to be driven. Payment was at the rate of $1 per 1,000 feet for oak, 75 cents per 1,000 feet for other logs, 3 cents for cross-ties driven to Bethel, and 5 cents for cross-ties driven to points below Bethel. A flood carried a considerable proportion of the logs past the Johnstown (D) boom, and Johnstown (D) refused to pay on the contract. Gill (P) sued, and a directed verdict was entered for Johnstown (D). Gill (P) appealed.

ISSUE: If a contract consists of several and distinct items and the price to be paid is apportioned to each item, can the contract be severed into its component parts?

HOLDING AND DECISION: (Heydrick, J.) Yes. If a contract consists of several and distinct items and the price to be paid is apportioned to each item, the contract can be severed into its component parts. However, if the consideration to be paid is single and entire, the contract is entire, even if the subject of the contract consists of distinct and independent items. In this case, it is clear that the contract apportioned payment among various items. They were distinct and separate from one another. Payment was to be made for the quantity of lumber delivered. Reversed and a *venire facias de novo* awarded.

> ▶ **ANALYSIS**

Defining contracts as severable allows for more equitable decisions. It affords courts an opportunity to dispense a fair solution in a situation where all but a few specific items of a contract have been completed before some breach or intervening event prevented complete performance. Payment for completed items can be rendered, and unjust enrichment is avoided.

Quicknotes

ASSUMPSIT An oral or written promise by one party to perform or pay another.

INSTALLMENT CONTRACT A contract pursuant to which the parties are to render performance or payment in periodic intervals.

SEVERABLE CONTRACT A divisible contract so that the performance of one of its promises is not dependent upon the other and failure to perform one promise does not result in a breach of the total contract.

UNJUST ENRICHMENT The unlawful acquisition of money or property of another for which both law and equity require restitution to be made.

VENIRE FACIAS DE NOVO The summoning of a new jury in order to retry a case in which no judgment can be entered due to some impropriety or where a verdict is defective or otherwise erroneous.

Ramirez v. Autosport

Buyer of camper (P) v. Seller (D)

N.J. Sup. Ct., 88 N.J. 277, 440 A.2d 1345 (1982).

NATURE OF CASE: Appeal from rescission of contract.

FACT SUMMARY: The Ramirezes (P) sought the rescission of their contract to purchase a camper with defects from Autosport (D), and the return of a trade-in van they had tendered pursuant to the sales agreement.

🏛 RULE OF LAW
Under a contract for the sale of goods, the seller is required to furnish a "perfect tender" of the subject matter of the contract, and the buyer may reject any nonconforming goods.

FACTS: The Ramirezes (P) entered into a contract with Autosport (D) for the purchase of a camper and the trade-in of their van. When the camper arrived, it had several defects including scratched paint, no electric and sewer hookups, and no hubcaps. The Ramirezes (P) intended to use the van for their summer vacation. On August 14, they went to Autosport (D) to pick up the van. However, the interior cushions were wet and the paint was not finished. The Ramirezes (P) refused to accept the camper. On August 15, Autosport (D) transferred title of the camper to the Ramirezes (P). They were notified the van would be ready September 1. On September 1 when the Ramirezes (P) arrived to pick up the van, they waited in vain for one and a half hours and left without the van. On October 5, the Ramirezes (P) returned to Autosport (D) with an attorney and requested the return of their trade-in van. Autosport (D) did not return their trade-in, and subsequently sold it for $4,995. The Ramirezes (P) initiated suit seeking to rescind the contract. Autosport (D) brought a counterclaim for breach of contract. The trial court awarded the Ramirezes (P) the fair market value of their trade-in van. The appellate division affirmed, and Autosport appealed.

ISSUE: May a buyer reject defective goods that do not conform to the requirements of the sales agreement?

HOLDING AND DECISION: (Pollock, J.) Yes. Under a contract for the sale of goods, the seller is required to furnish a "perfect tender" of the subject matter of the contract, and the buyer may reject the goods based on any nonconformity prior to acceptance. However, such rejection does not terminate the contract. Rather, the seller has an absolute right to cure the defect within the time specified for performance under the contract. If the buyer rejects the nonconforming goods after this time period, the seller may cure the defects within a reasonable time as determined by the circumstances. Where the buyer has accepted the nonconforming goods, revocation is only available where the defect substantially impairs their worth. If the seller does not cure the defects, then the buyer may terminate the contract. Here the record demonstrates that the Ramirezes (P) rejected the nonconforming van within a reasonable time, and Autosport (D) failed to cure the defects. Thus, the Ramirezes (P) properly exercised their right to terminate the contract. Affirmed.

▶ ANALYSIS

Traditionally, the "perfect tender rule" required a seller to tender goods that conformed exactly pursuant to the contract provisions. More recently, both the common law and statutory provisions began to recognize the buyer's right to rescind a contract for the sale of goods only where the nonconformity amounted to a material breach of the agreement. The Uniform Commercial Code (UCC) § 2-106 preserves the perfect tender rule, allowing the buyer to reject any nonconforming goods. However, the UCC mitigates the severity of the rule by providing the seller with the recourse of curing such defects.

━■□■━

Quicknotes

CURE In a commercial transaction, the seller has a right to correct a delivery of defective goods within the time originally provided for performance as specified in the contract.

PERFECT TENDER Goods tendered pursuant to a contract for sale, which conform precisely to the contract's requirements.

RESCISSION The canceling of an agreement and the return of the parties to their positions prior to the formation of the contract.

REVOCATION The cancellation or withdrawal of some authority conferred or an instrument drafted, such as the withdrawal of a revocable contract offer prior to the offeree's acceptance.

━■□■━

Baker v. Ratzlaff

Buyer (P) v. Seller (D)

Kan. Ct. App., 1 Kan. App. 2d 285, 564 P.2d 153 (1977).

NATURE OF CASE: Appeal of award of damages in breach of contract action.

FACT SUMMARY: Baker (P) agreed to purchase a crop of popcorn from Ratzlaff (D) in three installments, with payment to be made upon delivery; some corn was delivered, no payment was tendered, and rather than asking for payment, Ratzlaff (D) gave notice of termination.

RULE OF LAW
The duty of good faith extends even to termination clauses, and as a result, a seller will have acted in bad faith if he abuses his discretion in utilizing a termination provision without first attempting to secure performance from the buyer.

FACTS: Baker (P) was a buyer and distributor of popcorn. Ratzlaff (D) agreed to raise 380 acres of popcorn and Baker (P) would buy the crop in three installments. They agreed upon a price of $4.75 per hundredweight. The contract also provided that Baker (P) was to pay for the popcorn when delivered and Ratzlaff (D) was permitted in the contract to withhold remaining popcorn if payment was not made. Two truckloads of popcorn were delivered, and each time a weight voucher was given to the seller. At neither time did Ratzlaff (D) request payment. Baker (P) called to ask about further delivery schedules, and Ratzlaff (D) said he was having equipment problems. But at no time did he mention the payments due. Seven days later, Ratzlaff (D) sent notice of termination, citing the payment clause. Baker (P) immediately sent payment. It was his practice to send weight slips to his offices and disperse checks each week. Ratzlaff (D), meanwhile, entered into a contract to sell to a third party at $8.00 per hundredweight. Baker (P) had to pay $10.30 for replacement popcorn. Baker (P) filed suit for breach of contract, and he was awarded $52,000 in damages as the difference between contract price and the $8.00 selling price Ratzlaff (D) received for some 1,600,000 pounds. Baker (P) appealed the damage calculation and Ratzlaff (D) appealed the findings.

ISSUE: If an installment contract contains a termination provision for failure to pay upon delivery, has the seller acted in bad faith if the contract is terminated without requesting payment first?

HOLDING AND DECISION: (Rees, J.) Yes. The duty of good faith extends even to termination clauses, and as a result, a seller will have acted in bad faith if he abuses his discretion in utilizing a termination provision without

first attempting to secure performance from the buyer. The requirement for good faith covers performance and enforcement aspects of a contract. Ratzlaff (D) argues that termination does not fall into these two categories. But it requires tortured reasoning to find that the termination clause is not an inseparable incident of enforcement of substantive provisions of the contract. The duty of good faith required Ratzlaff (D) to demand payment in accordance with the terms of the contract, which he did not do. The facts strongly suggest that he saw an opportunity to get out of the contract and sell at a higher price. Affirmed.

ANALYSIS

Having a term included in a contract does not necessarily mean that it can be applied as literally written. Contract terms help specify the nature of the agreement, but each party is under a duty to perform in good faith and to enforce his rights in good faith. The goal is to have parties to contracts settle differences without resorting to litigation at the first sign of a disagreement.

Quicknotes

FAIR DEALING An implied warranty that the parties will deal honestly in the satisfaction of their obligations and without an intent to defraud.

GOOD FAITH An honest intention to abstain from any unconscientious advantage of another.

Brown v. AVEMCO Investment Corp.

Buyers (P) v. Creditor (D)

603 F.2d 1367 (9th Cir. 1979).

NATURE OF CASE: Appeal of a denied motion for a new trial in a diversity action alleging conversion and a successful counterclaim for interference with contractual rights.

FACT SUMMARY: An airplane used as security for a loan was going to be purchased by a group of buyers, ready and willing to pay the remainder of the loan debt, but AVEMCO Investment Corp. (D) refused to accept payment of the remaining debt and repossessed the plane.

> ### 🏛 RULE OF LAW
> The Uniform Commercial Code (UCC) requires that options to accelerate a debt be exercised with a good faith belief that the prospect of payment or performance is impaired.

FACTS: Herriford borrowed $6,500 from AVEMCO (D) and secured the debt with his airplane. The loan agreement provided in part that if Herriford sold, leased, or otherwise encumbered the plane without written consent, AVEMCO Investment Corp. (AVEMCO) (D) could accelerate the debt or seize the airplane. One year later, Herriford entered into a lease agreement with Brown and two others (P) to use the plane. After payment of the mortgage on the plane, they would have the option to purchase the plane. AVEMCO (D) was notified of the lease and accepted timely payments for one year. After a year of payments, Brown (P) notified AVEMCO (D) of their intention to purchase the plane from Herriford, and the entire remaining sum of $4,859 on Herriford's debt was offered to AVEMCO (D). AVEMCO (D) refused and declared that it would accelerate the debt. Brown (P) advised AVEMCO (D) that AVEMCO's rejection was not accepted. AVEMCO (D) then used a passkey and took the plane. AVEMCO (D) then filed a bill of sale on the plane for an amount of $7,000. Brown (P) filed an action for conversion, and a counterclaim for interference with contract rights was filed by AVEMCO (D). A jury found for AVEMCO (D) on all claims, but no damages were awarded. Brown (P) moved for a new trial and was denied. He then appealed.

ISSUE: Does the UCC impose a duty of reasonableness and fairness when a creditor invokes an acceleration clause for the claimed purpose of reacting to an impairment of property held in security for a debt?

HOLDING AND DECISION: (Ferguson, J.) Yes. The UCC requires that options to accelerate a debt be exercised with a good-faith belief that the prospect of payment or performance is impaired. Acceleration clauses are designed to protect the creditor from actions by the debtor, which jeopardize or impair the creditor's security. They are not intended to be used offensively, for commercial gain. In this case, payments were made to AVEMCO (D) in a timely manner for two years. The remainder of the mortgage was then offered in full. It is unclear how AVEMCO (D) could justify a claim that it had a good faith belief that its interest was in danger. The attempt to sell the seized plane for well more than was owed on the loan indicates further the commercial aspect to invoking the acceleration. Reversed and remanded for a new trial.

▶ ANALYSIS

A better justification exists for the result reached by the court in this case. The offer to pay off the mortgage could have been construed as meeting the condition precedent for release of the security interest. Since AVEMCO (D) refused performance, the result was that they were in breach by revocation. The security interest would have been lifted by the breach.

■═■

Quicknotes

ACCELERATION CLAUSE A contract provision that upon the happening of a specified event an interest will immediately vest.

CONVERSION The act of depriving an owner of his property without permission or justification.

DIVERSITY ACTION An action commenced by a citizen of one state against a citizen of another state or against an alien, involving an amount in controversy of $10,000 or more, over which the federal court has jurisdiction.

INTERFERENCE WITH CONTRACT RIGHTS An intentional tort whereby a defendant intentionally elicits the breach of a valid contract resulting in damages.

■═■

Burne v. Franklin Life Insurance Co.

Injured (P) v. Insurance company (D)

Penn. Sup. Ct., 451 Pa. 218, 301 A.2d 799 (1973).

NATURE OF CASE: Appeal from an order denying plaintiff's motion for summary judgment and granting defendant's motion for summary judgment on an action, in assumpsit, for the recovery of accidental death benefits.

FACT SUMMARY: After Burne (P) was struck by a car, suffered severe brain damage, and remained in a hospital in a vegetative state for over four years before dying, his insurance company refused to pay on the double indemnity accidental death portion of the policy.

🏛 RULE OF LAW
Public policy concerns mitigate against the enforcement of an insurance contract term that prohibits accidental death benefits if death occurs more than ninety days after an accident.

FACTS: In 1949, Burne (P) was issued a life insurance policy with a face value of $15,000, and a double indemnity term for an additional $15,000 if death was purely accidental. The double indemnity clause required that death occur within ninety days of the accident causing death. In 1959, Burne (P) was struck by a car. Tremendous brain damage was caused by the accident. Burne (P) was kept alive in a vegetative state for over four years. Burne's (P) estate filed suit to receive the double indemnity payment, but a motion for summary judgment was issued against Burne (P). Burne (P) appealed.

ISSUE: Does it violate public policy to enforce an insurance contract provision that denies payment of double indemnity accidental death benefits where death occurs more than ninety days after the accident?

HOLDING AND DECISION: (Roberts, J.) Yes. Public policy concerns mitigate against the enforcement of an insurance contract term that prohibits accidental death benefits if death occurs more than ninety days after an accident. Decades of rapid advances in the field of medicine have allowed doctors to become amazingly adept at delaying death. The gruesome paradox of a time limit on accidental death benefits is that a person who dies instantly in an accident receives the benefits, but someone who lingers on in agony, expending more resources in an attempt to sustain life, receives nothing. Such an offensive concept as a time limit on accidental death benefits defies the very purpose of the insurance and is contrary to public policy. Hence, in this case, the ninety-day limitation on the double indemnity term is unenforceable. Reversed.

DISSENT: (Pomeroy, J.) This court has rewritten a contract to provide a benefit where none was intended.

When the insurance contract was made, both parties included the ninety-day provision as their intent. The contract was reasonable when it was entered into, and the courts should abstain from rewriting with the benefit of hindsight.

▶ ANALYSIS

The outcome in this case might be more acceptable from a legal standpoint had the court focused on an unconscionability argument. As it stands, the case substantially undermines the freedom to contract and the certainty of what constituted a bargain.

Quicknotes

ASSUMPSIT An oral or written promise by one party to perform or pay another.

DOUBLE INDEMNITY Payment of double the benefit or policy amount for harm sustained as a result of particular circumstances.

PUBLIC POLICY Policy administered by the state with respect to the health, safety and morals of its people in accordance with common notions of fairness and decency.

The Boundaries of Autonomy

Quick Reference Rules of Law

Taylor v. Caldwell

Lessee (P) v. Lessor (D)

Q.B., 3 B.&S. 826, 122 Eng. Rep. 309 (1863).

NATURE OF CASE: Action for damages for breach of a contract for letting of premises.

FACT SUMMARY: Taylor (P) contracted to let Caldwell's (D) hall and gardens for four fetes and concerts, for four days, for 100 pounds per day. Taylor (P) expended money in preparation and for advertising, but Caldwell (D) could not perform when the hall burned down without his fault.

RULE OF LAW
In contracts in which the performance depends on the continued existence of a given person or thing, a condition is implied that the impossibility of performance arising from the perishing of the person or thing shall excuse the performance.

FACTS: By written agreement Caldwell (D) agreed to let the Surrey Gardens and Musical Hall at Newington, Surrey, for four days for giving four "Grand Concerts" and "Day and Night Fetes." Taylor (P) was to pay 100 pounds at the end of each day. Before any concerts were held, the hall was completely destroyed by fire without any fault of either of the parties. Taylor (P) alleged that the fire and destruction of the hall was a breach and that it resulted in his losing large sums in preparation and advertising for the concerts and fetes.

ISSUE: Was Caldwell (D) excused from performance by the accidental destruction of the hall and gardens which had made his performance impossible?

HOLDING AND DECISION: (Blackburn, J.) Yes. Caldwell (D) was excused from performance. First, the agreement was not a lease but a contract to "let." The entertainments that were planned could not be made without the existence of the hall. Ordinarily, when there is a positive contract to do something that is not unlawful, the contractor must perform or pay damages for not doing it even if an unforeseen accident makes performance unduly burdensome or even impossible. This is so when the contract is absolute and positive and not subject to either express or implied conditions. If it appears that the parties must have known from the beginning that the contract could not be fulfilled unless a particular, specified thing continued to exist and there is no express or implied warranty that the thing shall exist, the contract is not positive and absolute. It is subject to the implied condition that the parties shall be excused in case, before breach, performance becomes impossible from the perishing of the thing without fault of the contractor. This appears to be within the intention of the parties when they enter into a contract. The excuse from the contract's performance is implied in law because from the nature of the contract it is apparent it was made on the basis of the continued existence of the particular, specified thing. Judgment for the defendants.

ANALYSIS

It was important for Judge Blackburn not to find the agreement to be a lease, otherwise the decision would come within direct conflict with *Paradine v. Jane*, K.B., 1647, 82 Eng. Rep. 897, which held that a lease must be performed to the letter despite unforeseen hardship or good fortune. Next, performance is excused only if the destruction of the specified thing is without fault. Had Caldwell (D) been shown to be guilty of arson in the destruction of the hall, he would not have been excused. If there is impossibility of performance due to no one's fault, the one seeking to enforce performance takes the risk. It might be said that the court was actually apportioning the loss if the contract was, in effect, a joint venture with Taylor (P) paying Caldwell (D) 100 pounds out of each day's admission fees to the concerts (Caldwell [D] was supplying the band). The modern view of this case is found in Uniform Commercial Code § 2-613 where for total destruction of the specified thing the contract is avoided, or if the specified thing is goods which have so deteriorated as to no longer conform, the contract can be avoided or the goods can be accepted with an allowance for their lesser value. Note that there is not a satisfactory distinction between a contract to let and a lease.

Quicknotes

DOCTRINE OF IMPOSSIBILITY A doctrine relieving the parties to a contract from liability for nonperformance of their duties thereunder, if the subject matter of the contract ceases to exist, a person essential to the performance of the contract is deceased, or the service or goods contracted for has become illegal.

IMPLIED CONDITION A condition that is not expressly stated in the terms of an agreement, but which is inferred from the parties' conduct or the type of dealings involved.

Krell v. Henry

Licensor (P) v. Licensee (D)

K.B. Ct. App., 2 K.B. 740 (1903).

NATURE OF CASE: Action for damages for breach of a contract for a license for use.

FACT SUMMARY: Henry (D) paid a deposit of £25 to Krell (P) for the use of his apartment in Pall Mall, London, for the purpose of a viewing sight for King Edward VII's coronation procession. The King became ill, causing a delay of the coronation upon which Henry (D) refused to pay a £50 balance for which Krell (P) sued.

🏛 RULE OF LAW
Where the object of one of the parties is the basis upon which both parties contract, the duties of performance are constructively conditioned upon the attainment of that object.

FACTS: In two letters of June 20, 1902, Henry (D) contracted through Krell's (P) agent, Bisgood, to use Krell's (P) flat in Pall Mall, London, to view the coronation procession of King Edward VII which had been advertised to pass along Pall Mall. The contract made no mention of this purpose. The period of use of the flat was the daytime only of June 26, 27, 1902, for £75, £25 paid in deposit with the £50 remainder due on June 24, 1902. Henry (D) became aware of the availability of Krell's (P) flat as an announcement to that effect had been made which was reiterated by Krell's (P) housekeeper who showed Henry (D) the rooms. When the king became very ill, the coronation was delayed, and Henry (D) refused to pay the £50 balance for which Krell (P) brought suit.

ISSUE: Where the object of one of the parties is the basis upon which both parties contract, are the duties of performance constructively conditioned upon the attainment of that object?

HOLDING AND DECISION: (Lord Williams, J.) Yes. Where the object of one of the parties is the basis upon which both parties contract, the duties of performance are constructively conditioned upon the attainment of that object. It can be inferred from the surrounding circumstances that the rooms were taken for the purpose of viewing the processions, and that was the foundation of the contract. It was not a lease of the rooms—they could not be used at night—but a license for use for a particular purpose. With the defeat of the purpose of the contract, the performance is excused. Appeal dismissed.

▮ ANALYSIS

This case is an extension of *Taylor v. Caldwell*, Q.B., 3 B.&S. 826, 122 Eng. Rep. 309 (1863), and as in that case it was necessary to remove the roadblock of a lease in order to avoid a conflict with *Paradine v. Jane*, K.B., 1647, 82 Eng. Rep. 897. The rule explained here is "frustration of purpose" or "commercial frustration." It has not been made clear whether this doctrine rests upon the failure of consideration or the allocation of the risks. While there is a frustration, performance is not impossible. No constructive condition of performance has failed as Krell (P) made no promise that the condition would occur. Rather, a constructive condition based upon the attainment of the purpose or object has arisen. Note that the frustration should be total or nearly total, though that is a matter of degree.

▬▬▬

Quicknotes

CONSTRUCTIVE CONDITION A condition that is not expressly stated in or implied by the terms of an agreement, but is imposed by law.

FRUSTRATION OF PURPOSE A doctrine relieving the parties to a contract from liability for nonperformance of their duties thereunder when the purpose of the agreement ceases to exist due to circumstances not subject to either party's control.

LICENSE A right that is granted to a person allowing him or her to conduct an activity that without such permission he or she could not lawfully do, and which is unassignable and revocable at the will of the licensor.

▬▬▬

Northern Indiana Public Service Co. v. Carbon County Coal Co.

Utility company (P) v. Coal mining company (D)

799 F.2d 265 (7th Cir. 1986).

NATURE OF CASE: Cross-appeals of an award of $181 million in damages for breach of contract.

FACT SUMMARY: Northern Indiana Public Service Co. (P) claimed it was excused from its obligations under its contract with Carbon County Coal Co. (D) when the state made it more expensive to use coal.

> ### 🏛 RULE OF LAW
> Performance under a fixed-price contract is not excused when circumstances cause the contract to be less profitable than originally planned.

FACTS: In 1978, Northern Indiana Public Service Co. NIPSCO (P), a utility company, entered into a contract with Carbon County Coal Co. (Carbon) (D) whereby NIPSCO (P) agreed to purchase approximately 1.5 million tons of coal every year for twenty years at a price of $24 a ton subject to various provisions for escalation which by 1985 had driven the price up to $44 a ton. In 1983, NIPSCO (P) requested permission from the state to raise its rates to reflect the increased cost of fuel. While the state granted the increase, it also mandated through "economy purchase orders" that NIPSCO (P) seek out less-expensive forms of energy and that any long-term contract which provided more expensive fuel would not be passed on to consumers. Subsequently, when NIPSCO (P) was able to purchase electricity at a cost less than coal, it stopped accepting coal from Carbon (D). NIPSCO (P) alleged that it was excused from the contract due to force majeure, impossibility, or frustration of purpose. Carbon (D) counterclaimed against NIPSCO (P) for breach of contract and sought a preliminary injunction requiring NIPSCO (P) to accept the coal. The court granted the preliminary injunction and then, after trial, the court ordered NIPSCO (P) to pay Carbon (D) $181 million, but the court did not enforce specific performance of the contract. Both parties appealed.

ISSUE: Can performance under a fixed-price contract be excused when circumstances cause the contract to be less profitable than originally planned?

HOLDING AND DECISION: (Posner, J.) No. Performance under a fixed-price contract is not excused when circumstances cause the contract to be less profitable than originally planned. The purpose of a fixed-price contract is to shift the risk of the contract to the buyer. Performance may only be excused when there are unforeseeable circumstances that make performance impossible. Here, NIPSCO (P) is now able to buy electricity at a cheaper rate than coal. However, it assumed that risk when it entered into the contract with Carbon (D).

NIPSCO (P) cannot claim that government regulations prevented it from buying the contracted coal. The regulations simply made the purchases more expensive. This was a risk that NIPSCO (P) assumed. Affirmed.

▶ ANALYSIS

A force majeure clause is a provision that excuses nonperformance for causes beyond the control of the parties. Typically, this could include natural disasters or government acts. The contract at issue allowed NIPSCO (P) out if a government order banned the use of coal.

Quicknotes

FORCE MAJEURE CLAUSE Clause, pursuant to an oil and gas lease, relieving the lessee from liability for breach of the lease if the party's performance is impeded as the result of a natural cause that could not have been prevented.

FRUSTRATION OF PURPOSE A doctrine relieving the parties to a contract from liability for nonperformance of their duties thereunder when the purpose of the agreement ceases to exist due to circumstances not subject to either party's control.

IMPOSSIBILITY A doctrine relieving the parties to a contract from liability for nonperformance of their duties thereunder, if the subject matter of the contract ceases to exist, a person essential to the performance of the contract is deceased, or the service or goods contracted for has become illegal.

PRELIMINARY INJUNCTION A judicial mandate issued to require or restrain a party from certain conduct; used to preserve a trial's subject matter or to prevent threatened injury.

Transatlantic Financing Corp. v. United States

Ship operator (P) v. Federal government (D)

363 F.2d 312 (D.C. Cir. 1966).

NATURE OF CASE: Action for unforeseen costs in execution of a contract for carriage.

FACT SUMMARY: Transatlantic Financing Corp. (Transatlantic) (P), under charter of the United States (D), contracted to ship a full cargo of wheat from Galveston, Texas, to Iran. Shipment was contemplated on Transatlantic's (P) SS Christos through the Suez Canal, but war broke out between Egypt and Israel, forcing the closure of the canal. The SS Christos had to steam an extra 3,000 miles around the Cape of Good Hope.

🏛 RULE OF LAW
When the issue of impossibility is raised, the court must construct a condition of performance based on changed circumstances involving the following: (1) a contingency, something unexpected, must have occurred, (2) the risk of unexpected occurrence must not have been allocated either by agreement or custom, and (3) occurrence of the contingency must have rendered performance commercially impracticable.

FACTS: Transatlantic Financing Corp. (Transatlantic) (P), under charter to the United States (D), contracted to carry a full cargo of wheat on its SS Christos from Galveston, Texas, to a safe port in Iran. On July 26, 1956, Egypt nationalized the Suez Canal. During the international crisis resulting from this, the parties contracted on October 2, 1956, for Transatlantic (P) to ship the wheat as described. The charter stated the termini of the voyage but not the route. The SS Christos sailed October 27, 1956, on a planned route through the Suez Canal. On October 29, 1956, war between Egypt and Israel broke out. On October 31, 1956, Great Britain and France invaded the Suez Canal Zone. On November 2, 1956, Egypt obstructed the canal with sunken vessels, closing it to traffic. Transatlantic (P) sought an agreement for additional compensation for a voyage around the Cape of Good Hope from a concededly unauthorized department of agriculture employee who advised Transatlantic (P) that it had to perform the charter according to its terms but could always file a claim. The SS Christos changed course for the Cape of Good Hope, arriving in Bandar Shapur, Iran, on December 30, 1956. The planned 10,000 mile voyage was increased by 3,000 miles. Transatlantic (P) sought the added expense of $43,972 over the $305,845 contract price. The district court dismissed the libel (an action in admiralty).

ISSUE: Was the contract legally impossible, that is, only able to be done at an excessive and unreasonable cost?

HOLDING AND DECISION: (Wright, J.) No. While it was reasonable to assume that when no route was mentioned in the charter, the usual and customary route (through the Suez Canal) would be taken. But just because this means of performance was impossible, the court must find whether the risk of the contingency (the closure of the canal) was allocated and, if not, whether performance by alternate routes was rendered impracticable. Allocation of risk of the contingency's occurrence may be expressed or implied in the agreement or found in the surrounding circumstances, including custom and usages of the trade. Nothing in the charter specified the Suez route or implied continued availability of that route for performance. Nothing in custom or trade usage, or in the surrounding circumstances, supported such a condition of performance. An implied expectation of the Suez route was hardly adequate proof of an allocation to the promises of the risk of closure. Circumstances instead seemed to place the risk on Transatlantic (P), as the parties knew or should have known of the crisis. Freight rates were most likely affected by the increased risk of voyage in the Suez area. While one might not have foreseen that nationalization of the canal would have brought about a subsequent closure, the circumstances did indicate Transatlantic's (P) willingness to assume abnormal risks. That legitimately causes the court to judge impracticability of performance by alternative route in stricter terms. Impracticability did not appear as the goods could be shipped in the less temperate climate. The ship and crew were fit for the longer voyage, and Transatlantic (P) was no less able than the Government (D) to purchase insurance. In fact, the ship's operator would be more reasonably expected to cover the hazards of war. To justify relief there must be more of a variation between expected cost and the cost of performing by alternative means than was present here as the promisor can be presumed to have accepted greater than normal risk and impracticability is argued on the basis of expense alone. Affirmed.

▌ ANALYSIS

In determining impossibility, the court will look first to see which party assumed the risk of unforeseen circumstances; if that cannot be determined, then to see whether performance was legally impossible. Legally impossible means impracticable, that is, at excessive and unreasonable cost. Knowledge of the crisis would tend to show assumption of the risk. The court, with respect to

Continued on next page.

unreasonable cost, examined Transatlantic's (P) theory of relief. If the contract was impossible, it was a nullity from the start. Transatlantic (P) asked for quantum meruit not for the total performance as it should have. The court believed that Transatlantic (P) wanted to avoid losing any of what appeared to be an advantageous contract price. The court would not place a burden on one party to preserve the other's profit. Note that when the court discussed foreseeability of the risk, that foreseeability is as much a fiction as implied conditions, and the parties might honestly have not foreseen the canal closure. Foreseeability is used as a tool in considering where the risk was to be allocated.

■≡■

Quicknotes

DOCTRINE OF IMPOSSIBILITY A doctrine relieving the parties to a contract from liability for nonperformance of their duties thereunder, if the subject matter of the contract ceases to exist, a person essential to the performance of the contract is deceased, or the service or goods contracted for has become illegal.

QUANTUM MERUIT Equitable doctrine allowing recovery for labor and materials provided by one party, even though no contract was entered into, in order to avoid unjust enrichment by the benefited party.

■≡■

Burger King Corp. v. Family Dining, Inc.

Burger company (P) v. Family restauranteurs (D)

426 F. Supp. 485 (E.D. Pa. 1977); *aff'd mem.* 566 F.2d 1168 (3d Cir. 1977).

NATURE OF CASE: Action to declare a contract unenforceable.

FACT SUMMARY: Burger King Corp. (P) sued to declare an exclusivity franchise contract unenforceable due to Family Dining Inc.'s (D) failure to meet a development schedule.

> ## 🏛 RULE OF LAW
> Whether words constitute a condition or a promise is a matter of the intention of the parties to be ascertained from a reasonable construction of the language used and the surrounding circumstances.

FACTS: Burger King Corp. (P) granted Family Dining Inc. (Family) (D) an exclusive territory within which to operate franchised restaurants. The contract allowed such exclusivity for as long as 80 years so long as Family (D) kept up with a development schedule requiring it to construct one restaurant a year for 10 years. Family (D) fell behind in its construction schedule yet ultimately built all 10. A controversy arose over the building of the final restaurant as Burger King (P) contended the failure to begin construction on one restaurant per year breached the contract and allowed it to cancel the exclusivity clause. Family (D) defended on the basis that the development schedule was a mere condition and not a promise.

ISSUE: Is the determination whether words in a contract constitute a promise or a condition based on the intention of the parties and the surrounding circumstances?

HOLDING AND DECISION: (Hannum, J.) Yes. Whether words in a contract are to be interpreted as constituting a promise or a condition is determined by the intention of the parties and the surrounding circumstances. In this case, it is clear from the record of dealings between the parties that the main focus of concern was the development of the restaurants and not the literal compliance with the schedule. Burger King (P) on several occasions waived the schedule. Therefore, it is clear that the intent was that the schedule be a condition subsequent and not a promise. As such, its breach did not give rise to cancellation of the contract. Judgment for Family (D).

▶ ANALYSIS

The court in this case also took into consideration the fact that to interpret the contract in a way so as to declare the schedule a promise, and its breach grounds for cancellation, would cause Family (D) to suffer forfeiture. As courts generally follow the maxim that the law of equity abhors forfeiture, this result was avoided.

■▬■

Quicknotes

CONDITION Requirement; potential future occurrence upon which the existence of a legal obligation is dependent.

CONDITION PRECEDENT The happening of an uncertain occurrence, which is necessary before a particular right or interest may be obtained or an action performed.

CONDITION SUBSEQUENT Potential future occurrence that extinguishes a party's obligation to perform pursuant to the contract.

PROMISE The expression of an intention to act, or to forbear from acting, granting a right to the promisee to expect and enforce its performance.

■▬■

Bak-A-Lum Corp. of America v. ALCOA Bldg. Prods., Inc.

Distributor (P) v. Manufacturer (D)

N.J. Sup. Ct., 69 N.J. 123, 351 A.2d 349 (1976).

NATURE OF CASE: Action for breach of contract.

FACT SUMMARY: ALCOA Bldg. Prods., Inc. (D) canceled an exclusive distributorship agreement with Bak-A-Lum Corp. of America (Bak-A-Lum) (P) after it knew that a new warehouse lease had been entered into by Bak-A-Lum (P).

🏛 RULE OF LAW
An implied requirement of good-faith dealings is implied in franchise/exclusive dealings agreements, and its breach is actionable.

FACTS: ALCOA Bldg. Prods., Inc. (ALCOA) (D) entered into an exclusive distributorship agreement with Bak-A-Lum Corp. of America (Bak-A-Lum) (P) for it to distribute ALCOA's (D) products in a territory. ALCOA (D) terminated the agreement seven or eight years later. Bak-A-Lum (P) sued for damages from the failure to give adequate notice. Bak-A-Lum (P) also alleged that ALCOA (D) had kept its decision secret, knowing that it was expending a significant amount of money on the lease of a new warehouse, plus its remodeling. The court found that the notice given by ALCOA (D) was insufficient to terminate the agreement and awarded Bak-A-Lum (P) damages based on a seven-month notice period. Nothing in the award reflected the alleged bad faith of ALCOA (D) in failing to notify Bak-A-Lum (P) of cancellation so that it would not enter into the long-term lease.

ISSUE: Where an exclusive dealership agreement is being canceled, is there an implied good-faith requirement that notice should be given at a meaningful time so as to avoid unnecessary injury to the other party?

HOLDING AND DECISION: (Conford, J.) Yes. An implied requirement of good-faith dealings is inherent in all exclusive dealership/distributorship arrangements. A breach of this implied duty is actionable. ALCOA (D) knew of the long-term lease commitment that Bak-A-Lum (P) was contemplating. ALCOA (D) knew at that time that it was going to cancel the exclusive arrangement between it and Bak-A-Lum (P). ALCOA (D) not only did not warn Bak-A-Lum (P), but it encouraged Bak-A-Lum (P) to enter into the lease. Notice of termination of an exclusive arrangement must be meaningful and must be designed to minimize the other party's loss. ALCOA (D) breached this duty and should be liable for a portion of Bak-A-Lum's (P) losses. We find that 20 months' damages is appropriate. By the end of that period, Bak-A-Lum (P) should be able to use the warehouse for other purposes. Judgment is modified in part and affirmed in part.

▶ ANALYSIS

In every contract there is an implied duty that neither party shall do anything which will have the effect of destroying or injuring the right of the other party to receive the fruits of the contract. *Association Group Life, Inc. v. Catholic War Veterans of U.S.*, 61 N.J. 150 (1972). A party may not interpose barriers which will prevent the other party from obtaining the anticipated contractual benefits.

Quicknotes

GOOD FAITH An honest intention to abstain from any unconscientious advantage of another.

IMPLIED DUTY An obligation owed by one individual to another that arises from the particular relationship or circumstances.

Badgett v. Security State Bank

Debtor (P) v. Creditor (D)

Wash. Sup. Ct., 116 Wash. 2d 563, 807 P.2d 356 (1991).

NATURE OF CASE: Appeal from order denying summary judgment in a breach of contract action.

FACT SUMMARY: The Badgetts (P) contended that Security State Bank (D) had breached the duty of good faith by not considering their terms for loan renegotiation.

> ## 🏛 RULE OF LAW
> A failure to consider proposed renegotiation terms cannot serve as the basis for a breach of duty of good faith.

FACTS: The Badgetts (P), who had been in and out of the dairy industry for years, negotiated a loan with Security State Bank (the "Bank") (D). Subsequently, the Badgetts (P) proposed certain new terms so as to maximize their eligibility for federal monies. The Bank (D) declined the new terms, and the Badgetts (P) did not receive the benefits. They sued the Bank (D) for breach of the duty of good faith and fair dealing. The Bank (D) moved for summary judgment, which was granted. The court of appeals reversed. The state supreme court granted review.

ISSUE: Can a failure to consider proposed renegotiation terms serve as the basis for a breach of duty of good faith?

HOLDING AND DECISION: (Durham, J.) No. A failure to consider proposed renegotiation terms may not serve as the basis for a breach of duty of good faith. The duty of good faith and fair dealing goes only to the terms of a contract. To impose an amorphous duty with respect to renegotiation would entirely undercut the certainty that contract law seeks to promote. Therefore, a failure to consider new contract terms can never be a basis for a breach of the duty of good faith. Reversed.

▌ ANALYSIS

All jurisdictions mandate a duty of good faith in contracts. As the present case shows, there is room for disagreement as to its scope. The court here took a narrow view, which all courts do not share.

━━■

Quicknotes

FAIR DEALING An implied warranty that the parties will deal honestly in the satisfaction of their obligations and without an intent to defraud.

GOOD FAITH An honest intention to abstain from any unconscientious advantage of another.

━━■

Badgett v. Security State Bank

Financee (P) v. Financor (D)

Wash Ct. App., 56 Wash. App. 872, 786 P.2d 302 (1990).

NATURE OF CASE: Appeal from summary judgment dismissing action seeking damages.

FACT SUMMARY: The Badgetts (P) contended that Security State Bank's (D) prior dealings with them gave rise to a good-faith duty to consider new loan terms.

🏛 RULE OF LAW
Prior dealings between contractual parties may give rise to a good-faith duty to consider new terms.

FACTS: The Badgetts (P), in the dairy business, had a financing relationship with Security State Bank (the "Bank") (D). On at least one prior occasion they had asked for new terms, and received same. When the Badgetts (P) requested new financing again, so they could benefit from a government program, the Bank (D) denied the request. Approval was not given. The Badgetts (P) filed suit, contending that the Bank (D) unreasonably did not consider the request, in violation of the duty of good faith and fair dealing. The trial court granted summary judgment dismissing the action, ruling that the Bank (D) had no duty to consider the request. The Badgetts (P) appealed.

ISSUE: May prior dealings between contractual parties give rise to a good-faith duty to consider new terms?

HOLDING AND DECISION: (Petrich, J.) Yes. Prior dealings between contractual parties may give rise to a good-faith duty to consider new terms. The duty of good faith is the most important concept to be found in the Uniform Commercial Code. The duty does not require a party to accept material changes in contractual terms. However, if past dealings lead one party to assume that the other will consider proposed changes, and it does not, the good-faith duty is implicated. It is a question of fact as to whether such a situation exists, so summary judgment is improper. Reversed.

▌ANALYSIS

The court's opinion here leaves unanswered questions. On the one hand, it states that there is no duty to accept new terms. If this is so, it is unclear how a failure to consider new terms could proximately cause damages.

Quicknotes

FAIR DEALING An implied warranty that the parties will deal honestly in the satisfaction of their obligations and without an intent to defraud.

GOOD FAITH An honest intention to abstain from any unconscientious advantage of another.

J.J. Brooksbank Co. v. Budget Rent-A-Car Corp.

Franchisee (P) v. Franchisor (D)

Minn. Sup. Ct., 337 N.W.2d 372 (1983).

NATURE OF CASE: Appeal from grant of equitable relief.

FACT SUMMARY: Budget Rent-A-Car Corp. (D) contended it was no longer obligated to give J.J. Brooksbank Co. (P) free reservations because technological advancements had rendered the original contract impracticable.

RULE OF LAW
Impracticability will excuse performance of a contract only where an event occurs, the nonoccurrence of which was a basic assumption of the contract at the time it was made.

FACTS: Budget Rent-A-Car Corp. (Budget) (D) began operations in 1960, attracting franchisees such as J.J. Brooksbank Co. (Brooksbank) (P) by agreeing to give them reservations for car rentals out of New York, Los Angeles, and Chicago without charge. As the years went by, new franchisees were added, and their contracts were less favorable. As the company grew, a centralized reservations system was adopted, with each franchisee paying for each reservation received. Brooksbank (P) contended that the original agreement still applied, and it did not pay for reservations. Budget (D) contended that the technology rendered the original contract impracticable. Brooksbank (P) sued for a declaration that it owed nothing for reservations or that it was entitled to a reduction in such charges. The trial court entered judgment, granting Brooksbank (P) a 10 percent reduction. Both parties appealed.

ISSUE: Will impracticability excuse performance only where an event occurs, the nonoccurrence of which was a basic assumption of the contract?

HOLDING AND DECISION: (Peterson, J.) Yes. Impracticability will excuse performance of a contract only where an event occurs, the nonoccurrence of which was a basic assumption of the contract. In this case, the only event which occurred was the normal progression of technology. While clearly this was not specifically anticipated, it does not go to the essence of the contract. Thus, while the original contract controls, a reduction rather than an elimination of the fees is the equitable resolution. Judgment modified.

DISSENT: (Simonett, J.) No rule of contract construction applies to this case, and a court therefore should base its ruling in this case on equity. The cost-free-reservations provision of the 1962 contract has been irrelevant since 1970 because, in 1962, the parties did not foresee the technological changes made by Budget (D) in 1970.

Under the circumstances, Brooksbank (P) does deserve a reduction. The proper result in this appeal, though, is to reverse the trial court and remand for a reduction based on the equities of the parties' entire business relationship.

ANALYSIS

Neither party was pleased with the result in this case which seems to cut middle ground. Brooksbank (P) technically lost the benefit of its bargain, while Budget (D) must continue to supplement this one franchisee to the detriment of all others. The court essentially weighed the equities of the situation and answered with a compromise position.

Quicknotes

IMPRACTICABILITY A doctrine relieving the parties to a contract from liability for nonperformance of their duties thereunder, if the subject matter of the contract ceases to exist.

Gruenberg v. Aetna Insurance Co.

Insured (P) v. Insurance company (D)

Cal. Sup. Ct. (en banc), 9 Cal. 3d 566, 510 P.2d 1032 (1973).

NATURE OF CASE: Review of dismissal of action seeking contract and tort damages.

FACT SUMMARY: Gruenberg (P) contended that his property damage insurers breached the duty of good faith by encouraging a criminal investigation they knew to be unwarranted.

🏛 RULE OF LAW
An insurer violates the duty of good faith by encouraging a criminal investigation of its insured that it knows to be unwarranted.

FACTS: Gruenberg's (P) business was destroyed by fire. He was criminally investigated for arson. Gruenberg's (P) three casualty carriers, Aetna Insurance (D), Yosemite Insurance (D), and American Home Insurance (D) jointly mounted their own investigation. The insurers (D) concluded that Gruenberg (P) was overinsured which they considered to be evidence of intent to defraud. They relayed this information to authorities. Gruenberg (P) was charged with arson and insurance fraud. The insurers (D) refused to indemnify Gruenberg (P) for his losses. The criminal charges were eventually dismissed. Gruenberg (P) filed an action against the insurers (D) for breach of the duty of good faith and fair dealing. The trial court dismissed the complaint for failure to state a cause of action. Gruenberg (P) appealed.

ISSUE: Does an insurer violate the duty of good faith by encouraging a criminal investigation of its insured that it knows to be unwarranted?

HOLDING AND DECISION: (Sullivan, J.) Yes. An insurer violates the duty of good faith by encouraging a criminal investigation of its insured that it knows to be unwarranted. The duty of good faith imposes upon an insurer a duty not to do anything to put at risk the insurer's right to indemnity under the contract. Clearly, to encourage a criminal investigation of the insured with knowledge that the charges are baseless constitutes a violation of this duty since a finding of criminal conduct would nullify the policy. For purposes of pleading, such allegations are sufficient at the pleading stage. Reversed in part, affirmed in part, and remanded.

▌ ANALYSIS

Gruenberg (P) also sued various agents of the insurer. The dismissal was not reversed as to them. As they were not parties to the insurance contract, the agents did not have the same duty of good faith.

Quicknotes

FAIR DEALING An implied warranty that the parties will deal honestly in the satisfaction of their obligations and without an intent to defraud.

GOOD FAITH An honest intention to abstain from any unconscientious advantage of another.

Beck v. Farmers Insurance Exchange

Insured (P) v. Insurance company (D)

Utah Sup. Ct., 701 P.2d 795 (1985).

NATURE OF CASE: Appeal from dismissal of action based on breach of duty of good faith.

FACT SUMMARY: Beck (P) contended that Farmers Insurance Exchange (D) had breached its duty of good faith by unreasonably failing to investigate and negotiate.

RULE OF LAW
An insurer breaches its duty of good faith by unreasonably failing to investigate and negotiate.

FACTS: Beck (P) was injured by an uninsured vehicle. He made an uninsured motorist claim with his first-party auto carrier, Farmers Insurance Exchange (Farmers) (D). He submitted a policy limit demand of $20,000, along with supporting documentation. The claim was rejected without a counter-offer. The parties later settled for $15,000, although Beck (P) reserved any claim he might have for bad faith. He filed a bad faith action, contending that Farmers (D) had breached the duty of good faith by failing to investigate and negotiate. The trial court granted summary judgment dismissing the action, citing authority that Farmers (D) had no duty to settle. Beck (P) appealed.

ISSUE: Does an insurer breach its duty of good faith by unreasonably failing to investigate and negotiate?

HOLDING AND DECISION: (Zimmerman, J.) Yes. An insurer breaches its duty of good faith by unreasonably failing to investigate and negotiate. This court has previously held that a carrier does not breach its duty of good faith by a mere failure to investigate and negotiate. It is now clear that this approach effectively leaves an insured with no remedy, as the financial and emotional problems that often accompany an accident can weaken the insured and force him into a low settlement. Consequently, this court now holds that an unreasonable failure by a carrier to investigate and negotiate a first-party claim results in a breach of the duty of good faith. However, this court believes that this cause of action arises from contract, not tort. The parties to an insurance policy stand in a contractual relationship, and the insured's action should be sound in contract. Those jurisdictions allowing for a tort action appear to do so for policy reasons, believing that a contract action alone will not motivate carriers to act fairly. This court disagrees. A contract action will allow consequential damages, which can include a loss of business, attorney's fees, and even mental anguish. This court believes that the prospect of such damages is sufficient to deter insurer misconduct. Reversed and remanded.

ANALYSIS

The court here limited its ruling to first-party actions. Its language indicated that it would allow tort actions in third-party cases. The insurer there stands as a fiduciary, said the court, which it does not do in a first-party case.

Quicknotes

DUTY OF GOOD FAITH OF FAIR DEALINGS An implied duty in a contract that the parties will deal honestly in the satisfaction of their obligations and without intent to defraud.

Rights of Third Parties

Quick Reference Rules of Law

Lawrence v. Fox

Creditor (P) v. Debtor (D)

N.Y. Ct. App., 20 N.Y. 268 (1859).

NATURE OF CASE: Action by a third party to recover damages for breach of contract.

FACT SUMMARY: Fox (D) promised Holly for consideration that he would pay Holly's debt to Lawrence (P).

🏛 RULE OF LAW
A third party for whose benefit a contract is made may bring an action for its breach.

FACTS: One Holly owed Lawrence (P) $300. Holly loaned $300 to Fox (D) in consideration of Fox's (D) promise to pay the same amount to Lawrence (P), thereby erasing Holly's debts to Lawrence (P). Fox (D) did not pay Lawrence (P) and now Lawrence (P) brings this action for breach of Fox's (D) promise to Holly.

ISSUE: Is a third party precluded for want of privity of contract from maintaining an action on a contract made for his benefit?

HOLDING AND DECISION: (Gray, J.) No. [In the case of] a promise made to one for the benefit of another, he for whose benefit it is made may bring an action for its breach. This principle, which has been long applied in trust cases, is in fact a general principle of law. Affirmed.

DISSENT: (Comstock, J.) In general, there must be privity of contract. Here, Lawrence (P) had nothing to do with the promise on which he brought the action. "It was not made to him, nor did the consideration proceed from him. If [Lawrence (P)] can maintain the suit, it is because an anomaly has found its way into the law on this subject."

▶ ANALYSIS

This is the leading case which started the general doctrine of "third party beneficiaries." In the parlance of the original Restatement of Contracts, Lawrence (P) was a "creditor" beneficiary. Restatement, Second, § 133 has eliminated the creditor/donee distinction which the original Restatement fostered and has lumped both under the label of "intended" beneficiary. Although the court in the present case went to some effort to discuss trusts and agency, ultimately the court allowed Lawrence (P) to recover because it was manifestly "just" that he should recover. Such has been the creation of many a new legal doctrine. The dissenting justices were primarily worried about freedom of contract and the continuing ability of promisor and promisee to rescind or modify their contract. As the

doctrine has developed, various rules have arisen to handle these situations.

━■━

Quicknotes

CONSIDERATION Value given by one party in exchange for performance, or a promise to perform, by another party.

CREDITOR BENEFICIARY A creditor who receives the benefits of a contract between a debtor and another party, pursuant to which the other party is obligated to tender payment to the creditor.

INTENDED BENEFICIARY A third party who is the recipient of the benefit of a transaction undertaken by another.

PRIVITY OF CONTRACT A relationship between the parties to a contract that is required in order to bring an action for breach.

THIRD-PARTY BENEFICIARY A party who benefits from a promise made pursuant to a contract although he is not a party to the agreement.

━■━

Seaver v. Ransom

Beneficiary (P) v. Executor (D)

N.Y. Ct. App., 224 N.Y. 233, 120 N.E. 639 (1918).

NATURE OF CASE: Action by a third party to recover damages for breach of a contract.

FACT SUMMARY: Berman made a promise to his wife for the benefit of their niece, Seaver (P), who sued Berman's executor (D) for breach of that promise.

🏛 RULE OF LAW
A niece for whose benefit a promise was made to her aunt may successfully bring an action for breach of that promise.

FACTS: One Mrs. Berman, on her deathbed, wished to leave some property to her niece, Seaver (P). Her husband induced his dying wife to sign a will leaving all property to him by promising that he would leave a certain amount in his own will to Seaver (P). Mr. Berman died without making such a provision for Seaver (P). Seaver (P) brought suit against Ransom (D), as executor of Berman's estate, for Berman's breach of his promise to his dying wife.

ISSUE: Does a niece for whose benefit a promise was made to her aunt have an action for breach of that promise?

HOLDING AND DECISION: (Pound, J.) Yes. Although a general rule requires privity between a plaintiff and a defendant as necessary to the maintenance of an action on the contract, one of several exceptions to the rule is the case where a contract is made for the benefit of another member of the family. Here, Mrs. Berman was childless, and Seaver (P) was a beloved niece. However, "The constraining power of conscience is not regulated by the degree of relationship alone. The dependent or faithful niece may have a stronger claim than the affluent or unworthy son. No sensible theory of moral obligation denies arbitrarily to the former what would be conceded to the latter." The reason for this "family" exception (and other exceptions) to the rule is that it is just and practical to permit the person for whose benefit a contract is made to enforce it against one whose duty it is to pay. "The doctrine of *Lawrence v. Fox*, N.Y. Ct. App., 20 N.Y. 268 (1859), is progressive, not retrograde." Finally, in this particular case, the "equities" are with Seaver (P). Affirmed.

▶ ANALYSIS

In this case, the court (as does the original Restatement of Contracts) uses the term "donee beneficiary" to describe Seaver (P). The Restatement, Second, erases the creditor/donee distinction and labels both types of beneficiaries as "intended." Although the court here is very insistent on the close family relationship, subsequent New York cases have erased that requirement for donee beneficiaries as the doctrine governing third-party beneficiaries has expanded. These subsequent cases represent the now-prevailing view in the country.

Quicknotes

DONEE BENEFICIARY A third party, not a party to a contract, but for whose benefit the contract is entered with the intention that the benefits derived therefrom be bestowed upon the person as a gift.

INTENDED BENEFICIARY A third party who is the recipient of the benefit of a transaction undertaken by another.

PRIVITY OF CONTRACT A relationship between the parties to a contract that is required in order to bring an action for breach.

Bain v. Gillispie

Referee (P) v. Store owner (D)

Iowa Ct. App., 357 N.W.2d 47 (1984).

NATURE OF CASE: Appeal from grant of summary judgment in a suit requesting injunctive relief.

FACT SUMMARY: In Bain's (P) action against Gillispie (D) for injunctive relief, actual and punitive damages, Gillispie (D) contended, in his counterclaim, that Bain's (P) conduct as a referee in officiating a basketball game between the University of Iowa and Purdue University was below the standard of competence required of a professional referee and constituted malpractice which entitled Gillispie (D) to $175,000 plus exemplary damages as a beneficiary under Bain's (P) contract with the Big 10.

RULE OF LAW
The real test as to whether a party is a beneficiary under a contract is whether the contracting parties intended that a third person should receive a benefit which might be enforced in the courts.

FACTS: Bain (P), a referee employed by the Big 10 to officiate college basketball games, made a call during a University of Iowa-Purdue University game, which some University of Iowa fans asserted caused Purdue to win the game. Gillispie (D), who operated a novelty store near the University of Iowa, marketed, after the game, a T-shirt which was deprecatory of Bain (P). Bain (P) sued Gillispie (D) for injunctive relief and actual and punitive damages. Gillispie counterclaimed, contending that Bain's (P) conduct, in officiating the game, was below the standard of competence required of a professional referee and constituted malpractice which entitled Gillispie (D) to $175,000 plus exemplary damages as a beneficiary under Bain's (P) contract with the Big 10. The trial court found that Gillispie (D) had no rights and sustained a motion for summary judgment dismissing Gillispie's (D) counterclaim. Gillispie (D) appealed.

ISSUE: Is the real test as to whether a party is a beneficiary under a contract whether the contracting parties intended that a third person should receive a benefit which might be enforced in the courts?

HOLDING AND DECISION: (Snell, J.) Yes. The real test as to whether a party is a beneficiary under a contract is whether the contracting parties intended that a third person should receive a benefit which might be enforced in the courts. Here, because Gillispie (D) was not privy to the contract between Bain (P) and the Big 10, Gillispie (D) must be a direct beneficiary to maintain a cause of action against Bain (P). A direct beneficiary is either a donee or a creditor beneficiary. Gillispie (D)

makes no claim that he is a creditor beneficiary, and he does not come within the definition of a donee beneficiary. A donee beneficiary is one, other than the promisor or promisee, who will benefit from performance of a promise. The purpose of the promisee in obtaining such a promise from a promisor must be to make a gift to the beneficiary. It is clear that, here, any promise which Bain (P) might have made was not to confer a gift on Gillispie (D). Likewise, the Big 10 did not owe Gillispie (D) any duty. If a contract did exist between Bain (P) and the Big 10, Gillispie (D) can be considered nothing more than an incidental beneficiary, and, as such, unable to maintain a cause of action. Affirmed.

▌ ANALYSIS

Beneficiaries who can claim under a contract have been divided into donee or creditor beneficiaries. A promisee's intent to benefit the beneficiary named by her in a contract is clear in the case of the donee beneficiary. A creditor beneficiary is one for whom performance of a promise will satisfy an actual or supposed duty of the promisee to the beneficiary.

Quicknotes

ACTUAL DAMAGES Measure of damages necessary to compensate victim for actual injuries suffered.

COUNTERCLAIM An independent cause of action brought by a defendant to a lawsuit in order to oppose or deduct from the plaintiff's claim.

CREDITOR BENEFICIARY A creditor who receives the benefits of a contract between a debtor and another party, pursuant to which the other party is obligated to tender payment to the creditor.

EXEMPLARY DAMAGES Damages exceeding the actual injury suffered for the purposes of punishment, deterrence and comfort to plaintiff.

MALPRACTICE A failure to perform one's professional duties during the course of a client relationship, either intentionally or negligently; or the poor or improper discharge of one's professional obligations.

PUNITIVE DAMAGES Damages exceeding the actual injury suffered for the purposes of punishment, deterrence and comfort to plaintiff.

Lonsdale v. Chesterfield

Assignee (P) v. Land developer (D)

Wash. Sup. Ct., en banc, 99 Wash. 2d 353, 662 P.2d 385 (1983).

NATURE OF CASE: Appeal from dismissal of a class action suit for rescission and damages.

FACT SUMMARY: Lonsdale (P) claimed to be a third-party beneficiary of a contract between Chesterfield (D) and Sansaria (D).

🏛 **RULE OF LAW**
The parties must have intended that the promisor assume a direct obligation to the intended beneficiary at the time they entered into the contract in order to create a third-party beneficiary.

FACTS: In 1968, Chesterfield (D) developed certain portions of land and sold off certain tracts. The purchasers paid Chesterfield (D) to install a water system in the development. Chesterfield (D) then sold some of its vendor's interests to Lonsdale (P). Lonsdale (P) received an assignment of the vendor's interests together with a deed that corresponded to the particular parcel of land. Such deed was intended to secure payment of any outstanding balance on the real estate contract. Chesterfield (D) then sold the remaining undeveloped portion of the development to Sansaria (D). In this agreement, Sansaria (D) specifically promised to install a water system for the entire development. Ultimately, the water system was not installed. Lonsdale's (P) vendor's interests became worthless. Lonsdale (P) sued Chesterfield (D) and Sansaria (D) as a third-party beneficiary to the Chesterfield-Sansaria contract for failing to install the water system. The trial court determined that Lonsdale (P) was not a third-party beneficiary to the Chesterfield-Sansaria contract. The court of appeals affirmed. Lonsdale (P) appealed.

ISSUE: Does the creation of a third-party beneficiary require that the parties intend that the promisor assume a direct obligation to the intended beneficiary at the time they enter into the contract?

HOLDING AND DECISION: (Williams, C.J.) Yes. The parties must have intended that the promisor assume a direct obligation to the intended beneficiary at the time they entered into the contract in order to create a third-party beneficiary. Courts must look to the terms of the contract to determine whether performance would necessarily and directly benefit a third party. Paragraph 3 of the Chesterfield-Sansaria contract specifically describes an obligation on Sansaria (D) to confer a benefit to Lonsdale (P) by installing the water system. Despite their motives, this shows an intent to assume a direct obligation to a third party. Therefore, Lonsdale (P) should be considered a third-party beneficiary. Reversed and remanded.

▶ *ANALYSIS*

This case shows the issues that third parties face in contract disputes. In some cases, a third party may have the right to a contractual duty conferred upon him by the original holder of that benefit. And in other cases, a third party may be delegated the duties of performance under a contract by the original party that was obligated.

Quicknotes

CLASS ACTION SUIT A suit commenced by a representative on behalf of an ascertainable group that is too large to appear in court, who shares a commonality of interests and who will benefit from a successful result.

INTENDED BENEFICIARY A third party who is the recipient of the benefit of a transaction undertaken by another.

THIRD-PARTY BENEFICIARY A party who benefits from a promise made pursuant to a contract although he is not a party to the agreement.

The Cretex Companies, Inc. v. Construction Leaders, Inc.

Unpaid materialmen (P) v. General contractor (D)

Minn. Sup. Ct., 342 N.W.2d 135 (1984).

NATURE OF CASE: Appeal from summary judgment establishing liability under a performance bond.

FACT SUMMARY: Materialman Cretex Companies, Inc. (P) contended that it was entitled to payments from a performance bond.

🏛 RULE OF LAW
Third-party beneficiaries may only enforce contracts if they were an intended beneficiary of the agreement.

FACTS: Owners Northland Mortgage engaged Construction Leaders, Inc. (D) to provide general contractor services at a development. Travelers Indemnity (D) issued performance bonds naming Construction Leaders (D) as principal and Northland as obligee. Construction Leaders (D) obtained materials from, among others, Cretex Companies, Inc. (P). Construction Leaders (D) defaulted; and Cretex (P) sought payment under the bond. A trial court held Travelers (D) liable to Cretex (P) under the bond. Travelers (D) appealed.

ISSUE: May third-party beneficiaries enforce a contract if they were not intended beneficiaries?

HOLDING AND DECISION: (Simonett, J.) No. Third-party beneficiaries may only enforce contracts if they were intended to benefit from the agreement. As a general proposition, a performance bond only guarantees the principal's performance as to the obligee, usually the owner/developer. The surety is not liable to the contractors of the principal unless an obligation is owed to these parties by the owner, or the materialmen are intended beneficiaries. Generally, materialmen are not beneficiaries on a general contractor performance bond, so unless the bond specifically holds to the contrary, they will not be considered such beneficiaries. Here, Northland did not owe any payment to Cretex (P); nor was Cretex (P) an express third-party beneficiary. Therefore, Cretex (P) was not a qualified third-party beneficiary entitled to enforce the bond. Reversed.

DISSENT: (Yetka, J.) Travelers' (D) obligation to "faithfully perform the contract" included the incorporated obligation to "provide and pay for all materials, labor . . . [and related items] for the execution and completion of the work." Travelers (D) could have clearly stated an intention to limit its obligation to completing the project. Travelers (D) did not state such an intention, though, and the subcontractors therefore could legally rely on the general contract.

▶ ANALYSIS

Performance bonds are just that: They guarantee a principal's performance. Payment can be guaranteed through a payment bond. Cretex (P) would have had a much better chance of success if the bond in question had been a payment bond.

━━■

Quicknotes

INTENDED BENEFICIARY A third party who is the recipient of the benefit of a transaction undertaken by another.

PAYMENT BOND A type of contract bond that is required on construction contracts under the Miller Act.

PERFORMANCE BOND A bond that protects against the breach of contract typically by a contractor pursuant to a building contract.

SURETY A party who guarantees payment of the debt of another party to a creditor.

THIRD-PARTY BENEFICIARY A party who benefits from a promise made pursuant to a contract although he is not a party to the agreement.

━━■

Martinez v. Socoma Companies, Inc.

Citizen (P) v. Lessor (D)

Cal. Sup. Ct., en banc, 11 Cal. 3d 394, 521 P.2d 841 (1974).

NATURE OF CASE: Appeal from dismissal of a class action suit for damages for breach of contract.

FACT SUMMARY: Martinez (P) alleged that Socoma Companies, Inc. (D) failed to perform on contracts with the United States government under which Martinez (P) claimed he was a third-party beneficiary.

RULE OF LAW
Only creditor beneficiaries and donee beneficiaries qualify as third-party beneficiaries and have enforceable rights under contracts to which they are not parties.

FACTS: In January 1967, pursuant to changes in the Economic Opportunity Act, Socoma Companies, Inc. (D) entered into contracts with the federal government whereby Socoma (D) would lease certain spaces from the government for the purpose of establishing manufacturing companies and would hire and train designated low-income people, like Martinez (P), to work in the shops. The government in return would lease out the spaces and provide Socoma (D) with significant funds. Although the government paid significant funds to Socoma (D), Socoma (D) failed to perform under its respective contracts. Martinez (P) brought a class action suit against Socoma (D) for breach of contract, claiming he was a third-party beneficiary of the contract. Socoma (D) filed general demurrers to the complaints, admitting the truth to the factual allegations, but claiming that Martinez (P) did not have proper standing as a third-party beneficiary. The lower courts granted the demurrers and dismissed the complaints. Martinez (P) appealed.

ISSUE: Are creditor beneficiaries and donee beneficiaries the only ones who qualify as third-party beneficiaries and have enforceable rights under contracts to which they are not parties?

HOLDING AND DECISION: (Wright, C.J.) Yes. Only creditor beneficiaries and donee beneficiaries qualify as third-party beneficiaries and have enforceable rights under contracts to which they are not parties. Here, Martinez (P) was neither a creditor beneficiary (those persons on whom the promisor's performance of the contract will discharge some form of legal duty owed to the beneficiary by the promisee), nor a donee beneficiary (persons for whom the contractual intent is either to make a gift to them or confer on them a right against the promisor) to the contract. Martinez (P) consequently does not have proper standing to sue as a third-party beneficiary. Martinez (P) is not a creditor beneficiary because the government (the promisee of the contract) at no time

bore any legal duty toward Martinez (P) to provide the benefits set forth in the contracts and does not claim to be a creditor beneficiary. Martinez (P) is not a donee beneficiary either since the government did not intend to make a gift with this contract, nor did it intend to confer on Martinez (P) a right against Socoma (D). From the nature and the form of the contract and the accompanying circumstances, Socoma (D) never understood that it would be bound by duty to Martinez (P), nor did this contract with the government expressly describe such a duty. Additionally, the fact that a government program for social betterment confers benefits upon individuals who are not required to render contractual consideration in return does not necessarily imply that the benefits are intended as gifts. Such benefits are viewed not as gifts to the recipients, but rather as a means to an end of achieving a greater social good. Consequently, Martinez (P) does not have standing in this case as a third-party beneficiary. Affirmed.

DISSENT: (Burke, J.) Because Martinez (P) was the express, not incidental, beneficiary to the contract, the demurrers to his complaint were improper and should not have been allowed. The benefits conferred upon Martinez (P) were not simply the means to a greater social good, but were, in part, the ends of the contract as well— the provision of jobs to a specific group of people, as well as aiding an impoverished neighborhood. As a consequence, Martinez's (P) complaint asserts facts upon which a cause of action could rest and he should have been given the opportunity to prove that he was a donee beneficiary of the contract.

ANALYSIS

This case highlights the issues that arise when third parties claim a right to enforce a contract. Historically, the right of a third party to enforce a contract was traced by the privity of that beneficiary to the contract itself. Such privity has often been difficult to show and courts today are trying to clarify ways of determining third-party beneficiaries' rights.

Quicknotes

CLASS ACTION SUIT A suit commenced by a representative on behalf of an ascertainable group that is too large to appear in court, who shares a commonality of interests and who will benefit from a successful result.

Continued on next page.

CREDITOR BENEFICIARY A creditor who receives the benefits of a contract between a debtor and another party, pursuant to which the other party is obligated to tender payment to the creditor.

DEMURRER The assertion that the opposing party's pleadings are insufficient and that the demurring party should not be made to answer.

DONEE BENEFICIARY A third party, not a party to a contract, but for whose benefit the contract is entered into with the intention that the benefits derived therefrom be bestowed upon the person as a gift.

THIRD-PARTY BENEFICIARY A party who benefits from a promise made pursuant to a contract although he is not a party to the agreement.

Rouse v. United States

Purchaser of house (D) v. Federal government (P)

215 F.2d 872 (D.C. Cir. 1954).

NATURE OF CASE: Action by a third party to recover damages for breach of contract.

FACT SUMMARY: Rouse (D) promised to pay Bessie, Winston's creditor, but refused to do so after discovering flaws in his own contract with Bessie and in Bessie's contract with her creditor.

🏛 RULE OF LAW
(1) A promisor may assert against a third-party beneficiary a defense he would have against the promisee.
(2) A promisor may not assert against a third-party beneficiary a defense which the promisee would have against the beneficiary.

FACTS: The Government's (P) assignor sold a heating plant to Bessie, who gave her promissory note for $1,008.37 payable in monthly installments of $28.01. Bessie later sold her house to Rouse (D), who agreed in the contract of sale "to assume payment of $850 for the heating plant payable $28 per Mo." Bessie defaulted on her note, and the Government (P) sued Rouse (D) as a third-party beneficiary of Rouse's (D) contract with Bessie. Rouse (D) defended by alleging (1) that Bessie fraudulently misrepresented the condition of the heating plant and (2) that the Government's (P) assignor didn't install the heater properly in the first place.

ISSUE:
(1) May a promisor assert against a third-party beneficiary a defense that he would have against the promisee?
(2) May a promisor assert against a third-party beneficiary a defense which the promisee would have against the beneficiary?

HOLDING AND DECISION: (Edgerton, J.)
(1) Yes. The rights of the third-party beneficiary rise no higher than those of the promisee; or, in other words, one who promises to make a payment to the promisee's creditor can assert against the creditor any defense that the promisor could assert against the promisee. Thus, Rouse's (D) defense of fraud, which he would certainly have been entitled to show against Bessie, is equally effective against the beneficiary (or any valid assignee of the original beneficiary).
(2) No. Here, Rouse's (D) promise was to pay a specified sum of money to the beneficiary (P), and it is irrelevant whether or not the promisee (Bessie) was actually indebted in that amount. "Where the promise is to pay a specific debt . . . this interpretation will generally be the true one." 12 Williston, § 399. [The result would be

different if Rouse (D) had merely promised to discharge whatever liability the promisee was under. In that case, the promisor must certainly be allowed to show that the promisee was under no enforceable liability.] Reversed and remanded.

▶ ANALYSIS

This well-known case lays out what defenses are, and are not, available to a promisor in an action by a third party beneficiary. While the promisor usually may assert against the beneficiary any defense which he could assert against the promisee, he usually may not assert defenses which the promisee might have raised against the beneficiary. In support of its denial of Rouse's (D) second defense, the court rests on Williston's presumption as to the nature of the promisor's promise. Unless it is clearly indicated that a promisor is only undertaking to pay "the debt" of the promisee (whatever it may turn out to be), it will be presumed that the promise is to pay the specific amount, regardless of whether it is actually owed. [Whether this "presumption" necessarily effects a "just" result in all (or even most) ambiguous cases is open to some question.]

Quicknotes

CREDITOR BENEFICIARY A creditor who receives the benefits of a contract between a debtor and another party, pursuant to which the other party is obligated to tender payment to the creditor.

THIRD-PARTY BENEFICIARY A party who benefits from a promise made pursuant to a contract although he is not a party to the agreement.

United States v. Wood

Federal government (P) v. Homeowner (D)

877 F.2d 453 (6th Cir. 1989).

NATURE OF CASE: Appeal from summary judgment in a breach of contract action.

FACT SUMMARY: The federal Government (P) contended that it was a third-party beneficiary of a clause in a property settlement.

🏛 RULE OF LAW
Third parties may enforce contracts if they are the intended beneficiaries of a valid agreement.

FACTS: Wood (D) and her husband executed a property settlement agreement in their divorce proceedings. One provision was that Wood (D) would sell the house and use any available proceeds to pay her husband's $126,471 income tax arrearages. The house was sold at an auction, but Wood (D) exercised her statutory redemption rights. She later sold the house for $575,000 and did not pay the taxes to the Government (P). The Government (P) filed a breach of contract action. The district court entered summary judgment in favor of the Government (P), and Wood (D) appealed.

ISSUE: May third parties ever enforce contracts?

HOLDING AND DECISION: (Jones, J.) Yes. Third parties may enforce contracts if they are the intended beneficiaries of a valid agreement. A third-party beneficiary to a contract may enforce the agreement as long as there is consideration flowing from the promisee to promisor and the intent of the promisee is to directly benefit the third party. When one party to a valid contract agrees to pay the other's taxes, the collecting entity, the federal government qualifies as a third-party beneficiary. Therefore, the Government (P) had an enforceable right against Wood (D) due to her settlement agreement with her husband. Affirmed.

▌ ANALYSIS

Although this was a federal case, it was governed by state contract law. Not all states follow the same rules for third-party beneficiaries. Some, for instance, impose a reliance requirement.

■■■

Quicknotes

CONSIDERATION Value given by one party in exchange for performance, or a promise to perform, by another party.

RIGHT OF REDEMPTION The right of a mortgagor to reclaim forfeited property, following a default on mortgage payments, by the payment of the mortgage debt and any other interest, fees and costs.

■■■

Adams v. Merced Stone Co.

Heir (P) v. Debtor (D)

Cal. Sup. Ct., 176 Cal. 415, 178 P. 498 (1917).

NATURE OF CASE: Appeal from defense verdict in action on a debt.

FACT SUMMARY: Decedent T. Prather purported to convey a debt owed him to his brother, but did not make any delivery.

🏛 RULE OF LAW
A gratuitous transfer of the right to collect a debt is not valid absent delivery.

FACTS: Thomas Prather was owed a sum by Merced Stone Co. (D). Two days before he died, he verbally conveyed the debt to his brother Samuel Prather, who was also an officer of Merced (D). He delivered no papers or other tokens of the debt. Merced (D) raised the conveyance as a defense. The jury rendered a defense verdict, and Adams (P), an heir, appealed.

ISSUE: Is a gratuitous transfer of the right to collect a debt valid without delivery?

HOLDING AND DECISION: (Shaw, J.) No. A gratuitous transfer of the right to collect a debt is not valid absent delivery. For a transfer of a chose in action to be valid, there must be an actual or symbolic delivery, such as the handing of the note to the transferee. Absent such delivery, no transfer occurs. Here, Thomas Prather indicated an intention to give, but never effected the delivery. This was insufficient to transfer the right of payment. Reversed and remanded.

▌ANALYSIS

Prathers's would-be gift would have classified a gift causa mortis, or a gift in contemplation of death. The rules for such gifts differ somewhat from regular gifts. However, they both include a delivery requirement.

■■■■

Quicknotes

CHOSE IN ACTION The right to recover, or the item recoverable, in a lawsuit.

DELIVERY The transfer of title or possession of property.

■■■■

Delacy Investments, Inc. v. Thurman

Commissions factoring company (P) v. Real estate agent (D)

Minn. Ct. App., 693 N.W.2d 479 (2005).

NATURE OF CASE: Appeal from summary judgment for defendant in action for payment of account receivable.

FACT SUMMARY: Delacy Investments, Inc. d/b/a Commission Express (CE) (P), a commissions factoring company, contended that commissions generated by Thurman (D) on the sale of real estate that Thurman (D) had assigned to CE (P) belonged to CE (P) because Re/Max Real Estate Guide, Inc. (Re/Max) (D), the real estate broker through which Thurman (D) generated the commissions on the basis of an independent-contractor agreement, was on notice of the previously executed assignment agreement between CE (P) and Thurman (D).

RULE OF LAW
Under Uniform Commercial Code (UCC) § 9-404, a secured assignee is not entitled to payment of an account receivable where the assignor is not entitled to the account, but an account debtor is entitled to it, even where the account debtor has notice of a previously executed assignment agreement between the assignor and assignee.

FACTS: Thurman (D), a real estate agent, entered into an agreement with Delacy Investments, Inc. d/b/a Commission Express (CE) (P), a commissions factoring company, whereby he assigned his future commissions, or accounts receivable, to CE (P). CE (P) had a security interest in the accounts receivable and perfected this interest by filing a Uniform Commercial Code (UCC) financing statement with the state. Over a year later, Thurman (D) entered a standard independent-contractor agreement with Re/Max Real Estate Guide, Inc. (Re/Max) (D), a real estate broker. Under the agreement with Re/Max (D), Thurman agreed to pay certain overhead expenses and the agreement provided that Thurman (D) would be entitled to commissions only to the extent that they exceeded Thurman's (D) past-due financial obligations to Re/Max (D). Thus, under the agreement with CE (P), Thurman was the assignee, CE (P) was the assignor, and Re/Max (D) was an "account debtor," meaning that Re/Max had the potential right to receive that which Thurman (D) assigned to CE (P). A couple of months later, Re/Max (D) executed an acknowledgment of CE's (P) security interest in Thurman's (D) account receivable from the sale of certain real estate. Accordingly, Re/Max (D) directed that the commission be paid directly to CE (P). Subsequently, Thurman (D) and CE (P) entered an agreement whereby Thurman assigned to CE (P) $10,000 of a commission he anticipated earning on the sale of a different property. Less than a couple of

months later, Re/Max (D) terminated Thurman (D) for poor performance and other performance-related issues. At the time of his termination Thurman (D) owed Re/Max (D) over $11,000. Consequently, Re/Max (D) refused to pay the assigned receivable to CE (P) and, as per the independent-contractor agreement, applied the commission to Thurman's (D) balance. CE (P) brought suit for payment of $10,000 of Thurman's account receivable. The trial court granted summary judgment to Re/Max (D), finding that because Thurman (D) was not entitled to the commission, neither was CE (P). The state's intermediate appellate court granted review.

ISSUE: Under UCC § 9-404, is a secured assignee entitled to payment of an account receivable where the assignor is not entitled to the account, but an account debtor is entitled to it, even where the account debtor has notice of a previously executed assignment agreement between the assignor and assignee?

HOLDING AND DECISION: (Halbrooks, J.) No. Under UCC § 9-404, a secured assignee is not entitled to payment of an account receivable where the assignor is not entitled to the account, but an account debtor is entitled to it, even where the account debtor has notice of a previously executed assignment agreement between the assignor and assignee. This is a case of first impression in this jurisdiction. However, under UCC § 9-404, an assignee's rights are subject to all terms of the agreement between the account debtor and the assignor. Therefore, so long as Thurman (D) was not entitled to collect a commission while his fees were in arrears, CE (P) was not entitled to the commission because it did not have a greater right to the commission than Thurman (D) did. Or, as the official comment to the UCC indicates, an assignee generally takes an assignment subject to the defenses and claims of an account debtor. Moreover, it makes no difference whether the defense or claim accrues before or after the account debtor is notified of the assignment. Thus, under UCC § 9-404(a)(1), the rights of CE (P) are subject to all the terms of the independent-contractor agreement between Thurman (D) and Re/Max (D). This conclusion is supported by black-letter law that an assignee can take no greater rights than the assignor, and cannot be in a better position than the assignor, and is also supported by case law from other jurisdictions. For all these reasons, CE (P) is bound by the independent-contractor agreement and is not entitled to the commission. Nonetheless, CE (P) contends that under UCC § 9-404(a)(2), Re/Max (D), as an account

Continued on next page.

debtor, was not permitted to contract away the rights of Thurman (D) as assignee after having received notice of the previously executed assignment agreement. Although CE (P) is correct in asserting that Re/Max (D) had notice of the agreement, a perfected security interest is generally effective against creditors except as otherwise provided in the UCC. UCC § 9-404(a)(1) provides otherwise, so UCC § 9-404(a)(2) is inapplicable here. UCC § 9-404(a)(1) makes it clear that CE's (P) rights "are subject to . . . all terms of the agreement between the account debtor and assignor." Therefore, the trial court did not err by granting summary judgment to Re/Max (D). Affirmed.

▶ *ANALYSIS*

In keeping with the holding of this case, the Restatement, Second, of Contracts § 336, ct. b (1981) explains that an assignor can assign "only what he has" and "is subject to limitations imposed by the terms of that contract [creating the right] and to defenses which would have been available against the [account debtor] had there been no assignment."

■■■■

Quicknotes

ASSIGNEE A party to whom another party assigns his interest or rights.

ASSIGNOR A party who assigns his interest or rights to another.

SUMMARY JUDGMENT A judgment rendered by a court in response to a motion made by one of the parties, claiming that the lack of a question of material fact in respect to an issue warrants disposition of the issue without consideration by the jury.

■■■■

Crane Ice Cream Co. v. Terminal Freezing & Heating Co.

Assignee (P) v. Seller (D)

Md. Ct. App., 147 Md. 588, 128 A. 280 (1925).

NATURE OF CASE: Appeal from dismissal of a breach of contract action.

FACT SUMMARY: Terminal Freezing & Heating Co. (D) refused to perform a contract when Frederick attempted to assign its rights and delegate its duties to Crane Ice Cream Co. (P).

RULE OF LAW
A party may not delegate its duties under a contract unless performance by another is substantially the same.

FACTS: Frederick, an ice cream manufacturer, entered into a contract with Terminal Freezing & Heating Co. (Terminal) (D) whereby Frederick agreed to buy all of his ice needs from Terminal (D). In return, Terminal (D) agreed to sell to Frederick all of the ice he would need up to 250 tons per week. There was no minimum guaranty to the contract. Terminal (D) had a personal relationship with Frederick. Before the first year of the second term of the contract had expired, Frederick assigned his rights and duties under the contract to Crane Ice Cream Co. (Crane) (P), a large ice cream manufacturing company based in Philadelphia. Upon learning of the assignment, Terminal (D) notified Crane (P) that the contract was over and refused to deliver any ice. Crane (P) sued Terminal (D) for breach of contract, asserting third-party rights, and Terminal (D) demurred to the complaint. The court dismissed the complaint. Crane (P) appealed.

ISSUE: May a party delegate its duties under a contract to another party?

HOLDING AND DECISION: (Parke, J.) No. Parties may not delegate their duties under a contract unless performance by another would be substantially the same. Where rights and duties are personal in nature, they may not be assigned or delegated. In the present case, Crane (P) was a large corporation without any personal relationship with Terminal (D). Additionally, Frederick, as the owner of a sole company, was obliged to purchase all of his ice needs from Terminal (D). Thus, the contract depended on a personal relationship with Frederick. Only where an assignee would provide the same performance can rights and duties be transferred. Crane's (P) performance could not be the same as Frederick's. Accordingly, Frederick could not properly assign the contract to Crane (P). Affirmed.

ANALYSIS

This case highlights the conflict that arises between the autonomy of the parties and the freedom of contract in assignment cases. Assignments are the transfer of a contract right of one person to another person. Unlike contracts that deal strictly with the sale of goods, the assignment of contracts deals with the obligations various parties will have toward one another and how those obligations can shift.

Quicknotes

ASSIGNEE A party to whom another party assigns his interest or rights.

ASSIGNMENT A transaction in which a party conveys his or her entire interest in property to another.

The British Waggon Co. and the Parkgate Waggon Co. v. Lea & Co.

Assignee (P) v. Coal merchants (D)

Q.B., 5 Q.B.D. 149 (1880).

NATURE OF CASE: Breach of contract action.

FACT SUMMARY: Lea & Co. (D) contended that it was no longer bound by a rental/service contract because the other party had assigned the contract to another.

> ## 🏛 RULE OF LAW
> When a nonpersonal service contract is assigned, it remains enforceable.

FACTS: Parkgate Waggon Co. (Parkgate) (P) entered into two contracts with Lea & Co. (D) to provide wagons for hire and to provide repair service on the wagons. Subsequently, Parkgate (P) dissolved and transferred its liabilities and assets. The contracts with Lea (D) were assigned to the British Waggon Co. (P). Lea (D) then declared that it was no longer bound by the contracts as its agreement had been with Parkgate (P), not British (P). Parkgate (P) and British (P) sued for breach of contract.

ISSUE: Are nonpersonal service contracts assignable?

HOLDING AND DECISION: (Cockburn, C.J.) Yes. When a nonpersonal service contract is assigned, it remains enforceable. As a rule, contracts are assignable. The parties can alter this rule by express agreement. Also, if a contract contemplates that a certain person or company will perform a service because of unique skill, talent, or abilities, then the contract is considered personal and non-assignable. Here, the contract called only for competent repair and maintenance services. Thus, Parkgate (P) was not going to provide any personal and unique services to Lea (D). Therefore, Parkgate (P) was entitled to assign the contract to British (P). Judgment for plaintiffs.

▌ANALYSIS

The most well known types of personal service contracts are those involving entertainers. The services provided by such individuals are by definition unique, so the contracts are inherently personal. Measuring damages for breach can, however, be difficult.

■■■

Quicknotes

ASSIGNMENT A transaction in which a party conveys his or her entire interest in property to another.

SERVICE CONTRACT A written agreement to perform maintenance and/or repair service on a product for a specified duration.

■■■

Sally Beauty Co, Inc. v. Nexxus Prods. Co., Inc.

Distributor (P) v. Haircare product manufacturer (D)

801 F.2d 1001 (7th Cir. 1986).

NATURE OF CASE: Appeal from summary judgment in a breach of contract action.

FACT SUMMARY: Sally Beauty Co., Inc. (P) was assigned distributorship rights from Best for Nexxus Prods. Co., Inc.'s (D) products.

RULE OF LAW
The duty of performance under an exclusive distributorship may not be delegated to a competitor without the obligee's consent.

FACTS: In 1979, Nexxus Prods. Co., Inc. (Nexxus) (D), a manufacturer of hair care products, entered into a contract with Best, under which Best would be the exclusive distributor of Nexxus (D) products. Sally Beauty Co., Inc. (Sally) (P) acquired Best in a stock purchase, and Sally (P) succeeded to Best's rights on all of its contracts, including that with Nexxus (D). Sally (P) was a wholly owned subsidiary of Alberto-Culver, a manufacturer of hair care products that was a direct competitor with Nexxus (D). Nexxus (D) refused to allow Sally (P) to be the distributor and canceled the contract. In 1983, Sally (P) sued Nexxus (D) for breach of contract, and Nexxus (D) filed a motion for summary judgment on the breach of contract claim. The court granted Nexxus's (D) motion for summary judgment on the grounds that the contract was one for personal services and was therefore not assignable to Sally (P). Sally (P) appealed.

ISSUE: May the duty of performance under an exclusive distributorship be delegated to a competitor without the obligee's consent?

HOLDING AND DECISION: (Cudahy, J.) No. The duty of performance under an exclusive distributorship may not be delegated to a competitor without the obligee's consent. Uniform Commercial Code § 2-210 provides that "a party may perform his duty through a delegate unless otherwise agreed to or unless the other party has a substantial interest in having his original promisor perform or control the acts required by the contract." In the instant case, Nexxus (D) had a substantial interest in not having a subsidiary of its direct competitor be the exclusive dealer of its products. Sally (P) could not guarantee the same efforts as Best could under the circumstances. Therefore, Nexxus (D) had the right to reject assignment of the contract by Best to Sally (P). The contract was not assignable without Nexxus's consent. Affirmed.

DISSENT: (Posner, J.) The contract issue was not a personal services contract and, because it was decided on a summary judgment motion, Sally (P) never had the opportunity to present evidence that it could distribute the Nexxus (D) products as effectively as Best. Sally (P) distributes products from other competitors and it should not be ruled as a matter of law that a wholly owned subsidiary of a competitor cannot effectively uphold an exclusive-dealing contract.

ANALYSIS

The majority rejected the grounds for summary judgment adopted by the lower court. But instead of remanding the case, it found another basis for a summary ruling. The dissent was correct in pointing out the problems of this approach.

Quicknotes

DELEGATION The authorization of one person to act on another's behalf.

SUBSIDIARY A company a majority of whose shares are owned by another corporation and which is subject to that corporation's control.

Glossary

Common Latin Words and Phrases Encountered in the Law

A FORTIORI: Because one fact exists or has been proven, therefore a second fact that is related to the first fact must also exist.

A PRIORI: From the cause to the effect. A term of logic used to denote that when one generally accepted truth is shown to be a cause, another particular effect must necessarily follow.

AB INITIO: From the beginning; a condition which has existed throughout, as in a marriage which was void ab initio.

ACTUS REUS: The wrongful act; in criminal law, such action sufficient to trigger criminal liability.

AD VALOREM: According to value; an ad valorem tax is imposed upon an item located within the taxing jurisdiction calculated by the value of such item.

AMICUS CURIAE: Friend of the court. Its most common usage takes the form of an amicus curiae brief, filed by a person who is not a party to an action but is nonetheless allowed to offer an argument supporting his legal interests.

ARGUENDO: In arguing. A statement, possibly hypothetical, made for the purpose of argument, is one made arguendo.

BILL QUIA TIMET: A bill to quiet title (establish ownership) to real property.

BONA FIDE: True, honest, or genuine. May refer to a person's legal position based on good faith or lacking notice of fraud (such as a bona fide purchaser for value) or to the authenticity of a particular document (such as a bona fide last will and testament).

CAUSA MORTIS: With approaching death in mind. A gift causa mortis is a gift given by a party who feels certain that death is imminent.

CAVEAT EMPTOR: Let the buyer beware. This maxim is reflected in the rule of law that a buyer purchases at his own risk because it is his responsibility to examine, judge, test, and otherwise inspect what he is buying.

CERTIORARI: A writ of review. Petitions for review of a case by the United States Supreme Court are most often done by means of a writ of certiorari.

CONTRA: On the other hand. Opposite. Contrary to.

CORAM NOBIS: Before us; writs of error directed to the court that originally rendered the judgment.

CORAM VOBIS: Before you; writs of error directed by an appellate court to a lower court to correct a factual error.

CORPUS DELICTI: The body of the crime; the requisite elements of a crime amounting to objective proof that a crime has been committed.

CUM TESTAMENTO ANNEXO, ADMINISTRATOR (ADMINISTRATOR C.T.A.): With will annexed; an administrator c.t.a. settles an estate pursuant to a will in which he is not appointed.

DE BONIS NON, ADMINISTRATOR (ADMINISTRATOR D.B.N.): Of goods not administered; an administrator d.b.n. settles a partially settled estate.

DE FACTO: In fact; in reality; actually. Existing in fact but not officially approved or engendered.

DE JURE: By right; lawful. Describes a condition that is legitimate "as a matter of law," in contrast to the term "de facto," which connotes something existing in fact but not legally sanctioned or authorized. For example, de facto segregation refers to segregation brought about by housing patterns, etc., whereas de jure segregation refers to segregation created by law.

DE MINIMIS: Of minimal importance; insignificant; a trifle; not worth bothering about.

DE NOVO: Anew; a second time; afresh. A trial de novo is a new trial held at the appellate level as if the case originated there and the trial at a lower level had not taken place.

DICTA: Generally used as an abbreviated form of obiter dicta, a term describing those portions of a judicial opinion incidental or not necessary to resolution of the specific question before the court. Such nonessential statements and remarks are not considered to be binding precedent.

DUCES TECUM: Refers to a particular type of writ or subpoena requesting a party or organization to produce certain documents in their possession.

EN BANC: Full bench. Where a court sits with all justices present rather than the usual quorum.

EX PARTE: For one side or one party only. An ex parte proceeding is one undertaken for the benefit of only one party, without notice to, or an appearance by, an adverse party.

EX POST FACTO: After the fact. An ex post facto law is a law that retroactively changes the consequences of a prior act.

EX REL.: Abbreviated form of the term "ex relatione," meaning upon relation or information. When the state brings an action in which it has no interest against an individual at the instigation of one who has a private interest in the matter.

FORUM NON CONVENIENS: Inconvenient forum. Although a court may have jurisdiction over the case, the action should be tried in a more conveniently located court, one to which parties and witnesses may more easily travel, for example.

GUARDIAN AD LITEM: A guardian of an infant as to litigation, appointed to represent the infant and pursue his/her rights.

HABEAS CORPUS: You have the body. The modern writ of habeas corpus is a writ directing that a person (body)

181

being detained (such as a prisoner) be brought before the court so that the legality of his detention can be judicially ascertained.

IN CAMERA: In private, in chambers. When a hearing is held before a judge in his chambers or when all spectators are excluded from the courtroom.

IN FORMA PAUPERIS: In the manner of a pauper. A party who proceeds in forma pauperis because of his poverty is one who is allowed to bring suit without liability for costs.

INFRA: Below, under. A word referring the reader to a later part of a book. (The opposite of supra.)

IN LOCO PARENTIS: In the place of a parent.

IN PARI DELICTO: Equally wrong; a court of equity will not grant requested relief to an applicant who is in pari delicto, or as much at fault in the transactions giving rise to the controversy as is the opponent of the applicant.

IN PARI MATERIA: On like subject matter or upon the same matter. Statutes relating to the same person or things are said to be in pari materia. It is a general rule of statutory construction that such statutes should be construed together, i.e., looked at as if they together constituted one law.

IN PERSONAM: Against the person. Jurisdiction over the person of an individual.

IN RE: In the matter of. Used to designate a proceeding involving an estate or other property.

IN REM: A term that signifies an action against the res, or thing. An action in rem is basically one that is taken directly against property, as distinguished from an action in personam, i.e., against the person.

INTER ALIA: Among other things. Used to show that the whole of a statement, pleading, list, statute, etc., has not been set forth in its entirety.

INTER PARTES: Between the parties. May refer to contracts, conveyances or other transactions having legal significance.

INTER VIVOS: Between the living. An inter vivos gift is a gift made by a living grantor, as distinguished from bequests contained in a will, which pass upon the death of the testator.

IPSO FACTO: By the mere fact itself.

JUS: Law or the entire body of law.

LEX LOCI: The law of the place; the notion that the rights of parties to a legal proceeding are governed by the law of the place where those rights arose.

MALUM IN SE: Evil or wrong in and of itself; inherently wrong. This term describes an act that is wrong by its very nature, as opposed to one which would not be wrong but for the fact that there is a specific legal prohibition against it (malum prohibitum).

MALUM PROHIBITUM: Wrong because prohibited, but not inherently evil. Used to describe something that is wrong because it is expressly forbidden by law but that is not in and of itself evil, e.g., speeding.

MANDAMUS: We command. A writ directing an official to take a certain action.

MENS REA: A guilty mind; a criminal intent. A term used to signify the mental state that accompanies a crime or other prohibited act. Some crimes require only a general mens rea (general intent to do the prohibited act), but others, like assault with intent to murder, require the existence of a specific mens rea.

MODUS OPERANDI: Method of operating; generally refers to the manner or style of a criminal in committing crimes, admissible in appropriate cases as evidence of the identity of a defendant.

NEXUS: A connection to.

NISI PRIUS: A court of first impression. A nisi prius court is one where issues of fact are tried before a judge or jury.

N.O.V. (NON OBSTANTE VEREDICTO): Notwithstanding the verdict. A judgment n.o.v. is a judgment given in favor of one party despite the fact that a verdict was returned in favor of the other party, the justification being that the verdict either had no reasonable support in fact or was contrary to law.

NUNC PRO TUNC: Now for then. This phrase refers to actions that may be taken and will then have full retroactive effect.

PENDENTE LITE: Pending the suit; pending litigation under way.

PER CAPITA: By head; beneficiaries of an estate, if they take in equal shares, take per capita.

PER CURIAM: By the court; signifies an opinion ostensibly written "by the whole court" and with no identified author.

PER SE: By itself, in itself; inherently.

PER STIRPES: By representation. Used primarily in the law of wills to describe the method of distribution where a person, generally because of death, is unable to take that which is left to him by the will of another, and therefore his heirs divide such property between them rather than take under the will individually.

PRIMA FACIE: On its face, at first sight. A prima facie case is one that is sufficient on its face, meaning that the evidence supporting it is adequate to establish the case until contradicted or overcome by other evidence.

PRO TANTO: For so much; as far as it goes. Often used in eminent domain cases when a property owner receives partial payment for his land without prejudice to his right to bring suit for the full amount he claims his land to be worth.

QUANTUM MERUIT: As much as he deserves. Refers to recovery based on the doctrine of unjust enrichment in those cases in which a party has rendered valuable services or furnished materials that were accepted and enjoyed by another under circumstances that would reasonably notify the recipient that the rendering party expected to be paid. In essence, the law implies a contract to pay the reasonable value of the services or materials furnished.

QUASI: Almost like; as if; nearly. This term is essentially used to signify that one subject or thing is almost analogous to another but that material differences between them do exist. For example, a quasi-criminal proceeding is one that is not strictly criminal but shares enough of the same characteristics to require some of the same safeguards (e.g., procedural due process must be followed in a parole hearing).

QUID PRO QUO: Something for something. In contract law, the consideration, something of value, passed between the parties to render the contract binding.

RES GESTAE: Things done; in evidence law, this principle justifies the admission of a statement that would otherwise be hearsay when it is made so closely to the event in question as to be said to be a part of it, or with such spontaneity as not to have the possibility of falsehood.

RES IPSA LOQUITUR: The thing speaks for itself. This doctrine gives rise to a rebuttable presumption of negligence when the instrumentality causing the injury was within the exclusive control of the defendant, and the injury was one that does not normally occur unless a person has been negligent.

RES JUDICATA: A matter adjudged. Doctrine which provides that once a court of competent jurisdiction has rendered a final judgment or decree on the merits, that judgment or decree is conclusive upon the parties to the case and prevents them from engaging in any other litigation on the points and issues determined therein.

RESPONDEAT SUPERIOR: Let the master reply. This doctrine holds the master liable for the wrongful acts of his servant (or the principal for his agent) in those cases in which the servant (or agent) was acting within the scope of his authority at the time of the injury.

STARE DECISIS: To stand by or adhere to that which has been decided. The common law doctrine of stare decisis attempts to give security and certainty to the law by following the policy that once a principle of law as applicable to a certain set of facts has been set forth in a decision, it forms a precedent which will subsequently be followed, even though a different decision might be made were it the first time the question had arisen. Of course, stare decisis is not an inviolable principle and is departed from in instances where there is good cause (e.g., considerations of public policy led the Supreme Court to disregard prior decisions sanctioning segregation).

SUPRA: Above. A word referring a reader to an earlier part of a book.

ULTRA VIRES: Beyond the power. This phrase is most commonly used to refer to actions taken by a corporation that are beyond the power or legal authority of the corporation.

Addendum of French Derivatives

IN PAIS: Not pursuant to legal proceedings.

CHATTEL: Tangible personal property.

CY PRES: Doctrine permitting courts to apply trust funds to purposes not expressed in the trust but necessary to carry out the settlor's intent.

PER AUTRE VIE: For another's life; during another's life. In property law, an estate may be granted that will terminate upon the death of someone other than the grantee.

PROFIT A PRENDRE: A license to remove minerals or other produce from land.

VOIR DIRE: Process of questioning jurors as to their predispositions about the case or parties to a proceeding in order to identify those jurors displaying bias or prejudice.

Casenote® Legal Briefs